AF564716

CONTESTING SYMBOLS AND STEREOTYPES

Essays on Indian History and Culture

Edited by

D.N. Jha

Contesting Symbols and Stereotypes: Essays on Indian History and Culture
Edited by D.N. Jha

First Published, 2013
Reprinted 2026

ISBN 978-93-5002-261-0

Published by
AAKAR BOOKS
28 E Pocket IV, Mayur Vihar Phase I
Delhi 110 091, India
www.aakarbooks.com

Printed at
D.K. Fine Art Press, Delhi

IN MEMORIAM

Nirmala Chaturvedi
Hem Chaturvedi
Bina Rao
Vijay Nath

Contents

SECTION IV
Nudity and Sexuality: Divine and Human

Preface

The construction of Hindu religious identity began in the nineteenth century, and, has continued unabated ever since. Accompanied by the demonization of minorities, especially Muslims, and the creation and propagation of absurd ideas about Hinduism, the Hindu identity has become increasingly aggressive in its manifestations in recent years. Its ideologues have been trying to redefine the boundaries of Hinduism by creating stereotypes which have no basis in historical evidence. They project Rama as the supreme god, who, in the words of L.K. Advani, is "the unique symbol of our oneness", deny the diversity of religious beliefs and practices negating even the plurality of epic traditions, appropriate and even invent cultural symbols of questionable Hindu association, burn books that do not endorse their view, vandalize the art they consider blashphemous and agitate against films that go against their irrational notions of cultural purity. The essays in the present anthology argue against their distorted view of Indian history and culture on the basis of empirical historical evidence.

I am thankful to the contributors who cooperated with me by sending in their articles in time but, have, hopefully forgiven me for the inordinate delay in the publication of the book. I must place on record my gratitude to Antara Dev Sen for permission to reproduce Nabaneeta Dev Sen's paper on the *Rāmāyaṇa* from the *Little Magazine* and to the editor,

Frontline, for reprinting K.M. Shrimali's paper on *triśula*.

I have received help from several friends and well wishers in the preparation of the book. Professor Amar Farooqui read portions of it and offered valuable comments. Professor Niraj K. Jha helped me obtain many references from Princeton University Library and Ms Toshie Awaya was kind enough to send the PDFs and the xerox copies of many articles from Tokyo University of Foreign Studies. Dr Jyotsna Arora, Ms Malavika Gulati and Ms Noorshabina Aziz of the library of the Indian Council of Historical Research, New Delhi, were always helpful in accessing the internet resources for me. Ajeet, Amol, Mihir and Shankar rendered much needed bibliographical assistance and Praveen Kumar (Pintoo) drove me even at odd hours so as to enable me to honour my commitments. Mr K.K. Saxena of Aakar Books took pains to publish this anthology expedetiously. My wife, Rajrani, as usual stood by me in moments of stress. I am grateful to all of them.

5 October 2013 **D.N. Jha**

Section I

STEREOTYPES AND HISTORY

1

Stereotyping Hindu Identity

D.N. Jha

The formation of a religious Hindu identity has been a matter of much debate among scholars interested in the construction of Hinduism and there has been no consensus on the issue so far. But in spite of the divergent approaches to the problem, it is difficult to deny that the beginning of the census operations in 1872, the application of categories of "Hindus" and "Muhammadans" to classify and divide the people of the Indian colony on religious lines and to keep these religious groups constantly at loggerheads played a crucial role in creating the notion of a Hindu identity as distinct from Muslim or Christian. An equally, if not more, important factor in the initial phase of Hinduism's construction was the acceptance and dissemination of the term "Hindu" by religious thinkers and reformists of the nineteenth century. Ram Mohan Roy (1772–1833), who founded the Brahmo Samaj in 1828, vindicated Hinduism against the expansion of Christianity, even though he was in favour of certain Western reformist ideas like the abolition of *satī*. The religion based on the Vedas and Upaniṣads, he argued, was monotheistic and egalitarian, and it was only in course of time that decline set in and retrograde practices like polytheism, the caste system and the suppression of women crept into it. The notion of the Vedic age as a "golden age" was thus "embodied in the doctrine of the Brahmo Samaj"[1] and it anticipated the ideas of subsequent religious reformers.

Like him Dayananda Saraswati (1824–1883), who founded the reformist organisation, Arya Samaj, in 1875, also harked back to the Vedic "golden age" in *āryāvarta* where the first men were born and where Sanskrit, the mother of all tongues, was spoken.[2] He "maintained that the Aryas of the Vedas were the autochthonous people of Bhārat."[3] Unlike Roy, however, he treated the Vedas as a divine revelation and accorded them the status of a fixed and clearly demarcated canon—a status which the *Bible* and *Quran* enjoyed in Christianity and Islam respectively. This gave a "specifity and distinction" to the Arya Samajist ideology in relation to Hinduism, which, according to it, was a degraded form of Vedic religion—a reason why the followers of Dayananda preferred to register themselves as "Aryas" and not Hindus in the 1891 Punjab census.[4] Thus, apparently Dayananda would not initially appear to be a proponent of Hindu nationalism, but judging from his activities, he was certainly a forerunner of the later Hindu chauvinism and xenophobia. For example, he fully shared the militant Hinduism's concern for cow-protection, and founded the Gorakhsini Sabha in 1881. So strong was his commitment to the movement for cow-protection that despite his sharp ideological antagonism with the adherents of the anti-reformist and orthodox brāhamaṇical religious practices called the Sanātanists, the Arya Samajists felt no uneasiness of conscience in collaborating with them over the issue. The idea of protecting the cow thus gained popularity among a wide cross-section of the people, galvanized and unified them as Hindus[5] and strengthened their separate identity as against that of the Muslims who were stereotyped as kine killers and beef eaters. Similarly, Dayananda's ardour and enthusiasm for the purification/reconversion (*śuddhi*) of those who or whose ancestors had converted to Islam and Christianity,[6] clearly recognized their followers as enemies. Although his missionary activity was initially opposed by the orthodox Sanātanists who projected Hinduism as a non-proselytizing religion,[7] it soon received their endorsement, notably from persons like Madan Mohan Malaviya, in the early twentieth century, and thus tended to reinforce the idea of Hindu identity.

Some of the ideas of Dayananda found an echo in those of Vivekananda (1863–1902), though his background and career trajectory were different from those of his predecessors. Like them, he glorified the Vedas and Upaniṣads, and referred nostalgically to the earliest period of Indian past as one of "Vedic harmony"—a period when the people were "ruled according to the principles of the *Veda*s and India enjoyed 2000 years of uninterrupted peace, tranquility and prosperity;"[8] in contrast, he spoke, with a *cri de coeur*, of the period of the Muslim rule as one of oppression of the Hindus. He did not share the concern of Dayananda for cow-protection and, even advised "young men in India to eat beef in order to develop muscles",[9] but like him, he was interested in converting members of other faiths to his own, which in his case, was the Advaita Vedānta, and which he used to unify the Hindus. He founded the Rama Krishna Mission in 1897 for its promotion and propagation through Maths and Ashrams in different parts of India as well as through international missionary activity.[10] Despite their different views on issues relating to social and religious reform, Dayananda and Vivekananda shared a revivalist perception of India's past and an exclusivist notion of Hinduism, which were echoed by their contemporaries in different parts of the country. In Bengal, Rajnarain Basu (1826–1899), a close associate of Debendranath Tagore, stood for the triumph of *sanātanadharma*, spoke forcefully of the superiority of Hindu religion and culture in contrast to Christainity and Islam, and asserted that "his Hindu Mahasamiti... could not have a place for Muslims."[11] Chandranath Basu (1844–1910), who was intimate to Bankim Chandra Chattopadhyaya and was a champion of reform through revivalism, published his *Hindutva—An Authentic History of Hindus* in Bengali as early as 1892, in which he portrayed Hinduism "in terms of its glorious archaic past" and as superior to Christianity, and presented his spirited defense of traditional brāhmaṇical ritualism, child marriage, caste system, patriarchal values, etc.[12] Essentially anti-Islamist at the core, the Hindutva idea popularized by him was conspicuously present in Bankim Chandra's (1838–94) influential novel *Anandamath* (1882), which refers to Muslims as "dirty bastards."[13]

The demonization of Muslims was a prominent theme also in the works of many writers outside Bengal. In Hindi, Bharatendu Harishchandra (1850-85), often considered to be the father of modern Hindi literature, thus, depicted Muslim characters as cruel, coward, treacherous, bigots and depraved, and his contemporaries described Muslim rule "as a chronicle of rape and abduction of Hindu women, the slaughter of sacred cows, and the defilement of temples."[14] The Marathi writers displayed a similar attitude to Muslims and described them as "bullies and fanatics" and the period of their rule as one of "the overall degradation of the Hindus" and of the spread of the "pernicious influence of Islam on their social customs."[15] The most influential of the Marathi writers was the nationalist and social reformer Bal Gangadhar Tilak (1856–1920) who made "a conscious choice of historical figures and symbols" to strengthen the notion of a Hindu identity.[16] He reinvented a largely domestic festival of Ganesh by giving it a group character and used it as an instrument for mobilizing the Hindus. He revived the memories of Shivaji, promoted the celebration of Shivaji festivals and projected him as a pre-eminent symbol of Hindu militancy against Muslims. In 1893 he founded the Anti-Cow Killing Society and gave a direct challenge to Muslims. While Tilak thus sought to build an aggressive Maratha/Hindu identity leading often to Hindu-Muslim antagonism and tension, he emphatically asserted that the essence of Hinduism lay in its metaphysics and tolerance of other faiths,[17] though judging by his anti-Muslim sentiments and activities, these were mere fine words. His writings on the history of ancient Indian culture,[18] therefore, dwelt on the Hindu-Aryan primordialism and supported his notion of a future Hindu nation. He pushed the date of the Vedic period from 1500 BC first to 4000 BC and then to 8000 BC, glorified the Vedic Aryan race and religion and wove "a thread of cultural and religious continuity between the Aryans of the furthest antiquity and present-day Hindus."[19] Despite his view that the original home of the Aryans was in the Arctic, he underlined the importance of the Vedic Aryan heritage. "During Vedic times", Tilak asserted, "India was a self-contained country...

united as a great nation." He loudly proclaimed that the "common factor" in Indian society was "the feeling of Hindutva" and that all Hindus were one because of their adherence to *Hindudharma*."[20] Based on his reading of the *Bhagvadgītā*, on which he wrote an elaborate commentary, he espoused the use of violence as a higher duty.[21] Tilak's ideas, especially his anti-Muslim sentiments, assertion of Aryan/ Hindu primordiality, and his apologia for the use of violence had many takers during the extremist phase of India's freedom struggle, the most important of them being Aurobindo who declared that the Hindu religion was the eternal religion (*sanātanadharma*) preserved by the Aryan race through centuries, equated it with nationalism, and inspired by the *Gītā* like Tilak, justified the use of violence in its defense and in the nationalist resistance to the British rule.[22] It was, however, Tilak who was really the forerunner of militant Hinduism of the subsequent years expounded by V.D. Savarkar (1883–1966), K.B. Hedgewar (1889–1940) and M.S. Golwalkar (1906–1973) and others in the wake of an unprecedented communalization of Indian politics from the 1920s onwards.

V.D. Savarkar, seven-time president of the Hindu Mahasabha, the Right-wing Hindu political party, and founder of the modern day Hindutva movement, sought to provide a comprehensive definition of Hindu identity in his *Hindutva: Who is a Hindu?* published in 1923, and in doing so, he borrowed and elaborated several ideas of Tilak with whom he came in contact early in life. Although Tilak's commitment to the anti-cow slaughter movement was not much of an attraction for him, the Hindutva idea, to which Tilak had referred, became the central theme of his work in which he postulated that it was Hindutva (=Hinduness), rather than Hinduism, that constituted Hindu identity. But Hindutva itself, he tells us, "defies all attempts at analysis... [It] is not a word but a history. Not only the spiritual or religious history of our people, but a history in full."[23] Like Tilak, he accepted the belief that the Aryans originated outside India, migrated into the modern Punjab and called themselves Hindu (or Sindhu) for the first time and spread out to different parts of the subcontinent with their civilization, giving birth to a common race of the Hindus through miscegenation of Aryans and non-Aryans, and creating new 'colonies' on the way till the day Rāma made his triumphant entry into Ceylon, the day which was "the real birth-day of our Hindu people."[24] On the one hand, Savarkar primordialized Hindu identity and asserted that "the word Hindu dates its antiquity from a period... that even mythology fails to penetrate—to trace it to its source;"[25] and on the other, he declared that it was during the medieval period that Hindus "were welded into a nation to an extent unknown in our history" as a result of their "struggle of life and death" against the "Muslim invaders" and "tyrants". This perception of history was deeply flawed but he insisted that Hindus are a nation and India must be a land reserved for them. A Hindu, according to Savarkar, was one (i) who acquired citizenship by paternal descent, that is, who was born in India, (ii) who was born of Hindu parents and thus possessed Vedic Aryan blood and (iii) who shared a common *sanskriti* (culture) "...suggestive of that language, Sanskrit, which has been the chosen means of expression and preservation of that culture, of all that was best and worth-preserving in the history of our race."[26] In the ultimate analysis, however, a Hindu, according to Savarkar, was one who regarded India as his fatherland (*pitṛibhūmi*) and holy land (*puṇyabhūmi*),[27] one whose religion must have grown "out of the soil of India." This definition of a Hindu excluded Muslims and Christians whose holy lands were in Arabia and Palestine respectively and who were considered inherently treacherous. Savarkar's Hindu supremacism, not surprisingly, was best summed up in his call to "Hinduise all politics and Militarise all Hindudom"—a call that was to become a rallying cry of Hindu identity and nationalism.

Two years after Savarkar expounded his concept of Hindutva, Keshav Baliram Hedgewar (1889–1940), a Maharashtrian brāhmaṇ of Tilakite association, drawing inspiration from him but going a step further, proclaimed that long before recorded history, the Hindus were a mighty and prosperous nation and they ruled "over vast regions of the earth and our flag flew over many lands..."[28] But his real importance in promoting militant Hindu identity lay not in his ideas articulated through his occasional writings and speeches but in the fact that in 1925 he founded the Rashtriya Svayamsevak Sangh (National Volunteer Corps), popularly known as the RSS, whose network has grown steadily over the years and has now a large number of bodies including political parties affiliated to it.[29] This organization, with its martial character, has remained the vanguard of the Hindutva movement and has had its hand, directly or through its affiliates, in several communal conflagrations.[30]

While Savarkar provided an ideological *raison d'être* of the RSS, Hedgewar, supposedly endowed with supreme organizational skills, gave it a para-military and fascist character. However, it was for M.S. Golwalkar, who succeeded him in 1940 as chief of the RSS, to give it "the ideological charter it had previously lacked."[31] In 1939, a year before he took over from Hedgewar as the second chief of the RSS, he published his *We or Our Nationhood Defined*;[32] the collection of his essays and speeches came out in 1966 as *Bunch of Thoughts*. While Savarkar had claimed that the Hindu race originated four thousand years ago, Golwalkar, much like Tilak, pushed its antiquity back to 80 to 100 centuries. Inspired by Hitler's ethnic nationalism, he rejected the view that the Hindu-Aryans have been exogenous to India and asserted that "we Hindus came into this land from nowhere, but are indigenous children of the soil always, from time immemorial and are natural masters of the country."[33] It was from this indigenist Hindu-Aryan position that he asserted that "the foreign races in Hindusthan must either adopt the Hindu culture and language, must learn to respect and hold in reverence Hindu religion, must entertain no ideas but those of glorification of the Hindu race and culture... or may stay in the country, wholly subordinated to the Hindu nation, claiming nothing, deserving no privileges, far less any preferential treatment—not even citizen's rights."[34] Deeply committed to the supremacy of the Hindu religion and culture, Golwalkar enunciated his notion of "cultural nationalism" which was distinct from Savarkar's "territorial nationalism" and which, in his scheme of things, made it obligatory for Muslims and other religious minorities to respect and revere the Hindu religion. Unlike Savarkar, he attached great importance to the protection of the cow, considered this animal as "mother" and the emblem of Hindu devotion and protested against its slaughter.[35] According to him, the Muslims began the practice of cow killing in India and the Britishers continued it and since the practice began with foreign domination "it is a stigma on us."[36] Despite some differences in their ideas and attitude, both Savarkar and Golwalkar emphasized, in varying degrees, the primordialization and indigenization of Hindu identity. They also demonized religious minorities, especially the Muslims—a tendency whose pugnacious manifestations in the post-Nehruvian India culminated in the demolition of the sixteenth-century Muslim mosque at Ayodhya in 1992, triggering countrywide Hindu-Muslim riots and the genocide of Muslims in Gujarat in 2002, putting the country to shame. Even so, the RSS and its affiliates always deny their objective of establishing a religious Hindu state and claim that Hinduism is a "universalistic and tolerant religious philosophy."[37]

The divisive concept of Hindu identity propagated by the social and religious reformers, nationalist leaders and cultural nationalists has received much institutional support from modern university system and has found a prominent place in academic histories since the early twentieth century— a fact which calls for a detailed study but a few quick examples should serve our purpose here. Thus, the Calcutta University, the first modern university in India, established separate departments of ancient Indian history and culture and Islamic history, the first giving a boost to the supposed glories of ancient India and the second to the denigration of Muslims; and in order to bolster the idea of Hindu resistance to them, it also introduced separate courses on the history of Rajputs, Marathas and Sikhs who all fought against the Mughals. Many universities established after the one in Calcutta followed suit and set up separate departments for the teaching and research in ancient Indian history and culture, which invariably romanticized and glorified the ancient ('Hindu') period. This discouraged the study of an integrated history of the country, and encouraged the growth of a retrograde and revivalist historiography with primordialization and glorification of the Aryan/Hindu identity as its main agenda. Thus, almost at the same time as Savarkar was busy defining the contours of Hindu identity, Abinash Chandra Das, lecturer in ancient Indian history and culture in Calcutta University, argued that the Aryans were the original inhabitants of Sapta-Sindhu (modern Punjab) which, according to him, was "the oldest life-producing region in the whole of the Indian subcontinent", and assigned the Ṛgvedic hymns to 25,000 years ago or the Pleistocene Age.[38]

A majority of historians writing during the period of nationalist resistance to the British rule as well as after India's independence have oddly clung not only to the idea of autochthonous Aryans and their fantastic antiquity but also to their supposed civilizing role in the ancient world, especially in many Asian countries like Burma, Java, Cambodia, Bali and Vietnam, in which the ancient Indian adventurers established colonies and transmitted a "high culture to a mélange of unlettered primitives". A major source of inspiration to these historians has been the notion of a Greater India in ancient times. As is well known, an organization called the Greater India Society was founded in Calcutta in 1926 with the objective of organizing the study of the history and culture of Asian countries in which ancient Indians supposedly established colonies. A person no less than Rabindranath Tagore was its *purodhā* (spiritual head), but many scholars extended active support to it.[39] Of them, R.C. Majumdar was the most influential, industrious and prolific and it is to his revivalist and anti-Islamist writings that Hindu supremacists and cultural nationalists have often turned for legitimacy. A persistently polemic apologist of the greatness of ancient "Hindus" and a firm believer in the hinduization of the South-East Asian countries, he ignored their indigenous cultures and thus lent an ideological support to Hedgewar's vacuous claim that the Hindu "flag flew over many lands." As general editor of the multi-volume publication, *History and Culture of the Indian People,* Majumdar devoted more volumes to what he considered to be the periods of Hindu domination and less volumes to those that he considered to be phases of Muslim domination.[40] He credited the Hindus for their "spirit of religious toleration" and denigrated the Muslims for their intolerant and oppressive rule and for destroying Hindu temples. A similar anti-Muslim attitude is seen in the works of Jadunath Sarkar who wrote extensively on medieval Indian history. Like Majumdar, he perceived medieval period of Indian history as one of perpetual confrontation between the Hindus and Muslims and, asserted that the ideal of the Mughal state was "the conversion of the entire population to Islam." Listing all the individual acts of omission and commission during the "Muslim rule", he presented a negative picture of Muslim rulers[41] and spoke in glowing terms of the resistance to Muslims by Shivaji who, as a symbol of Maratha/Hindu chauvinism, has been a significant factor in even contemporary Indian politics—so much so that any critical reference to him may prove perilous! "Shivaji", Jadunath Sarkar tells us, "has shown that the tree of Hinduism is not really dead, that it can rise from beneath the seemingly crushing load of centuries of political bondage..."[42] Majumdar and Sarkar and other scholars of their ilk have projected the Muslims as oppressors and inherently intolerant of Hindus who, by contrast, are perceived as weak and tolerant. The latter feared the former and, according to an influential and respected historian, the Hindu women adopted the custom of veiling after 1200 AD so as to protect themselves "from the covetous eyes of the [Muslim] soldiery"—a patently erroneous and widely accepted view deeply embedded in popular consciousness so much so that even an aspirant for the Indian presidency could not get over it.[43] Muslims, we are also told, are vastly different from Hindus not only in religious beliefs and practices but also in dietary culture and social customs. The former have been stereotyped as beef eaters as against Hindus who are all thought of as vegetarians.[44] The modern historians have thus demonized the Muslim "Other" and fed into the dialectic of the aggressive

Hindu identity. But its cheerleaders remain the militant Hindutva organizations which have created many myths and misconceptions about it, including the fiction of an eternal Hinduism; in the riotous imagination of one of them, the Vedic Foundation based in the US, the Indian/Hindu civilization has existed in the Ganga valley uninterruptedly since 1972 million years![45]

In their cultural nationalist politics, the Hindutva organizations, which have mushroomed in recent years, have received considerable support from the electronic media whose numerous channels keep beaming religious soap operas which boost spurious religiosity and strengthen, even if unintentionally, Hindu communal consciousness. The misuse of television, in fact, started during the late eighties when it was fully state controlled, and in gross violation of the well established secular policy, it telecast two Hindu religious epics, *Rāmāyaṇa* and *Mahābhārata*, whose story lines totally ignored the temporal and spatial diversity in their renditions and tended to homogenize popular Hindu beliefs. The televising of the two epics between 1987 and 1989 coincided with the crescendo of the Hindutva cry for the "liberation" of several Hindu pilgrimage centres, especially Ayodhya, where the Sangh Parivar and its extended family later demolished the sixteenth-century mosque which, it believes, was built on the ruins of a Hindu temple. Ayodhya, the Hindu fanatics keep parroting, is the birth place of Rāma, and in accordance with this, their seniormost leader L.K. Advani, allegedly involved in the demolition of the mosque on 6 December 1992, unabashedly asserted: "Sri Rama is the unique symbol, the unequalled symbol of our oneness, or our integration, as well as of our aspiration to live the higher values. As Maryada Pursushottam Sri Rama has represented for thousands of years the ideal of conduct, just as Rama Rajya has represented the ideal of governance."[46] This is no different from a recent loud proclamation of the RSS chief, according to whom a temple to Rāma would establish the country's "self-identity".[47] Rāma is thus a hinduized and nationalized hero; he is the most political god of India today and devotion to him is a litmus test of one's loyalty to the nation and a means to consolidate and mobilize the Hindu society for the capture of political power.

The efforts of the Hindutva extremists to homogenize religious beliefs and practices by projecting Rāma as the god above other gods and the *Rāmāyaṇa* as the scripture over other religious texts have gone in tandem with their strong censorship of some important and interesting aspects of Indian culture and history. In 1993, not long after they demolished the mosque at Ayodhya, they attacked the Sahmat exhibition consisting of panels on the different versions of the Rāma legend, especially the one on the Buddhist text, *Daśaratha Jātaka*, which depicts Rāma and Sītā as brother and sister. The vandalization of the panel followed by its banning by the Delhi government at the instance of L.K. Advani and other BJP leaders[48] amounted to a denial of the plurality of the *Rāmāyaṇa* tradition. It was also a total rejection of the Buddhist origin myths according to which "the founding family [of ancient Indian republics] resulted from an incestuous union between brother and sister."[49] Few years later, in 1998, the Hindutva hoodlums demonstrated against Deepa Mehta's film, *Fire*, whose story revolved round the same-sex love, though it was not unknown in ancient Indian literature. The most important example of censorship in contemporary India by Hindu extremists is related to the paintings by Maqbool Fida Husain, who was unquestionably the greatest painter of modern India. In 1996, they questioned the legitimacy of nudity in Hindu religious art and raised a huge hue and cry over the depiction of Hindu goddesses in nude by him. The first target of attack was a line drawing of the goddess Saraswatī which was "hauled up as an insult and offense to Hindu religious sensibilities by a Muslim artist"; his naming of nude female bodies after divinities like Pārvatī, Lakṣmī or Saraswatī, according to the Hindu fundmentalists, was tantamount to "the rape of Hindu goddesses."[50] The Hindutva forces barged into art galleries in Ahmedabad in 1996 and later in 2004 at Surat to vandalize Husain's paintings and slapped numerous court cases on him. Combining their "coercive use of law" with threats of various kinds, they forced him to leave the country and die in exile. He became the victim as much of the communal politics as of the cultural terrorism unleased by the Hindu fanatics.

The Hindu extremists have also tried to appropriate and even invent cultural symbols of questionable exclusive Hindu association. For instance, when, in 2005, the European Union initiated the move to ban the swastika, a reminder of the Holocaust, the Indian diaspora strongly protested and claimed the symbol as the "most ancient and Hindu", despite its provenance in different parts of the ancient world. At home, they have been distributing trident (*triśūla*), Siva's weapon, in different states of India, and have called it *triśūla-dikṣā* (initiation through *dikṣā*). The trident is not specifically Indian; possibly an import from the north-west, its association with Śiva is very late. The *triśūla-dikṣā* is likewise unknown to Indian tradition, and is an invention of the Sangh Parivar. Though projected as "a venture of glorious cultural resurgence" to reinvigorate the "Hindu" ethos, it is, in reality, an effort to symbolically weaponize the Hindus against religious minorities.

The Hindutva ideologues and their followers have been trying to redefine the boundaries of Hinduism, and examples of this can be multiplied to almost any length. They censure anything that does not fit into their scheme. They burn books that do not endorse their view, vandalize objects of art which they consider blashphemous, and demonstrate against films which present a counter point to their propaganda. They distort Indian history and religion, and nurture a culture of intolerance. The essays that follow are intended to counter some of the many distortions they have introduced in the common man's perception of Indian identity, religion and culture, and thus damage the rich mosaic of social and cultural diversity which India represents.

ENDNOTES

1. Christophe Jaffrelot, *Hindu Nationalism: A Reader*, Permanent Black, Delhi, 2007, pp. 7–8.
2. J.T.F. Jordens, *Dayanand Saraswati: His Life and Ideas*, Oxford University Press, Delhi, 1978, p. 110.

3. Jaffrelot, *Hindu Nationalism*, p. 9
4. K. Jones, "Religious Identity and the Indian Census", in N.G. Barrier, ed., *The Census in British India*, Manohar, Delhi, 1981, p. 87.
5. John Zavos, *The Emergence of Hindu Nationalism*, Oxford University Press, Delhi, 2000, pp. 87–8
6. J.E. Llewellyn, *The Arya Samaj as a Fundamentalist Movement*, Manohar, Delhi, 1993, pp. 99–103; Zavos, *The Emergence of Hindu Nationalism*, pp. 87–92.
7. Since caste system *(varṇāśramadharma)* has always occupied a central position in the orthodox sanātanist Hindu religion, and since the Arya Samajist ideology preached the necessity to recognize merit-based caste and not the traditional hereditary caste system, questions were raised about how a convert could be looked upon as a Hindu unless he or she was assigned a place in the caste hierarchy. This added a controversial dimension to *śuddhi* (reconversion) but in the early twentieth century leaders like Madan Mohan Malaviya lent support to this movement (Jaffrelot, *Hindu Nationalism*, pp. 68–9)
8. Amalendu Misra, *Identity and Religion: Foundations of Anti-Islamism in India*, Sage Publications, New Delhi, 2004, p. 37
9. Jyotirmaya Sharma, *Cosmic Love and Human Apathy: Swami Vivekananda's Restatement of Religion*, Harper Collins India, Delhi, 2013, p. 272
10. Torkel Brekke, *Makers of Modern Indian Religion in the Nineteenth Century*, Oxford University Press, New York, 2002, p. 47.
11. Chetan Bhatt, *Hindu Nationalism, Ideologies and Modern Myths*, Oxford, Berg, 2001, p. 24.
12. Ibid., pp. 25–6.
13. Tanika Sarkar, "Imaginning Hindu Rashtra: The Hindu and the Muslim in Bankim Chandra's Writings", in David Ludden, *Making India Hindu*, Oxford University Press, Delhi, 1996, p. 175. This portrayal of Muslims, however, was contested by intellectuals like Bhudev Mukhopadhyaya (1827–94) and others (Mushirul Hasan, "The Myth of Unity: Colonial and National Narratives", in David Ludden, op. cit., p. 201.)
14. Hasan, op. cit., p. 200
15. Ibid., p. 200.
16. Ibid.
17. Shanta Sathe, *Lokmanya Tilaka: His Social and Political Thoughts*, Ajanta, Delhi, 1994, p. 166.
18. Bal Gangadhar Tilak authored several books, the most well-known of them being the *Orion or Researches into the Antiquity of*

the Vedas, Arctic Home in the Vedas (1903) and the *Gītārahasya* (1915).

19. Vasant Kaiwar, "The Aryan Model of History and the Oriental Renaissance: The Politics of Identity in an Age of Revolutions, Colonialism and Nationalism", in Vasant Kaiwar and Sucheta Mazumdar, eds., *Antinomies of Modernity, Essays on Race, Orient, Nation*, Tulika Books, Delhi, 2003, p. 45.
20. Bhatt, op. cit, p. 36; Kaiwar, op. cit, p. 45.
21. Robert N. Minor, *Modern Indian Interpreters of the Bhagvadgītā*, Sri Satguru Publications, Delhi, 1991, pp. 44–60.
22. Kaiwar, op. cit., p. 42; Minor, op. cit., pp. 61–87.
23. V.D. Savarkar, *Hindutva: Who is a Hindu?*, Hindi Sahitya Sadan, Delhi, 2005, reprint, 1923, p. 3.
24. Savarkar, op. cit, pp. 11–2; Bhatt, op. cit., p. 87.
25. Savarkar, op. cit., p. 10.
26. Ibid., p. 92.
27. Ibid., p. 115
28. Pralay Kanungo, *RSS'S Tryst with Politics: From Hedgewar to Sudarshan*, Manohar, Delhi, 2002, p. 42.
29. Christophe Jaffrelot, *The Nationalist Movement and Indian Politics 1925 to the 1990s*, Panguin Books India, Delhi, 1996; idem, *Sangh Parivar: A Reader*, Oxford University Press, Delhi, 2007.
30. The martial brand of Hinduism represented by the RSS is buttressed by its hierachical and dictatorial organizational structure, and the daily morning/evening meeting of its basic unit called *shākhās* (branch) where the young recruits are imparted physical and mental training more or less on the model of the traditional *akhārā*, a place where the young men of a locality gather daily for body building, exercise and sports-mainly wrestling and weight-lifting (Jaffrelot, *Sangh Parivar*, pp. 2–5, 56–102).
31. Ibid., p. 97
32. Some years ago the RSS and the Hindu Right-wing parties tried to dissociate themselves from Golwalkar's book. But this has been based on falsehoods which generally go with their functioning (Shamsul Islam, *Golwalkar's We or Our Nation Defined: A Critique with the Text of the Book*, Pharos and Media Publishing, New Delhi, 2006, 44–52).
33. M.S. Golwalkar, *We or Our Nationhood Defined*, Bharat Publications, Nagpur, 1939, p. 6.
34. Ibid.
35. Golwalkar, *Bunch of Thoughts*, Sahitya Sindhu Prakashan,

Bangalore, 1966, pp. 59, 232, 363.
36. Ibid., p. 496.
37. Kanungo, op. cit., p. 126.
38. A.C. Das, *Ṛgvedic India*, University of Calcutta, Calcutta, 1971 [1920], pp. 22–3.
39. Susan Bayly, "Imagining 'Greater India': French and Indian Visions of Colonialism in the Indic Mode", *Modern Asian Studies*, vol. 38, no. 3 (2004), pp. 703–44. Among scholars directly involved in the establishment and activities of the Geater India Society were P.C. Bagchi, Suniti Kumar Chatterji, Phanindra Nath Bose, Kalidas Nag, U.N. Ghoshal, Nalinaksha Datta and R.C. Majumdar.
40. R.S. Sharma, "Communalism and India's past", *Social Scientist*, vol. 18, nos. 1–2 (1990), p. 6.
41. S.K. Srivastava, *Sir Jadunath Sarkar: The Historian at Work*, Anamika Prakashan, Delhi, 1989, p. 86.
42. Jadunath Sarkar, *Shivaji and His Times*, Orient Longman, Calcutta, 1973 [1919], p. 390.
43. Many pre-Islamic Sanskrit texts refer to the veiling of women. The word *avaguṇṭhana* (veil), for instance, occurs in the *Rāmāyaṇa* of Vālmīki, *Mudrārākṣasa* of Viśākhadatta, *Mṛchhakaṭika* of Śūdraka, *Abhjnānaśākuntalam* and *Kumārsambhava* of Kālidāsa, and *Veṇīsamhāra* of Bhaṭṭanārāyaṇa etc.; it is also mentioned at several places in a late text, the *Sāhityadarpaṇa* (15th century) of Viśvanātha Kavirāja. Pratibha Patil, the presidential candidate, was obviously ill advised to state publicly on 18 June 2007, that "the purdah system was introduced to protect them [women] from the Muslim invaders." *The Indian Express*, 19 June 2007.
44. A specialist in medieval Indian history tells us that the "Hindus in general were vegetarians...and abhorred beef" and the Muhammadans, on the other hand, "were almost cent per cent non-vegetarians, and were not prepared to give up cow slaughter and beef-eating." (A.L. Srivastava, *The Sultanate of Delhi*, 711–1526, Shivalal Agrawal and Company, Agra, 1984, p. vii).
45. See the website of the Vedic Foundation (USA).
46. BJP White Paper 1993
47. *The Hindu*, 8 February, 2013.
48. Rajeev Dhavan, "Ban, Burn and Destroy", *Outlook*, January 23, 2004
49. Romila Thapar, *A History of India*, vol. 1, Penguin, 1992 1966), p. 51; idem, *Early India: From Origins to 1300 AD*, University of California Press, 2002, p. 148.

50. The Husain controversy was triggered by Om Nagpal's article "Ye Chitrakar Hai Ya Kasai" published in *Vichār Mimānsā*, September, 1996. For a discussion of its various aspects see Monica Juneja, "Reclaiming the Public Sphere: Husain's Portrayals of Saraswati and Draupadi", *Economic and Political Weekly*, vol. 32, no. 4, January 25-31, 1997, pp. 155-7. Tapati Guha-Thakurta, *Monuments, Objects, Histories: Institutions of Art in Colonial and Postcolonial India*, Permanent Black, New Delhi, 2004, pp. 245-6. Rajeev Dhavan, *Harassing Husain: Uses and Abuses of the Law of Hate Speech*, Sahmat, Delhi, 2007.

2

Eternal India and Timeless Hinduism

D.N. Jha

The quest for India's national identity through the route of Hindu religious nationalism began in the nineteenth century and has continued ever since. In recent years, however, it has received an unprecedented boost from the communal forces which have brought a virulent version of Hindu cultural chauvinism to the centre stage of contemporary politics and produced a warped perception of India's past buttressed by a huge corpus of propaganda literature supporting the myth of Aryan autochthony, demonization of religious minorities (Muslims and Christians), and upholding the perception of India and Hinduism as eternal. There has been a crazy insistence on the idea that the people who composed the Vedas called themselves Aryans and were indigenous to India. They are also projected as the authors of the Harappan civilization[1] which the xenophobes and communalists have been trying to rechristen after the Vedic Saraswatī. Such views have received strong support from the paralogistic writings of Indian archaeologists like B.B. Lal[2] and foreign scholars like David Frawley; the latter, in his frenzied search for antiquity, even asserts that the history of Hinduism begins in an idyllic age initiated at the end of the last Ice Age along the banks of the "Vedic Saraswatī."[3]

The obduracy to prove that the Indian ("Hindu" is no different in the communal lexicon!) civilization is older than all others and was therefore free from any possible contamination in its early formative phase presents a historiographical format in which India, i.e., Bhārata, is timeless. The first man was born here; its people were the authors of the first human civilization, the Vedic (which is the same as the Indus-Saraswatī); they had reached the highest peak of achievement in both the arts and the sciences, and were conscious of belonging to the Indian nation, which has existed eternally. Views such as these are churned out of the cultural nationalist mill day in and day out, and are peddled to the credulous who accept them as a matter of faith. But, as I argue in the sequel, India as a country evolved over a long period, that the formation of its identity was linked with the changing perceptions of the people who migrated into the subcontinent at different times, and that Indian nationalism developed mostly as a response to Western imperialism.[4]

II

The geographical horizon of the early Aryans was limited to the north-western part of the Indian subcontinent, referred to as Saptasindhava,[5] and the word Bhārata in the sense of a country is absent from the entire Vedic literature, though the Bharata tribe is mentioned at several places in different contexts. In the *Aṣṭādhyāyī* of Pāṇini (500 BC) we find a reference to Prācya Bharata in the sense of a territory (*janapada*) which lay between *Udīcya* (north) and *Prācya* (east).[6] It must have been a small region occupied by the Bharatas and cannot be equated with the Akhaṇḍabhārata or Bhārata of the Hindutva camp. The earliest reference to Bhāratavarṣa (Prākrit *Bharadhavasa*) is found in the inscription of Khāravela (first century BC),[7] who lists it among the territories he invaded: but it did not include Magadha, which is mentioned separately in the record. The word may refer here in a general way to northern India, but its precise territorial connotation is vague. A much larger geographical region is visualized by the use of the word in the *Mahābhārata* (200 BC to 300 AD), which provides a good deal of geographical information about the subcontinent, although a large part of the Deccan and the far south does not find any place in it. Among the five divisions of Bhāratavarṣa named, Madhyadeśa finds frequent mention in ancient Indian texts; in the *Amarakośa* (also known as the *Nāmalingānuśāsana*), a work of the fourth or fifth centuries, it is used synonymously with Bhārata and *Āryāvarta*;[8] the latter, according to its eleventh-century commentator Kṣīrasvāmin, being the same as Manu's holy land situated between the Himalayas and the Vindhya range.[9] But in Bāṇa's *Kādambarī* (seventh century), at one place, Bhāratavarṣa is said to have been ruled by Tārāpīḍa, who "set his seal on the four oceans" (*dattacatuḥsamudramudraḥ*);[10] and at another, Ujjaini is indicated as being outside Bhāratavarṣa,[11] which leaves its location far from clear. Similarly, in the *Nıtivakyāmṛta* of Somadeva (tenth century), the word *bhāratīyāḥ* cannot be taken to mean anything more than the inhabitants of Bhārata, which itself remains undefined.[12]

Bhāratavarṣa figures prominently in the Purāṇas, but they describe its shape variously. In some passages, it is likened to a half-moon, in others it is said to resemble a triangle; in yet others it appears as a rhomboid or an unequal quadrilateral or a drawn bow.[13] The *Mārkaṇḍeya Purāṇa* compares the shape of the country with that of a tortoise floating on water and facing east.[14] Most of the *Purāṇas* describe Bhāratavarṣa as being divided into nine *dvīpas* or *khaṇḍas*, which, being separated by seas, were mutually inaccessible. The Purāṇic conception of Bhāratavarṣa has much correspondence with the ideas of ancient Indian astronomers like Varāhamihira (sixth century AD) and Bhāskarācārya (eleventh century). However, judging from their identifications of the rivers, mountains, regions and places mentioned in the Purāṇas, as well as from their rare references to areas south of the Vindhyas, their idea of Bhāratavarṣa does not seem to have included southern India. Although a few inscriptions of the tenth and eleventh centuries indicate that Kuntala (Karnataka) was situated in the land of Bhārata,[15] which is described in a fourteenth-century record as extending from the Himalayas to the southern sea,[16] by and large the available textual and epigraphic references to it do not indicate that the term stood for India as we know it today.

An ambiguous notion of Bhārata is also found in the *Abhidhānacintāmaṇi* of the Jain scholar Hemacandra (twelfth century), who describes it as the land of *karma* (*karmabhūmi*), as opposed to that of *phala* (*phalabhūmi*).[17] Although he does not clarify what is meant by the two, his definition of *Āryāvarta* (which may correspond with Bhārata) is the same as that found in Manu.[18] In fact, *Āryāvarta* figures more frequently than Bhārata in the geohistorical discourses found in early Indian texts. It was only from the 1860s that the name Bhāratavarṣa, in the sense of the whole subcontinent, found its way into the popular vocabulary. Its visual evocation came perhaps not earlier than 1905 in a painting by Abanindranath Tagore, who conceived of the image as one of Bangamātā but later, "almost as an act of generosity towards the larger cause of Indian nationalism, decided to title it 'Bhāratmātā'".[19] Thus it was only from the sixties and seventies of the nineteenth century that the notion of Bhārata was "forged by the self-conscious appropriation and transposition of discourse at once British-colonial, historical, geographical and ethnological, as well as received Purāṇic chronotopes".[20]

In many texts, Bhārata is said to have been a part of Jambūdvīpa, which itself had an uncertain geographical connotation. The Vedic texts do not mention it; nor does Pāṇini, though he refers to the *jambū* (the rose apple tree).[21] The early Buddhist canonical works provide the earliest reference to the continent called Jambūdvīpa (Jambūdīpa),[22] its name being derived from the *jambū* tree which grew there (having a height of one hundred *yojanas*, a trunk fifteen *yojanas* in girth and branches spreading to fifty *yojanas* in length), whose shade extended to one hundred *yojanas*.[23] It was one of the four *mahādīpas* (*mahādvīpas*) ruled by a Cakkavattī. We are told that Buddhas and Cakkavattīs were born only in Jambūdīpa, whose people were more courageous, mindful and religious than the inhabitants of Uttarakuru.[24] Going by the descriptions of Jambūdīpa and Uttarakuru in the early Buddhist literature, they both appear to be mythical regions. However, juxtaposed with Sihaladīpa (Sinhaladvīpa=Sri Lanka), Jambūdīpa stands for India.[25] Aśoka thus uses the word to mean the whole of his empire, which covered nearly the entire Indian subcontinent excluding its far southern part.[26]

Ambiguity about the territorial connotation of Jambūdvīpa continued during subsequent centuries in both epigraphic and literary sources. In a sixth-century inscription of Toramāṇa, for instance, Jambūdvīpa occurs without any precise territorial connotation.[27] Similarly, the identification of Jambūdvīpa remains uncertain in the Purāṇic cosmological schema, where it appears more as a mythical region than as a geographical entity. The world, according to the Purāṇas, "consists of seven concentric *dvīpas* or islands, each of which is encircled by a sea, the central island called Jambūdvīpa...".[28] This is similar to the cosmological imaginings of the Jains who, however, placed Jambūdvīpa at the centre of the central land (*madhyaloka*) of the three-tiered structure of the universe.[29] According to another Purāṇic conception, which is similar to the Buddhist cosmological ideas, the earth is divided into four *mahādvīpas*, Jambūdvīpa being larger than the others.[30] In both these conceptions of the world, Bhāratavarṣa is at some places said to be a part of Jambūdvīpa but at others the two are treated as identical.[31] Since these differently imagined geographical conceptions of Bhārata and Jambūdvīpa are of questionable value, to insist that their inhabitants formed a nation in ancient times is sophistry. It legitimates the Hindutva perception of Indian national identity as located in remote antiquity, accords centrality to the supposed primordiality of Hinduism and thus spawns Hindu cultural nationalism. All this draws sustenance from, a systematic abuse of archaeology by a number of scholars, notably B.B. Lal.[32]

III

Those obsessed with the incredible antiquity of the Indian nation, have also created several stereotypes about Hinduism over the years, especially recently; and these have percolated down to textbooks. A few sample statements from two books, randomly picked from among a large number, adequately illustrate the point:

> Hinduism [is] a *very* old religion ... sanatana dharma i.e. the Eternal Spiritual Tradition of India.[33] The Vedas are ... recognised ... as the most ancient literature in the world. The term 'sanatana' is often used to highlight this quality[34] ... freedom of thought and form of worship is unique to Hinduism[35]... In Hindu history no example of coercion or conversion can be found[36]... there is no conflict [in Hinduism] between science and religion.[37]

The above passage contains several clichés which lend support to militant Hindu cultural nationalism. One of these—the imagined "oldness" of what has come to be known as Hinduism—has been a parrot-cry of Hindu rightist groups and needs to be examined in the light of historical evidence. It is not necessary to go into the etymological peregrinations of the word "Hindu", derived from "Sindhu", on which much has been written; suffice it to say that the earliest use of the word, as is well known, can be traced back to the *Zend Avesta*, which speaks of Hapta Hindu (identical with the Ṛgvedic Saptasindhava) as one of the sixteen regions created by Ahur Mazda. The word retained its territorial connotation for a long time and did not acquire any religious dimension. According to one scholar, [38] the earliest use of the word "Hindu" in a religious sense is found in the account of Hsüan Tsang, who tells us that the bright light of "holy men and sages, guiding the world as the shining of the moon, have made this country eminent and so it is called In-tu"[39] (the Chinese name for India being Indu, moon). But the religious affiliation, if any, of these "holy men and sages" remains unknown, which hardly supports the view that Hsüan Tsang used the word In-tu (Hindu) in a specifically religious sense: indeed, the later Chinese pilgrim I-tsing questioned the veracity of the statement that it was a common name for the country.[40] Similarly, the suggestion that the use of the word "Hindu" in a religious sense began immediately after the conquest of Sind by Muhammad ibn Qasim in 712 is unacceptable. It has been asserted that the "Hindu" was "now identified on a religious basis" and that "conversion from this Hindu religion" was now possible.[41] The sources bearing on eighth-century Sind indicate the existence of several non-Islamic religions and sects of

Brāhmaṇism and Buddhism denoted by the Arabic compound *barhimah-sumaniyah* used by the classical Muslim writers,[42] but the word "Hindu" in their writings had a geographic, linguistic, or ethnic connotation. In the *Chachnāma*, for example, *hinduvān* means Indians in general and *hindavī* stands for the Indian language.[43] The word "Hindu" continued to have several meanings in subsequent times. The classical Persian poets used the word in various senses—the black complexion of the Indian, the beloved's tresses, a mole on the cheek, or the planet Sarurn—to describe anything black.[44] "Hindu" also implied slavery in contradistinction to the Turkish rulership but Sultan Mahmūd's protégé Firdausī, in his *Shāhnāma*, portrayed Alexander the Great as addressing a letter to an Indian ruler with the salutation "Best of the Hindus, wise, knowing and clear minded."[45] The wide range of connotations of the term in classical Persian thus presents a conundrum, though Alberuni, another protégé of Mahmūd, is widely believed to be the first to have mentioned it as a religious designation in his *Kitāb-al-Hind* written in Arabic (AD 1030).[46]

Alberuni evinced a sustained interest in Indian religion and philosophy and translated a number of Sanskrit works into Arabic (including portions of Patañjali's *Yogasūtra* and the *Bhagvadgītā*). He states that "they (Hindus) totally differ from us in religion"[47] and distinguishes them from Buddhists at one place but holds the distinction to be between Śramaṇs (Buddhists) and brahmaṇs at another.[48] His understanding seems to have been limited to brāhmaṇical religious beliefs and practices, and, if he used the word "Hindu" in religious sense,[49] its meaning remains far from clear and coherent.[50] It is therefore not possible to credit him with any definite and essentialist view of a Hindu religion,[51] much less treat his perception of it as a landmark in the development of Hindu religious identity. The ambivalence surrounding the word "Hindu", in fact, continued for a long time. Even three centuries after him, Ziāuddīn Baranī (1285–1357), in his major historical work on medieval India, *Tārīkh-i-Firūzshāhī*, makes frequent references to Hindus (Hunūd and Hindu'ān) either as a religious category or as a political one and sometimes as both,[52] and his contemporary, 'Abdal Malik' Iṣāmī, in his *Futūhu-s-Salāṭīn* (1350), uses "Hindu" in the sense of the follower of the Hindu religion without discussing its connotation.[53] In the sixteenth century, despite Akbar's familiarity with and patronage of non-Islamic religions of India, Abū-l Faẓl could do no better than "merely give resumés of Brahmanism ... presumably because this was the most prestigious"[54] and these are nowhere near the notion of a Hindu religion. Half a century after his death, the author[55] of the *Dabistān-i-Mazāhib*, who claimed to present a survey of all religions and sects, devoted one full chapter to the religion of the Hindus and other Indian sects but failed to provide a clear understanding of what was intended by the use of the term "Hindu". In his work, the word means the orthodox brāhmaṇical groups ("*smartians*") as well as the non-Islamic belief systems of various schools, sects, castes and religions of India. At some places the rubric "Hindu" includes Jains and at others it excludes them, along with the Yogīs, Sanyāsīs, Tapasīs and Cārvākas.[56] In the eighteenth century, Mirzā Mazhar Jan-I Janan (1699–1781), a prominent revivalist thinker and a major figure in the late *naqshbandī* Sufism, tried to explain some aspects of Hindu religious beliefs and practices through the prism of distinctly Islamic categories.[57] But a vagueness in the connotation of the word "Hindu" seems to have continued so that his contemporary Alī Muhammad Khān (1761) in his *Mirāt-i-Ahmadī*, uses it "as a term of reference for people of all religions, castes, sub-castes, and professions who can be classified as a group different from the Muslims" and "reckons the Jain clergy (Shevra) and the laity (Shravak) as Hindus even though he is aware of the difference in the religious persuasions of, as well as the antagonism between, the Jains and the Vaishnavites (Maishris)".[58] The fuzziness of definitions of "Hindu" and "Hinduism" is thus unquestionable and it derives largely from the fact that Arabic and Persian scholarship describes all non-Muslim Indians as Hindus.

What possibly added to the ambiguity surrounding the word is the fact that no Indians described themselves as Hindus before the fourteenth century. The earliest use of the word in the Sanskrit language occurs in a 1352 inscription of Bukka, the second ruler of Vijayanagara's first dynasty, who described himself with a series of titles, one of them being *hindurāya suratrāṇa* (Sultan among Hindu kings). His successors continued to use this title for 250 years, "until as late as the opening years of the seventeenth century."[59] In north India, Rāṇa Kumbha was the first to style himself as *hindusuratrāṇa* in an inscription dated 1439[60] to be followed more than two centuries later by Harihar Sen, a ruler of Nepal, who claimed the title *hindupati*.[61] Despite the use of the title by royalty, the word *hindu* does not occur in the mainstream Sanskrit literature until the early nineteenth century, with the rare exceptions of Jonarāja's *Rājataranginī*[62] (1455–9), which uses the word as part of the compound *hindughoṣa*, and Śrīvara's *Jain Rājataranginī* (1459–77), which refers to the social customs of the Hindus (*hindukasamācāra*)[63] and their language (*hindsthānavācā*)[64] as distinct from the Persian language (*pārasībhāsayā*) and also mentions a place called Hinduvāḍā[65] (modern Hindubata, 15 miles north of Sopore). The three Sanskrit texts of the Gauḍīya Vaiṣṇava tradition, ranging from the early sixteenth to the late eighteenth centuries, do not mention the word "Hindu" at all;[66] nor does it occur in the *Brahmasūtra* commentary written by the famous Gauḍīya Vaiṣṇava *ācārya* Baladeva Vidyābhūṣaṇa (1750).[67] It was not before the first half of the nineteenth century that the word "Hindu" begins to appear in the Sanskrit texts produced as a result of Christianity's encounters with brāhmaṇical religion. Among the religious debates and disputations of the early nineteenth century centring round the alleged superiority of Christianity vis-à-vis Brāhmaṇism, an important controversy was generated by John Muir's evangelist critique published as *Mataparīkṣā* (in Sanskrit) in 1839, which provoked three Indian pandits to defend their religion.[68] One of them, Haracandra Tarkapancānana, in his reply to Muir, impugned him as *hindudharmātivairin* (Hinduism's great foe)[69] and laid down conditions for becoming "eligible [*adhikārin*] for [Vedic] *dharma*, having become Hindus [*hindutvam prāpya*] in a subsequent birth."[70] But generally the occurrence of the word "Hindu" in Sanskrit texts remained rare, and the two nineteenth-century Bengali encyclopedists, Radhākānta Deb (1783–1867)[71] and Tārānātha Tarkavācaspati (1811–85)[72], could not cite any text other than the obscure and very late *Merutantra* (eighteenth century);[73] and they provided an extremely specious etymology of the word[74] based on it.

The word "Hindu" is rarely seen in the medieval vernacular *bhakti* literature as well. An examination of the ten Gauḍīya Vaiṣṇava texts in Bengali, ranging from the sixteenth to the eighteenth centuries, shows that it occurs forty-one times, and *Hindudharma* seven times, in the 80,000 couplets of only five of the ten texts. Apart from the small number of occurrences, the interesting aspect of the evidence is that there is no explicit discussion of what "Hindu" or *Hindudharma* means.[75] The word "Hindu" is also used in different contexts by the poet Vidyāpāti (1360–1450) in his *Kīrtilatā*,[76] medieval saint Kabīr (1450–1520) in his songs, Nānak (1469–1539) in his teachings, Ekanāth (1533–99) in his *Hindu-turka Samvāda*[77], Anantadās (sixteenth century) in his *Kabīr Parcai*[78], and many others. On this basis a scholar has argued that a Hindu religious identity defined itself primarily in opposition to Muslims and Islam and had a continuous existence through the medieval period.[79] This argument, however, is seriously flawed for it is based on the assumption that all non-Muslims were part of the postulated unified conceptual identity. It also ignores the basic fact that the medieval *sants* and *bhakti* poets used the term "Hindu" with reference to adherents of the caste-centric brāhmaṇical religion, against which they raised their voice.[80] The general absence of the words "Hindu" and *Hindudharma* in the precolonial Sanskrit texts and their limited connotation in the not-too-frequent occurrences in the *bhakti* literature clearly indicate that Indians did not create a Hindu religious identity for themselves, as is argued by some. Of course the word was in use in precolonial India, but it was not before the late eighteenth or early nineteenth centuries that it was appropriated by Western, especially British, scholars[81] whose writings helped the imperial administration to formulate and create the notion of Hinduism in the sense in which we understand it today. The British borrowed the word

"Hindu" from India, gave it a new meaning and significance, reimported it into India as a reified phenomenon called Hinduism, [82] and used it in censuses and gazetteers as a category in their classification of the Indian people,[83] paving the way for the global Hindu religious identity—a process perceptively equated with the "pizza effect", basically meaning that the Neapolitan hot baked bread exported to America returned with all its embellishments to Italy to become its national dish.[84] Given this background, Hinduism was a creation of the colonial period and cannot lay claim to any great antiquity.[85] Contrary to the view of those who locate its origins in the Indus valley civilization and in what they call Aryan culture,[86] Hinduism is among the youngest of religions, a nineteenth-century neologism popularised by the British.[87] That it has come to stay, despite the endless ambiguities of connotation in it,[88] is a different matter.

IV

Even though Hinduism as a religious category acquired much visibility in Christian missionary writings and in British administrative records,[89] not until the nineteenth century did it come to be labelled *sanātanadharma*. The term can be translated in a variety of ways: "eternal religion" or "eternal law,"[90] "unshakeable, venerable order",[91] "ancient and continuing guideline"[92] and "the eternal order or way of life"[93] are some of its English equivalents. It has been used by a variety of representatives of modern Hinduism, ranging from Ramakrishna-Vivekananda and Radhakrishnan to the leaders and followers of reform movements as well as their opponents. Although some scholars have tried to project it as having a "dynamic character", *sanātanadharma*[94] was basically an orthodox resistance to reform movements[95] and drew on references in ancient Indian literature. The earliest occurrence of the term is found in the Buddhist canonical work *Dhammapada*, according to which the eternal law (*esa dhamma sanātano*)[96] is that hatred and enmities cease through love alone; but it is mentioned frequently in the brāhmaṇical texts. The *Mahābhārata* often uses the expression *eṣa dharmaḥ sanātanaḥ* "as a sanctioning formula intended to emphasize the obligatory nature of social and religious rules",[97] but its use to justify Śvetaketu's mother's being snatched away by a brāhmaṇ would be far from palatable to modern sanatanists.[98] The *Gīta* uses the term in the plural to mean the "venerable norms for the families" (*kuladharmāḥ sanātanāḥ*)[99] and describes Kṛṣṇa as "protector of the established norms" (*śāśvatadharmagoptā sanātanaḥ*).[100] Similarly, in the law book of Manu, *sanātanadharma* stands for established "customs and statutes of the countries, castes and families, though the Purāṇas use the term in various senses. According to the *Matsyapurāṇa* it is rooted in virtues like the absence of greed and attachment, the practice of celibacy, forgiveness, compassion for living beings, etc.[101] The *Varāhapurāṇa* at one place refers to the eternal *dharma* promulgated by Varāha,[102] and, at another, states that according to the eternal law one should not sink into grief on seeing the fortunes of others and one's own distress (*eṣa dharmaḥ sanātanaḥ*).[103] In another Purāṇa, Śiva defines his eternal *dharma* (*dharmaḥ sanātanaḥ*)[104] as consisting of *jñāna, kriyā, caryā* and *yoga*, though in several epic and Purāṇic passages *sanātana* is used as an epithet for divinities like Kṛṣṇa, or for Dharma, who himself is thought of as a deity. The *Uttararāmacarita* of Bhavabhūti (eighth century), the earliest secular work to refer to *sanātanadharma*, mentions it in the sense of fixed laws and customs and the Khanapur plates (sixth century), which contain the earliest epigraphic reference to it, use it in speaking of rites and rituals prescribed by *śruti* and *smṛti* (*śrutismṛtivihitasanātanadharmakar-maniratāya*).[105] Although these textual references provide different connotations of the term *sanātanadharma*, it has generally been understood in the sense of traditionally established customs and duties of countries, castes and families also in texts as late as the *Mahānirvaṇatantra* (eighteenth century), by an unknown author, and the *Śāstratattvavinirṇaya* (1844) of Nilakaṇṭha (Nehemia) Goreh. But when, in the nineteenth century, it emerged as a key concept in traditionalist self-assertion against Christianity as well as in the reform movements (Brahmosamaj and Aryasamaj), it came to be stereotyped as a venerable, "eternal", "all encompassing" and "inclusive" (*sarvavyāpaka*) religion, "with no temporal beginning, no historical founding figure", one which needed no innovations or reforms.[106] This added to the conceptual opacity and vagueness of the "timeless religion", which had to wait for its first codification by the Englishwoman Annie Besant who, in collaboration with Indian scholars like Bhagwan Das, drew up a textbook[107] on *sanātanadharma* for use at the Central Hindu College, Benares, whose establishment in 1898 owed much to her initiative.

V

Hinduism has often been viewed not only as eternal (*sanātanadharma*) but also as a monolithic religion in which there is "agreement about some static universal doctrine."[108] This stereotype has received support not only from Hindu right wing political groups but also from serious scholars of religion who define Hinduism as "the religion of those humans who create, perpetuate, and transform traditions with legitimising reference to the authority of the Vedas."[109] An early, though indirect, endorsement of the legitimizing authority of the Vedas comes from Yāska (fifth century BC), who describes Vedic "seers" as "having attained a direct experience of *dharma*" (*sākṣātkṛtadharma*).[110] Later, Manu categorically states that "the root of religion is the entire Veda" (*vedo'khilo dharmamūlam*),[111] and that the authority of the *śruti* and the *smṛti* is not to be questioned or reasoned about (*amimāṃsya*).[112] His assertion has received much support over time from the different philosophical systems, though their apologetic patterns have varied considerably. Nyāya and Vaiśeṣika, though not affiliated to the Veda, recognized it as a "source of knowledge" (*pramāṇa*), and their leading early medieval thinkers (Uddyotakara, Vācaspatimiśra and Udayana) defended it.[113] Much stronger support for the Vedic texts, however, came from the Mimāṃsā, whose "genuine affiliation with, and commitment to, the Veda are generally accepted."[114] Mimāṃsā thinkers like Kumārila, Prabhākara and Maṇḍanamiśra (all of the eighth century), for example, laid great emphasis on the principle that the *dharma* is justified by the Veda alone (*vedamūlatva*).[115] Similarly, Śaṅkara (eighth century) treated all the declarations of the Veda as authoritative[116] and defiance of it (*vedavirodha*) as heresy.[117] Indeed, the acceptance of the authority of the Vedas is an important feature of brāhmaṇical orthodoxy, but their number being only four, an amorphous category of the "fifth Veda" came into being as early as the later Vedic period,[118] leading to an open-endedness in the Vedic corpus, a phenomenon also in keeping with the general absence of and aversion to writing and the brāhmaṇical preference for the oral transmission of all knowledge.[119] The *Mahābhārata*,[120] the Purāṇas[121] and the Tantras[122] are called the "fifth Veda", just as the large body of Tamil devotional hymns in the Śaiva and Vaiṣṇava traditions, ranging in date from the sixth to the ninth centuries, claimed Vedic status.[123] Many religious teachers holding different opinions sought to legitimize their teachings with reference to the Vedas during the medieval period. Acceptance of the authority of the Vedas is in fact an important feature even of modern Hindu revivalist movements like the Arya Samaj of Dayananda.[124] But all this cannot be construed to mean that Hinduism acquired a monolithic character: for it has rightly been pointed out that allegiance to the Vedas was very often a fiction, nothing more than a mere "raising of the hat, in passing, to an idol by which one no longer intends to be encumbered later on."[125]

There is substantial evidence to show that the Vedas did not always enjoy a pre-eminent position in brāhmaṇical Hinduism or even outside it.[126] Anti-Vedic ideas, in fact, began to find expression in the *Ṛgveda* itself. The famous Ṛgvedic passage which equated brāhmaṇs with croaking frogs was an early attempt to ridicule the Vedas and their reciters.[127] In addition to the satirization of the brāhmaṇs, there is also evidence of the questioning of Vedic knowledge: "Who is the god whom we should worship with the oblation" (*kaṣmai devāya haviṣā vidhema*);[128] "Whence this creation developed is known only by him who witnesses this world in the highest heaven—or perhaps even he does not know."[129] At several places in the *Ṛgveda*, the very existence of the most important Vedic god Indra is questioned.[130] Thus in a hymn to Indra it is said: "to Indra, if Indra exists,"[131] and in another the question is asked: "about whom they ask, where is he? ... And they say about him, 'he is not'..."[132] Scepticism about the Vedic sacrifice was expressed by reviling it at the end of the *mahāvrata* Soma festival, as is evident from several Ṛgvedic passages.[133] In fact, the sanctity of the Vedas began to be questioned soon after their composition. The Upaniṣads contain several passages which deprecate the Vedas. The *Muṇḍaka Upaniṣad*, for example, regards the four Vedas as "lower knowledge" (*aparāvidyā*).[134] Similarly, in the *Nirukta*, Yāska (sixth to the fifth centuries BC) describes Kautsa as saying that "the Vedic stanzas have no meaning (*anarthaka*)" and that "their meaning is contradictory (*vipratisiddhārta*)."[135] Indications of the undermining of Vedic rituals are also found in the dharmaśāstra texts, which have been the main vehicle of Vedic thought. Baudhāyana, for instance, cites the view that "non-Vedic local practices may be allowed in their own territory", though his own opinion is that "one must never follow practices opposed to the tradition of learned authorities."[136] A general unwillingness to concede a legitimizing role to the Veda manifested itself in many texts representing the various strands of brāhmaṇical thought. For example, in the *Bhagavadgītā*, which has been the most popular Hindu religious text through the centuries, Kṛṣṇa tells Arjuna in unambiguous terms that those who delight in the eulogistic statements of the Vedas (*vedavādaratāḥ*) are full of worldly desires (*kāmātmānaḥ*),[137] and that the desire-ridden followers (*kāmakāmāḥ*) of the Vedic sacrificial rites stagnate in the world.[138] The Purāṇas often undermine the supremacy of the Vedas despite their general allegiance to them. While one Purāṇic text tells us that God thought of the Purāṇas before he spoke the Vedas, others state that the Vedas are "established" on the Purāṇas.[139] "There is no higher essence or truth than this", the *Agnipurāṇa* tells us, and "... there is no better book, ... there is no better *śāstra*, or *śruti* or ... *smṛti* ... for this Purāṇa is supreme."[140] The *Bhāgavatapurāṇa* was similarly said to have superseded and transcended the Vedas, and Jīva Goswāmī (sixteenth century) of the Gauḍīya Vaiṣṇava school vehemently denied that this text was based on them at all.[141] Despite the fact that the authors of the Tantric texts tried to base their doctrines on the Vedas, they also undermined their authority. For example, the *Mahānirvāṇatantra*, an eighteenth-century work, states that the Vedas, Purāṇas and śāstras are of no use in the *kaliyuga*[142] and "declares that all of the other religious traditions are encompassed by and disappear within the Tantric *kuladharma*, just as the tracks of all other animals disappear within the tracks of the elephant."[143] All this may not amount to a repudiation of the Vedas, but it certainly indicates that all post-Vedic brāhmaṇical religious traditions did not look to them for legitimacy.

Several religious movements within the fold of what is now known as Hinduism in fact rejected the authority both of the brāhmaṇs and that of the Vedas. Vīraśaivism, a Śaivite sect whose followers are also called Lingāyats and which gained prominence in Karnataka in the twelfth century, is a case in point. Its hagiographical texts bear ample testimony to the fact that, at least in the early phase, the Vīraśaivas ridiculed the Vedas and unequivocally rejected them.[144] Similarly, the adherents of the south Indian Śrīvaiṣṇava sect of Tenkalai rejected the Vedas and composed their own Veda, called the *Nālāyiraprabandham*.[145] This rejection of Vedic authority seems to have been a feature of other medieval religious movements as well. The Mahānubhāvas in Maharashtra and the Sahajiyas in Bengal also renounced the Vedas. So did individual medieval *bhakti* saints like Kabīr (fifteenth to the sixteenth centuries) and Tukārām (seventeenth century), to name only two.[146] As recently as the nineteenth century, precisely at the time when Dayananda Saraswati was propagating that the Vedas are the repository of all knowledge, Ramakrishna rejected them and said: "the truth is not in the Vedas, one should act according to the Tantras, not according to the Vedas, the latter are impure from the very fact of their being pronounced."[147] Evidently, thus, different religious sects have not had the same attitude towards the Vedic corpus, and even the texts of specific sectarian affiliations often express contradictory views about it. This being so, the stereotype of a monolithic Hinduism based on the Vedas must be seen as a myth deliberately propagated both by some scholars as well as by right wing Hindu groups, all of whom not only ignore the plurality of religious beliefs and practices covered by the umbrella term "Hinduism", invented in the colonial period, but who also deny the centuries-long process of their evolution.

ENDNOTES

1. N. Prinja, *Explaining Hindu Dharma: A Guide for Teachers*, Vishwa Hindu Parishad (UK), Norfolk, 1996, p. 10, cited in Sudeshna Guha, "Negotiating Evidence: History, Archaeology and the Indus Civilisation", *Modern Asian Studies*, vol. 39, no. 2, 2005, p. 399.
2. S.P. Gupta, *The Indus-Saraswati Civilization: Origins, Problems and Issues*, Pratibha Prakashan, Delhi, 1996, p. 142; B.B. Lal, "Rigvedic Aryans: The Debate Must Go On", *East and West*, vol. 48, nos. 3–4 (December 1998), pp. 439–48. For a rebuttal of Lal, see Ram Sharan Sharma, "Identity of the Indus Culture", *East and West*, vol. 49, nos. 1–4 (December 1999), pp. 35–45; Irfan Habib, "Imagining River Saraswati—A Defence of Commonsense", *Proceedings*, Indian History Congress, 61st session, Kolkata, 2001, pp. 65–92. Sudeshna Guha, op. cit., pp. 399–426.
3. Reza M. Pirbhai, "Demons in Hindutva: Writing a Theology for Hindu Nationalism", *Modern Intellectual History*, vol. 5, no. 1, 2008, p. 41
4. It is surprising that even some serious and respected historians tell us that the Purāṇic authors considered the inhabitants of the subcontinent as forming a nation and could be called "Bhāratī": B.N. Mukherjee, *Nationhood and Statehood in India: A Historical Survey*, Regency Publications, New Delhi, 2001, p. 6; Rajat Kanta Ray, *The Felt Community: Community and Mentality before the Emergence of Indian Nationalism*, Oxford University Press, New Delhi, 2004, pp. 49, 55 and p. 180 notes 33, 34.
5. *Ṛgveda*, VIII, 24, 27. This is the only Ṛgvedic passage where the word *saptasindhava* is used in the sense of territory; at all other places in the *Ṛgveda* it is used to mean the seven rivers (A.A. Macdonell and A.B. Keith, *Vedic Index of Names and Subjects*, Indian reprint, Motilal Banarsidass, Delhi, 1958, II, p. 324).
6. *Aṣṭādhyāyī*, IV.2.113. (ed. and trans., Srish Chandra Vasu, Motilal Banarsidass, Delh, 1962).
7. D.C. Sircar, *Select Inscriptions: Bearing on Indian History and Civilization*, I, Calcutta University, 1965, no. 91, line 10.

8. Krishnaji Govind Oka, ed., *The Nāmalingānuśāsana: Amarakośa of Amarasiṃha* (with the commentary of Kṣīrasvāmin), Law Printing Press, Poona, 1913; Upasana Prakashan, Delhi, 1981, p. 47.
9. *Manusmṛti*, II.22 (ed. V.N. Mandalik, Ganapat Krishnaji Press, Bombay, 1886). According to the *Kauṣītaki Upaniṣad* (II.13), āryavarta was bounded on the west by Adarsana near Kurukṣetra and on the east by Kālakavana near Allahabad. (S. Radhakrishnan, *The Principal Upaniṣads*, Motilal Banarsidass, Delhi, 1991).
10. *Kādambarī*, ed. & tr. M.R. Kale, Oxford University Press, Delhi, 1968, p. 290; V.S. Agrawal, *Kādambarī: Ek Sānskritik Adhyayan*, Chowkhamba, Varanasi, 1958, p. 188.
11. *Kādambarī*, p. 311; V.S. Agrawal, op. cit., 1958, p. 205.
12. *Nītivākyāmṛtam* of Somadeva Suri, *Prakīrṇaka* 78 (ed. & tr. Sudhir Kumar Gupta, Prakrita Bharati Academy, Jaipur, 1987).
13. S.M. Ali, *The Geography of the Purāṇas*, People's Publishing House, New Delhi, 1966, p. 109.
14. Ibid.
15. For references, see Israt Alam, "Names for India in Ancient Indian Texts and Inscriptions", in Irfan Habib, ed., *India: Studies in the History of an Idea*, Munshiram Manoharlal, Delhi, 2005, p. 43.
16. *Epigraphia Indica*, XIV, no. 3, lines 5–6.
17. IV.12. *Abhidhānacintāmaṇi*, with Hindi Commentary, ed., Haragovind Sastri, Varanasi, 1964, p. 235.
18. Ibid., IV.14.
19. Sugata Bose, "Nation as Mother: Representations and Contestations of 'India' in Bengali Literature, " in Sugata Bose and Ayesha Jalal, eds., *Nationalism, Democracy and Development: State and Politics in India*, Oxford University Press, Delhi, 1997, pp. 53–4. For a discussion of the Tamil mother and Bhāratamātā, see Sumathi Ramaswamy, "The Goddess and the Nation: Subterfuges of Antiquity, the Cunning of Modernity", in Gavin Flood, ed., *The Blackwell Companion to Hinduism*, Indian reprint, Blackwell, 2003, pp. 551–68.
20. Manu Goswami, *Producing India*, Permanent Black, Delhi, 2004, chapters 5 and 6.
21. *Aṣṭādhyāyī*, IV.3.165.
22. G.P. Malalasekera, *Dictionary of Pāli Proper Names*, II, 1st Indian edition, Delhi, 1983, pp. 941–2, sv. Jambudipa.
23. Ibid., p. 941.
24. Ibid., p. 942.
25. *Mahāvamsa*, V.13 (ed., W. Geiger, London, 1958); *Cūlavamsa*,

XXXVII. 216, 246 (tr. W. Geiger, Delhi, 1996); Malalasekera, op. cit., p. 942.

26. Sircar, *Select Inscriptions*, no. 2, line 2.
27. Ibid., no. 56, line 9.
28. D.C. Sircar, *Studies in the Geography of Ancient and Medieval India*, Motilal Banarsidass, Delhi, 1960, pp. 8–9.
29. Pravin Chandra Jain and Darbarilal Kothia, eds., *Jaina Purāṇa Kośa* (in Hindi), Jain Vidya Samsthan, Srimahavirji, Rajasthan, 1993, pp. 256, 259. According to some it is divided into six parts (*khaṇḍas*), of which one is *āryakhaṇḍa* and is the same as Bhārata, the remaining five being *mlecchakhaṇḍas*. Among the Jain texts, the *Jambūdvīpaprajñapti* provides the most detailed account of Jambūdvīpa and Bhārata. See *Jambūddivpaññattisuttam*, ed. Kanhailalji Kamal et al., Shri Agam Prakashan Samiti, Vyavara, Rajasthan, 1986. The Jain texts had several geographical categories in common with the Purāṇic ones, but they had many unique spatio-temporal conceptions too.
30. Ibid., p. 9, note 1.
31. D.C. Sircar, *Geography of Ancient and Medieval India*, pp. 6, 8.
32. B.B. Lal, *The Earliest Civilization of South Asia: Rise, Maturity and Decline*, Aryan Books International, Delhi, 1997; idem, *The Saraswati Flows On*, Aryan Books International, Delhi, 2002; S.P. Gupta, *The Indus-Saraswati Civilization: Origins, Problems and Issues*, Pratibha Prakashan, Delhi, 1996; For a reasoned critique of their views, see K.M. Shrimali, "Constructing an Identity: Forging Hinduism into Harappan Religions", *Social Science Probings*, vol. 15, nos.1–2 (2003), pp. 1–59; Sudeshna Guha, "Negotiating Evidence: History, Archaeology and The Indus Civilisation", *Modern Asian Studies*, vol. 39, no. 2 (2005), pp. 399-426.
33. Makhan Lal et al., *India and the World for Class VI*, National Council of Educational Research and Training, New Delhi, September 2002, p. 133.
34. Nawal K. Prinja, *Explaining Hindu Dharma: A Guide for Teachers*, Vishwa Hindu Parishad, Norwich, 1996, p. 7. The book was produced by the Vishwa Hindu Parishad. The history textbooks used in the RSS-run Shishu Mandirs and other schools abound in similar pearls of wisdom about Hinduism.
35. Ibid., p. 13.
36. Ibid., p. 54.
37. Ibid., p. 153.

38. Arvind Sharma, "Of Hindu, Hindustan, Hinduism and Hindutva", *Numen*, vol. 49 (2002), pp. 3–4.
39. Samuel Beal, *Si-Yu-Ki: Buddhist Records of the Western World*, Delhi, 1969, p. 69.
40. J. Takakusu, tr., *A Record of Buddhist Religion as Practised in India and the Malay Archipelago (AD 671–695) by I-tsing*, Munshiram Manoharlal, Delhi, 1966, p. 118.
41. Arvind Sharma ("Of Hindu, Hindustan..." p. 6) points out that Muhammad ibn Qāsim appointed his adversary Dāhir's minister Siskar as his advisor after the latter's acceptance of Islam. Since conversion from what he calls "Hindu religion" became possible, he seems to imply that a Hindu identity had already emerged. Similarly, the brāhmaṇ princes of Sind, Jaysīyah b. Dāhir and his brother Śaṣṣah, accepted Islam at the invitation of the Caliph 'Umar b. 'Abd al-Aziz (Derryl N. Maclean, *Religion and Society in Arab Sind*, E.J. Brill, Leiden, 1989, pp. 33, 48) But mere acceptance of Islam by certain Sindis does not justify a reified perception of Hinduism as early as the eighth century.
42. Several Arab travellers and geographers refer to the existence of large number of religious sects in India. For example, Ibn Khurdādbih refers to the existence of forty-two sects among the people of India and al-Gardizi, a contemoprary of Alberuni, tells us that the Indians were divided into ninety-nine religious communities. See Bruce B Lawrence, *Shahrastānī on the Indian Religions*, Mouton The Hague, 1976, p. 20; Yohanan Friedman, "Muslim Views of Indian Religions", *Journal of the American Oriental Society*, vol. 95, no. 2, 1975, p. 216.
43. Maclean, op. cit., pp. 12–3; Irfan Habib, *Linguistic Materials from Eighth-Century Sind: An Exploration of the Chachnāma*, Symposia Papers 11, Indian History Congress, Aligarh, 1994, pp. 8–9.
44. Carl W. Ernst, *Eternal Garden: Mysticism, History and Politics at a South Asian Sufi Center*, Oxford University Press, Delhi, 2004, p. 23
45. Ibid. Annemarie Schimmel traces, though unconvincingly, the origins of modern communal divide to the Turk-Hindu dichotomy as found in the early Persian and Turkish poetry ("Turk and Hindu: A Poetical Image and its Application to Historical Fact", in Speros Vryonis, ed., *Islam and Cultural Change in the Middle Ages*, Otto Harrassowitz,Wiesbaden, 1975, pp. 107–26).
46. Alberuni's reference to Hindu religion has been treated as a landmark in the "religious semantic journey" of the word

"Hindu", just as the sack of Somanatha by Mahmūd has been blown out of proportion by some scholars, e.g., Arvind Sharma, "Of Hindu, Hindustan...", pp. 6–7

47. Edward C. Sachau, tr., *Alberuni's India*, Trübner & Co., London, 1910, I, pp. 7, 21, cited in Irfan Habib, "India: Country and Nation—An Introductory Essay," in idem, ed., *India: Studies in the History of an Idea*, p. 5, note 14.
48. *Alberuni's India*, p. 19
49. The fact that Alberuni used "Hindu" in a religious sense has been contested by a scholar according to whom the word does not occur in the Arabic text and the word "hind" which finds mention in it does not have a religious connotation: Syed Farid Alatas, "Intellectual and Structural Challenges to Academic Dependency", Keynote Address: ADRI-SEPPHIS Seminar on Coping with Academic Dependency, Patna, 2008, p. 16.
50. For a detailed though biased view of Alberuni's perception of brāhmaṇical religion, see Arvind Sharma, *Studies in "Alberuni's India"*, Otto Harrassowitz, Wiesbaden, 1983. Cf. D.N. Jha, *Rethinking Hindu Identity*, Equinox, London, 2009, pp. 16–7.
51. The general absence of an essentialist view of the religion of the Hindus may be inferred from the many inscriptions including the one from Veraval discussed by Anwar Hussain ("The 'Foreigners' and the Indian Society: c. Eighth Century to Thirteenth Century", unpublished M. Phil. dissertation, Centre for Historical Studies, Jawaharlal Nehru University, 1993, Chapter IV). Basing on his data B.D. Chattopadhyaya (*Representing the Other: Sanskrit Sources and the Muslims*, Manohar, Delhi, 1998, p. 78) rightly points out that whatever essentialism may be there in Alberuni's description is contradicted by many records including the Veraval inscription, which speaks of the reconstruction of a demolished mosque by Jayasiṃha Siddharāja.
52. Baranī mentions Hindus forty times in his *Tārīkh-i-Firūzshāhī*: Qeyamuddin Ahmad, "Baranī's References to the Hindus in the *Tārīkh-i-Firūzshāhī*—Territorial and Other Dimensions", *Islamic Culture*, LVI (1982), pp. 295–302. The Moroccan traveller Ibn Battūtah, a contemporary of Baranī, interpreted the name Hindu Kush as "Hindu killer" because the Indian slaves passing through its mountainous terrain perished in the snows. Ibn Battūtah's derivation of the word, however, may have been based on folk etymology, and the name Hindukush possibly originated from the Arabic Hindu Koh, meaning the "mountains of India." I am thankful to Dr Najaf Haider for this suggestion.

53. David Lorenzen, *Who Invented Hinduism? Essays on Religion in History*, Yoda Press, New Delhi, 2006, p. 33.
54. Romila Thapar, "Syndicated Hinduism", in Günther-Dietz Sontheimer and Hermann Kulke, eds., *Hinduism Reconsidered*, Manohar, Delhi, 1997, p. 73.
55. The author of the *Dabistān* has been variously identified, e.g., as "Mobad", Muhsin Fani, Mirza Zulfiqar Beg and Kaikhusrau Isfandyar.
56. Manisha Mishra, "Perception of the Hindus and their Religious Systems as Described in the Dabistān-i-Mazāhib", unpublished M.Phil. dissertation, Department of History, University of Delhi, 2003.
57. Sher Ali Tareen, "Reifying Religion While Lost in Translation: Mirza Mazhar Jan-i Janan (d.1781) on the Hindus", *Macalester Islam Journal*, vol. 1 (2006), Issue. 2, Art. 3, pp. 19-29.
58. Najaf Haider, "A 'Holi Riot' of 1714: Versions from Ahmadabad and Delhi", in Mushirul Hasan and Asim Roy, eds., *Living Together Separately: Cultural India in History and Politics*, Manohar, Delhi, 2005.
59. Philip B. Wagoner, "Sultan among Hindu Kings: Dress, Titles, and the Islamicization of Hindu Culture at Vijayanagara", *Journal of Asian Studies*, vol. 55, no.4 (November 1996), p. 862. Cf. Hermann Kulke, *Kings and Cults: State Formation and Legitimation in India and Southeast Asia*, Manohar, Delhi, 1993, pp. 208–39
60. B.D. Chattopadhyaya, op. cit., p. 54.
61. Richard Burghart, "The Category of "Hindu" in the Political Discourse of Nepal" in C.J. Fuller and Jonathan Spencer, eds., *The Conditions of Listening*, Oxford University Press, Delhi, 1996, p. 264.
62. *Hindughoṣa* may be taken to mean the Hindukush mountain (*Rājataranginī* of Jonarāja, ed. and tr. Raghunath Singh, Chowkhamba, Varanasi, 1972, verse 381).
63. *Jaina Rājataranginī* of Śrīvara, tr., Raghunath Singh, Chowkhamba, Varanasi, 1977, 3.218.
64. Ibid., 2.215.
65. Ibid., 2.51.
66. Joseph T. O'Connell, "The word 'Hindu' in Gauḍīya Vaiṣṇava Texts", *Journal of the American Oriental Society*, vol. 93, no. 3 (1973), pp. 340–43; idem, "Vaiṣṇava Pereceptions of Muslims in Sixteenth Century Bengal", in Milton Israel and N.K. Wagle, eds., *Islamic Society and Culture*, Delhi, 1983, pp. 289–313.
67. Wilhelm Halbfass, *India and Europe: An Essay in Philosophical*

Understanding, Motilal Banarsidass, Delhi, 1990, p. 193.

68. The pandits were Somanātha (Subaji Bapu), Haracandra Tarkapancānana and Nilakantha Goreh, the last of whom ultimately converted to Christianity and was baptized as Nehemiah Goreh. For a discussion of the material produced in the context of the controversy, see Richard Fox Young, *Resistant Hinduism: Sanskrit Sources on Anti-Christian Apologetics in Early Nineteenth Century India*, Reberto de Nobili Research Library, Vienna, 1981.
69. Haracandra Tarkapancānan, *Mataparīkṣottaram*, Samachurn Chandrica, Calcutta, 1940, p. 1, cited in Young, op. cit., p. 93.
70. Young, op. cit., p. 150.
71. His multi-volume lexicon *Śabdakalpadruma* appeared between 1819 and 1858.
72. *Vācaspatyam*.
73. The crucial passage is given by V.S Apte (*Practical Sanskrit English Dictionary*, sv. *hindu*): *hindudharmapraloptāro jāyante cakravarttinaḥ/ hīnam ca duṣayatyeṣa hinduritiucyate priye//* He dates the text to the eighth century AD, but one is intrigued by its reference to *tāntriks* born in London who will become lords of the earth.
74. *hīnam dūṣayati iti hindu*: the Hindu "spoils" (*dūṣayati*) what is "inferior" (*hinam*). Halbfass, *India and Europe*, p. 515, note 96. The twentieth-century text *Dharmapradīpa*, written by three leading pandits in the 1930s, discusses in detail the rules laid down for the purification of those Hindus who joined or were forced to join other religions: *atra kevalam balād eva mlecchadharmam svīkāritānām hindūnām... vividhaḥ prāyascīttavidhayo nirdiṣṭā dṛṣyante*, p. 219, cited in Halbfass, *India and Europe*, p. 534, note 66. The word also occurs in the *Dharmatattvavinirṇaya* by Vasudeva Sastrin Abhyankara (Anandasrama Press, Poona, 1929).
75. Joseph T. O'Connel, "The Word 'Hindu' in Gauḍīya Vaiṣṇava Texts", pp. 340–4.
76. Peter Gaeffke, "Muslims in Hindi Literature", *Beitrage zur Indienforschung*, Museum fur Indische Kunt, Berlin, 1977, pp. 119–26.
77. Eleanor Zelliot, "A Medieval Encounter Between Hindu and Muslim: Eknāth's Drama-Poem Hindu-Turk Samvad", in Fred W Clothey, ed., *Images of Man: Religion and Historical Process in South Asia*, Madras, 1982, pp. 171–95.
78. David Lorenzen, *Who Invented Hinduism?: Essays on Religion in History*, Chapter 5.

79. David N. Lorenzen, "Who Invented Hinduism", *Comparative Studies in Society and History*, vol. 41, no. 4 (October 1999), pp. 630–59. Also see idem, ed., *Bhakti Religion in North India: Community Identity and Political Action*, Manohar, Delhi, 1996, Introduction.
80. R.P. Bahuguna, "Recent Western Writings on Medieval Indian Sant Movement", ICHR Seminar on Dialogue with the Past: Trends in Historical Writings in India, Bangalore, 14–16 February 2003; idem, "Symbols of Resistance: Non-Brahmanical Sants as Religious Heroes in Late Medieval India", in Biswamoy Pati *et al.*, eds., *Negotiating India's Past: Essays in Memory of Parthasarathi Gupta*, Tulika, Delhi, 2003.
81. Charles Grant used the term "Hindooism" first in a letter to John Thomas in 1787 and subsequently in his *Observations on the State of Society among the Subjects of Great Britain*, written in 1792 (Will Sweetman, *Mapping Hinduism: Hinduism and the Study of Indian Religions 1600–1776*, Verlag der Franckcschen Stiftungen zu Halle, Halle, 2003, p. 56, note 12). William Jones also used the term "Hindu" in the religious sense in 1787 (S.N. Mukherjee, *Sir William Jones: A Study in Eighteenth-century British Attitudes to India*, Cambridge University Press, Cambridge, 1968, p. 119; Dermot Killingley, "Modernity, Reform, and Revival," in Gavin Flood, ed., *The Blackwell Companion to Hinduism*, op. cit., p. 513). Rammohun Roy was, however, perhaps "the first Hindu" to use the word "Hindooism" in 1816 (Dermot Killingley, *Rammohun Roy in Hindu and Christian Tradition: The Teape Lectures* 1990, Newcastle upon Tyne, 1993, p. 60, cited in Richard King, *Orientalism and Religion*, Oxford University Press, Delhi, 1999, p. 100.)
82. Several scholars have argued that Hinduism was a colonial construct which finally took shape when the imperial administration engaged in the classification of the Indian people into religious categories through the mechanism of the census. Among them are Vasudha Dalmia ("The Only Real Religion of the Hindus: Vaiṣṇava Self-Representation in the Late Nineteenth Century", in Vasudha Dalmia and Heinrich von Stietencron, eds., *Representing Hinduism: The Construction of Religious Traditions and National Identity*, Sage Publications, New Delhi, 1995, pp. 176–210); Robert Frykenberg ("The Emergence of Modern 'Hinduism' as a Concept and as an Institution", in Günther-Dietz Sontheimer and Hermann Kulke, eds., *Hinduism Reconsidered*, Manohar, Delhi, 1997, pp. 82–107); John Stratton Hawley ("Naming

Hinduism", *Wilson Quarterly*, Summer 1991, pp. 20–32); Harjot Oberoi (*The Construction of Religious Boundaries: Culture, Identity and Diversity in the Sikh Tradition*, Oxford University Press, Delhi, 1994, pp. 16–7); and Heinrich von Stietencron ("Hinduism: On the Proper Use of a Deceptive Term", in Sontheimer and Kulke, op. cit., pp. 32–53). Their views have been contested in recent years by quite a few scholars, e.g., Will Sweetman, op. cit., and Brian K. Pennington, *Was Hinduism Invented? Britons, Indians and the Colonial Construction of Religion*, Oxford University Press, New York, 2005. Their main source of inspiration is David Lorenzen ("Who Invented Hinduism?", *Comparative Studies in Society and History*, vol. 41, no. 4, October 1999, pp. 630–59), who has argued that "a Hindu religion ... acquired a much sharper self-conscious identity through the rivalry between Muslims and Hindus in the period between 1200 and 1500, and was firmly established before 1800" (p. 631). While he thus assigns primary agency to "rivalry between Muslims and Hindus" in the construction of Hinduism, he also pronounces: "Hinduism wasn't invented by anyone, European or Indian. Like Topsy, it just grow'd" (ibid., p. 655). One wonders if this comparison to a character from the nineteenth-century anti-slavery novel *Uncle Tom's Cabin* is not a mere muddying of the waters of history.

83. The role of census in the creation of the Hindu religious identity cannot be denied; for the "census procedures often involved the imposition of the order, rather than simple recording of realities on the ground" as is evident from the fact that the census commissioner Edward Gait, being dismayed at the recording of 35000 "Hindu Mohammadans" in Gujarat by a census superintendent, ordered "the location of persons concerned to the one religion or the other as best as he could" (*Census* 1911, vol. I. I, India, Report, p. 118 cited in Sumit Sarkar, "Hindutva and the Question of Conversions", in K.N. Panikkar, ed., *The Concerned Indian's Guide to Communalism*, Viking, Delhi, 1999, p. 85). Also see K.W. Jones, "Religious Identity and the Indian Census", in N.G. Barrier, ed., *The Census in British India*, Manohar, Delhi, 1981, pp. 73–101; Michael Haan, "Numbers in Nirvan: How the 1872–1921 Censuses helped Operationalise 'Hinduism'", *Religion*, vol. 35, No.1 (2005), pp. 13-30; R.B. Bhagat, "Census and the Construction of Communalism", *Economic and Political Weekly*, vol. XXXVI, nos. 46–7 (2001).

84. Agehananda Bharati, "The Hindu Renaissance and its Apologetic Patterns", *Journal of Asian Studies*, 29 (1970), pp. 267–87.

85. Recently Brian K. Pennington (op. cit.) has vehemently opposed the view that Britain invented Hinduism on the grounds, first, that that argument "grants ... too much power to colonialism" and, second, that denying the existence of Hinduism prior to the arrival of the British "introduces an almost irreparable disruption in Indian traditions that can only alienate contemporary Indians from their own traditions" (p. 5). He seems to forget that colonialisms everywhere have manipulated facts to suit their interests. Worse, must historians cease to work because their reasoned conclusions show that "traditions", held to be crucial to the psychic welfare of today's people, are concocted?
86. Gavin Flood, *An Introduction to Hinduism*, first South Asian edition, Foundation Books, Delhi, 2004, p. 50.
87. Richard H. Davis, "A Brief History of Religions in India", Introduction, in Donald S. Lopez, Jr, ed., *Religions of India in Practice*, Indian reprint, Munshiram Manoharlal, Delhi, 1998, p. 5. Also see John Stratton Hawley, "Naming Hinduism", *Wilson Quarterly*, (Summer 1991), pp. 20–3; and Wendy Doniger, "Hinduism by Any Other Name", ibid., 35–41.
88. The only clarity about Hinduism is that it is used as a catch-all category for all non-Abrahamaic religions (Islam, Judaism, Christianity) and is thus a negative appellation. In the Hindu Marriage Act (1955), "Hindu" includes not only Buddhists, Jains and Sikhs but also all those who are not Muslims, Christians, Parsees or Jews. There is therefore much substance in Frits Staal's view that no meaningful notion of Hinduism can be obtained except by exclusion and in his argument that it fails to qualify both as a religion and as "a meaningful unit of discourse" (*Rules Without Meaning: Ritual, Mantras and the Human Sciences*, Peter Lang, New York, 1989, p. 397).
89. Bernard S. Cohn, *An Anthropologist among the Historians and Other Essays*, Delhi, 1987, pp. 224–54.
90. Klaus Klostermaier, *A Survey of Hinduism*, SUNY Press, Albany, 1989, pp. 31, 531.
91. Halbfass, *India and Europe*, p. 344.
92. Julius Lipner, *Hindus: Their Religious Beliefs and Practices*, Routledge, London, 1994, p. 221.
93. Julius Lipner, "On Hinduism and Hinduisms: The Way of the Banyan", in Sushil Mittal and Gene Thursby, eds., *The Hindu World*, Routledge, New York, 2004, Indian reprint, Raplika Press, Kundli, Haryana, 2005, p. 19.

94. John Zavos, "Defending Hindu Tradition: Sanātana Dharma as a Symbol of Orthodoxy in Colonial India", *Religion*, 31 (2001), pp. 109–23. Also see Vasudha Dalmia, *Nationalisation of Hindu Traditions: Bharatendu Harischandra and Nineteenth Century Benaras*, Oxford University Press, Delhi, 1997, pp. 2–4, note 5.
95. It is not surprising that early twentieth-century pandits like V.S. Abhyankara, Anantakṛṣṇa Sastri, Sitaram Sastri and Srivijaya Bhattacharya were against the introduction of "new sectarian traditions" (*nūtanasampradāya, Dharmapradīpa*, p. 64) and described themselves as "followers of eternal religion" (*sanātanadharmīya, sanātanadharmāvalambin, Dharmapradīpa*, pp. 207, 219: *Dharmatattvavinirṇaya*, pp. 39ff). See W. Halbfass, *India and Europe: An Essay in Understanding*, p. 260.
96. *Dhammapada*, I.5. It has been suggested the word *sanātana* may have some connection with *sanatā*, which occurs in the Vedic literature twice. At one place in the *Ṛgveda* (2.3.1d) it occurs along with *dharma* and at another, without it (2.3.6ab). In both cases the word *sanatā* means "from old times" or "always." I am thankful to Professor Shingo Einoo, who drew my attention to these references.
97. *Mahābhārata*, XII.96.13; 128.30; 131.2; XIII.44.32; 96.46; XIV.50.37. Cited in Halbfass, *India and Europe*, p. 558, note 56.
98. According to the story, when his mother was being led away by a brāhmaṇ he flew into a rage and was calmed down by his father, who told him not to get angry because this was the eternal law (*eṣa dharmaḥ sanatanaḥ*), *Mahābhārata*, I.113, verses 11–14.
99. *Bhagvadgītā*, I.40.
100. Ibid., XI.18.
101. *Matsyapurāṇa*, 143.32, Anandasramagranthavali, 1981, p. 269.
102. *Varāhapurāṇa*, 126.7 (ed. Panchanan Taskarasna, Vangavasi Press, Calcutta, BS1313).
103. Ibid., 126.43.
104. *Śivapurāṇa*, 7.2.10.30-72 (ed. Panchanan Taskarasna, Vangavasi Press, Calcutta, BS1314).
105. *Epigraphia Indica*, vol. XXVII, no. 49, line 7.106, Halbfass, *India and Europe*, p. 343.
107. *Sanātanadharma: An Elementary Text-book of Hindu Religion and Ethics*, Central Hindu College, Benares, 1910. This was followed by several works on the *sanātanadharma*, e.g., *Sanātanadharma-dipikā* by Hamsayogin, Madras, 1917; Ganga Prasad, *The Fountainhead of Religion*, 1909; Shri Bharat Dharma Mahamandala, ed., *The World's Eternal Religion*, Benares, 1920; etc.

108. Julius Lipner, *Hindus: Their Religious Beliefs and Practices*, p. 221.
109. Brian K. Smith, *Reflections on Resemblance, Ritual and Religion*, Oxford University Press, 1989, pp. 13–4.
110. *Nirukta*, I.20.
111. *Manu*, II.6. Cf. *Manu*, XII. 95–6.
112. Ibid., II.10.
113. Wilhelm Halbfass, *Tradition and Reflection: Exploration in Indian Thought*, SUNY Press, Albany, 1991, pp. 24–7.
114. Ibid. p. 33.
115. Brian K. Smith, op. cit., p. 18; Halbfass, *India and Europe*, pp. 326–9, 359. Cf. Louis Renou, *The Destiny of the Veda in India* (English tr. Dev Raj Chanana), Motilal Banarsidass, Delhi, 1965, pp. 40–6.
116. Renou, op. cit., p. 37.
117. Brian K. Smith, op. cit., p. 18.
118. *Itihāsapurāṇam pañcamam vedānām vedam*, *Chāndogya Upaniṣad*, 7.2, (S. Radhakrishnan, *The Principal Upaniṣads*, Delhi, 1991, p. 470). For a discussion of the claim of the *Mahābhārata* to be the "fifth Veda", see John Brockington, *The Sanskrit Epics*, E.J. Brill, Leiden, 1998, p. 7. According to some scholars even the *Atharvaveda* did not belong to the "revealed" Vedic corpus and its followers invented legends and allegories to prove the superiority of the text and earn for it the status of a "divine revelation" (Lakshman Sarup, *The Nighantu and the Nirukta*, Indian edition, Motilal Banarsidass, Delhi, 1984, pt. 1, pp. 72–3.
119. Frits Staal, "The Concept of Scripture in the Indian Tradition", in Mark Juergensmeyer and Gerald Barrier, eds., *Sikh Studies: Comparative Perspectives on a Changing Tradition*, Graduate Theological Union, Berkeley, 1979, pp. 121–4. For a different point of view, see C. Mackenzie Brown, "Purāṇas as Scripture: From Sound to Image of the Holy Word in the Hindu Tradition", *History of Religions*, 26 (1986), pp. 68–86.
120. *The Mahābhārata* (I.56.33) claims: *yad ihāsti tad anyatra, yan nehāsti na tat kvacid* ("That which is found herein exists elsewhere; that which is not here, is nowhere").
121. The Purāṇas often claim to be the essence of all the Vedas (*sarvavedasāra*, *akhilaśrutisāra*, *sarvavedārthasāra*), or the soul of the Vedas: *Bhāgavata Purāṇa* 1.2.3, 1.3.42, 12.13.15; *Nāradīya Purāṇa* 1.1.36, 1.9.97; *Skanda Purāṇa* 5.3.1.22. Cited in Brian K. Smith, op. cit., p. 26.
122. Halbfass, *India and Europe*, p. 366.
123. Brian K. Smith, op. cit., pp. 20–9. The tradition of extending the use of the word *veda* is seen in the description of Nammalvar's

Tiruvaymoli as *Draviḍaveda*. It was in keeping with this old practice that the "Tranquebar Bible" was called *Vedapustagam* and B. Ziegenbalg described the Bible and the Christian religion as *satyavedam* or "the true Veda" (Halbfass, *India and Europe*, p. 340).

124. J.E. Llewellyn, *The Arya Samaj as a Fundamentalist Movement*, Manohar, Delhi, 1993, chapter 2. Also see J.T.F. Jordens, *Dayanand Saraswati: His Life and Causes*, Delhi, 1981.
125. Renou, op. cit., p. 2.
126. Although we do not wish to discuss the various forms and levels of atheism and heresies in India, it is necessary to recall that among those who repudiated the authority of the Vedas outside the brāhmaṇical fold and earned the epithets *pāṣandas* (heretics) and *nāstikas* (non-believers in the Vedas), the important ones are the Jains, the Buddhists and the Cārvākas (also known as *lokāyatikas)*. The Vedas, according to the Jains, were *anāryavedas*, which they replaced with their own scriptures, calling them *āryavedas*. They also describe the Vedas as *mithyāsūtras* (*micchāsūya*) (Renou, op. cit., p. 87). Gautama Buddha is equally unsparing in his denunciation of the Vedas and says that "... the talk of the Brāhmaṇas versed in the three Vedas turns out to be ridiculous, mere words, a vain and empty thing", *Dīghanikāya* (London, 1967, vol. I, p. 240, Tevijjasutta 15). Further, he describes the three Vedas as "foolish talk", "a waterless desert", and their threefold wisdom as "a pathless jungle" and "a perdition" (ibid., p. 248, Tevijjasutta 15). The strongest condemnation of the Vedic texts, however, came from the Cārvākas. According to them the Veda is "tainted with the three faults of untruth, self-contradiction, and tautology... the incoherent rhapsodies of knaves" (*dhūrtapralāpa*)", *Sarva-darśana-saṃgraha*, tr. E.B. Cowell and A.E. Gough, London, 1914, p. 4.
127. *Ṛgveda*, VII.103.
128. Ibid, X.121.
129. Ibid, 10.129.7.
130. J.C. Heesterman, *The Inner Conflict of Tradition*, Oxford University Press, Delhi, 1985, p. 77.
131. *Ṛgveda*, VIII.100.3
132. Ibid, II.12
133. Heesterman, op. cit., p. 75; *Ṛgveda*, V.30.1, VI.18.3, VI.27.3, VIII.64.7, VIII.100.3, X.22.1 (cited in ibid., p. 224). Also see Wendy Doniger O'Flaherty, "The Origin of Heresy in Hindu Mythology", *History of Religions*, 10 (May 1971), p. 284, note 83.

134. *Muṇḍaka Upaniṣad*, I.1.4-5. Lakshman Sarup, op. cit., pp. 74–5) lists several anti-Vedic Upaniṣadic passages: *Muṇḍaka Upaniṣad*, III.2.3; *Kaṭha Upaniṣad*, I.2.23; *Bṛhadāraṇyaka Upaniṣad*, I.5.23; *Kauṣītaki Upaniṣad*, II.5; *Chāndogya Upaniṣad*, V.11–24; *Taittirīya Upaniṣad*, II.5.
135. Lakshman Sarup, op. cit., I.15.
136. Wendy Doniger O'Flaherty, "The Origin of Heresy in Hindu Mythology", p. 286.
137. *Bhagavadgītā*, II.41–6.
138. Ibid., IX.21. Cf. XI.48, 53.
139. *Matsyapurāṇa*, 53.3.20, 5.3.1.20; *Nāradīyapurāṇa*, 2.24.16. Cited in Brian K. Smith, op. cit., p. 26.
140. *Agnipurāṇa*, 383, 47–50, cited in C. Mackenzie Brown, op. cit., pp. 70–1.
141. Halbfass, *India and Europe*, p. 366.
142. N.N. Bhattacharyya, *History of Tantric Religion*, Manohar, Delhi, 1982, p. 75.
143. Halbfass, *India and Europe*, p. 366. The *Mahānirvāṇatantra* is "probably the most widely known" and the most recent of the Tantras. Written in the second half of the eighteenth century, it contains much material on such varied themes as marriage, conjugal ethics, inheritance, caste rules and slavery, though it has been described as a "well-intentioned fraud". (J.D.M. Derrett, *Essays in Classical and Modern Hindu Law*, Leiden, 1977, vol. 2, pp. 197–242). Also see N.N. Bhattacharyya, *History of the Tantric Religion*, pp. 74–5; Teun Goudriaan and Sanjukta Gupta, *Hindu Tantric and Śākta Literature*, Otto Harrassowitz, Wiesbaden, 1981, pp. 98–101;
144. R.N. Nandi, "Origin of the Vīraśaiva Movement", in D.N. Jha, ed., *The Feudal Order*, Manohar, Delhi, 2000, p. 485, note 47. The smārtas, who joined the Vīraśaiva movement in large numbers, retained their superiority, undermined its fraternalism and paved the way for the growth of the brāhmaṇical caste system among its followers. Not surprisingly, the Vīraśaivas, in the later phase of their movement, preached loyalty to the *varṇāśramadharma*, as is evident from the works of Bhīmakavi and Śripati Paṇḍita (both of the fourteenth century). The latter even said that only the performance of caste duties and Vedic rites could purify a person and prepare him for final liberation (ibid., p. 477; Suvira Jaiswal, "Semitising Hinduism: Changing Paradigms of Brahmanical Integration", *Social Scientist*, vol. 19, no. 12 (1991), p. 22.). The Vīraśaiva emphasis on the observance of caste duties as well as on the necessity of seeking legitimation

from the Vedas is evident from one of their basic texts, the *Lingadhāraṇacandrikā*: Louis Renou, op. cit., p. 61, note 1.

145. Louis Renou, op. cit., p. 2.
146. Ibid., p. 2. Giovanni, Verardi, *Hardships and Downfall of Buddhism in India*, Manohar, Delhi, 2011.
147. Ibid., p. 3.

3

Of Conflict, Conversion, and Cow

D.N. Jha

An imporatant myth which, through repetition, has been made to stick to the artefact called Hinduism is that it is a tolerant religion. Peddled perpetually by the Hindu Right and accepted easily by Hindus in India and abroad, the idea is rooted, to a significant extent, in the Western writings on India. Francois Bernier, the French doctor who traveled widely in India during the 1660s, was one of the early Europeans to perceive Hindus as a tolerant people and to state that they "did not claim that their law is universal".[1] Similarly Herder (1744–1803), the forerunner of the Romantic glorification of India, referred to the Hindus as "mild" and "tolerant" and as "the gentlest branch of humanity"; and Immanuel Kant (1724–1804) said that they "do not hate the other religions but they believe they are also right." Such views find a more prominent place in the writings of Orientalists like William Jones, according to whom "the Hindus...would readily admit the truth of the Gospel but they contend that it is perfectly consistent with their Sastras."[2] In the nineteenth century, religious reformers emphasized the idea of tolerance in Hinduism. Ramakrishna (1836–1886), for example, spoke of the equality of religions and listed all faiths—Hinduism, Islam and Christianity—without privileging any, though in his view "the Hindu religion alone is the Sanātana Dharma."[3] His disciple Vivekananda (1863–1904) also laid emphasis on toleration and picked up the famous Ṛgvedic passage *ekaṃsad viprā vahudhā vadanti* to support his vision that "India alone [was] to be...the land of toleration"—a vision which, in reality, did not conform to his view that "all creeds may be equal but Hinduism [was] more equal" and to his description of Hinduism as a "religion" and of Islam and Christianity as mere "sects"[4] as well as to his perception of Hinduism as a "standard by which to measure both the theological and philosophical content as well as the histories of the other religions."[5] The Ṛgvedic quote, which has been "milked for all its worth" since the time of Vivekananda, has become a cliché, and his prophecy itself, if seriously meant, has repeatedly been shown to be ill-founded.[6]

During the period of the Indian freedom struggle the supposed inclusive and tolerant nature of Hinduism was emphasized by many leaders. Bal Gangadhar Tilak (1856–1920), despite his espousal of militant Hinduism, quite often cited the above Ṛgvedic passage to lay stress on religious tolerance; several decades later, even the Muslim hater M.S. Golwalkar, spoke of the Hindus as the most tolerant people of the world, though this sounded like devil quoting scriptures for, in his view, it was their "spirit of broad catholicism, generosity and toleration" which entitled them to have the land of India to themselves disenfranchizing the Muslims. Mohandas Karamchand Gandhi, who lived and died for religious harmony in India, found Hinduism to be the most tolerant of all religions known to him, though by taking pride in its inclusivism he made it exclusive—a position similar to that of the greatest Indian philosopher S. Radhakrishnan. Jawaharlal Nehru, who is rightly considered to be the architect of a secular state in modern India, asserted that Hinduism's "essential spirit seems to be to live and let live".

The perception of Hinduism as a tolerant religion has predictably elicited conflicting responses from the scholarly community. On the one hand are scholars like the late Nirad C. Chaudhuri, who almost ruled out the idea of religious tolerance and asserted that "if the familiar words about the tolerance and capacity for synthesis were true, one would be hard put to it to explain why there are such deep suspicions and enmities among the human groups in India..."[7] On the other hand, there are many historians and social scientists who have emphasized the inclusive character of Hinduism. The influential literature generated by them in recent years, most notably by Amartya Sen, has glorified religious tolerance and inclusiveness in early India.[8]

Admittedly religious sects in India have showed a certain degree of mutual accommodation in the past, and one may offer several examples to illustrate this process. Thus, judging from the Purāṇic evidence, much of which belongs to the early medieval or even the later period, the Buddha, founder of a heretic religion, emerged as an *avatāra* of Viṣṇu around the middle of the sixth century AD[9] and figured as such in several *Purāṇas*[10] and other sources including the *Daśāvatāracarita* of Kṣemendra (eleventh century) and *Gītagovinda* of Jayadeva[11] (twelfth century) as well as inscriptions,[12] and interestingly, in Alberuni's *Kitābu-ul-Hind.*[13] Similarly, Ādinātha (Ṛṣabha), the first *tīrthaṅkara* of another heretic religion, Jainism, was accepted as an incarnation of Viṣṇu in the *Bhāgavatapurāṇa.*[14] Although sacrifice to the Buddha was recommended for those desirous of beauty (*rūpakāmo yajed buddhaṃ,*)[15] and a way was thus opened for brāhmaṇ priests to officiate at Buddhist temples,[16] it is forgotten that he was also reviled as a thief and atheist[17] and Śiva is believed to have appeared on earth in the form of Śaṅkara to combat the Buddha *avatāra* just as it is suppressed that Nārāyaṇācārya described Śaṅkara as an illegitimate child in his *Maṇimañjarī.*[18] Likewise, the acceptance of Ṛṣabhanātha as an *avatāra* of Viṣṇu was an effort at Vaiṣṇavizing a Jain deity and an ingenious, albeit unsuccessful, "drive towards the syncretism of the two rival faiths."[19] Further, the Vedāntist philosopher Mādhava Ācārya (fourteenth century) is often said to have displayed an exemplary tolerance of opposing points of view in his *Śarvadarśanasaṃgraha* (Collection of All Systems), which begins by presenting the school of Cārvākas, criticizes it and ends with Śaṅkara's Advaita "as the conclusion and crown of all philosophical systems."[20] What, however, is missed is that this was in keeping with the traditional Indian practice of presenting the opponent's view before refuting it and similar examples from subsequent periods can be multiplied. Christ was sometimes included in the incarnations of Viṣṇu[21] and the Muslim sect of Imām Shāhīs believed that the Imām was himself the tenth *avatāra* of Viṣṇu and that the Quran was a part of the *Atharvaveda*.[22] Akbar was some times thought of as the tenth *avatāra* of Viṣṇu[23] and Queen Victoria was accepted as a Hindu goddess when a plague broke out in Mumbai following an insult to her statue by some miscreants.[24] It is, however, ignored in all this, that neither the Imām, nor Christ, nor Akbar and nor Victoria occupied an important place in the brāhmaṇical scheme of things.

Even if we accept these instances as indicating that Brāhmaṇism gave space to heterodoxies, there is considerable historical evidence to question the stereotype of India as a land of religious tolerance. Apart from the fact that a religion with a caste system and untouchability as characteristic features was and is inherently incapable of promoting tolerance, sources show that there were antagonisms between the various brāhmaṇical sects as well as between Brāhmaṇism, which accepted the authority of the Vedas, and the heterodox non-brāhmaṇical sects which rejected it. Thus the legend of Dakṣa, which evolved from the *Ṛgveda* through several *Brāhmaṇas* (*Taittirīya, Śatapatha, Aitareya, Gopatha*) to the *Mahābhārata* and the Purāṇas (*Bhāgavata, Kūrma* and *Devī-Bhāgavata*), has been interpreted by scholars as a saga of conflict between Vaiṣṇavism and Śaivism.[25] It has also been suggested that the core of the Dakṣa legend describes the struggle between adherents of the two cults for control over a holy place called Kanakhala near Hardwar on the Ganga.[26]

The Purāṇic and other early Indian texts are, in fact, quite unambiguous about the Śaiva-Vaiṣṇava antagonism. The *Viṣṇupurāṇa* claims the superiority of Viṣṇu over Brahmā and Śiva[27] *(Viṣṇupurāṇa*, I.9.56), and the *Kūrmapurāṇa* considers the various Śaiva sects—Bhairavas, Kāpālikas, Vāmas–as deserving to be censured for deluding the world.[28] Similarly, the *Varāhapurāṇa* devotes two chapters to the negative portrayal of the Śaiva sect of the Pāśupatas,[29] and the *Padmapurāṇa*

(6.234.27) makes the general statement that even a brāhmaṇ is a *pāṣaṇḍa* if he is not a Vaiṣṇava (*avaiṣṇas tu yo vipraḥ sa pāṣaṇḍaḥ prakīrtitaḥ*)—an exclusivist position also supported by the *Vṛddhahārita*, a medieval legal text, according to which a Vaiṣṇava reciting a *mantra* received from a non-Vaiṣṇava guru will be cooked in the fire of hell for millions of years.[30] The *Śaṅkaradigvijaya* recalls a meeting between Mādhava and Śaṅkara, accompanied respectively by the king Sudhanvan and the Kāpālikas. The Kāpālika preceptor reproached the philosopher Mādhava for not worshipping Bhairava, leading to a fight between king Sudhanvan and the Kāpālikas, who were all killed.[31] Some early medieval legal authorities even prescribed purificatory rites for those touching a Śaiva or entering a Śaiva or Buddhist temple.[32] The Vaiṣṇava aversion to the Śaivas is evident from the practice that a "good" Vaiṣṇava would not use even the common word "to sew" (*siv*) because it resembled the name of Śiva—a practice which prevailed among Vaiṣṇavite families till recently.[33]

The Śaivas seem to have reciprocated the Vaiṣṇava contempt in full measure. They regarded Viṣṇu sometimes as a sorcerer;[34] and the *Saurapurāṇa* (3.6) seeks to prove the superiority of Śiva, who gave the *sudarśanacakra* to Viṣṇu. The *Padmapurāṇa*, which extols the worship of Vāsudeva at one place but discourages it strongly at another, states "let not the name of Viṣṇu ever be pronounced".[35] The followers of Śaṅkara "opposed and persecuted" the Vaiṣṇava philosopher Madhu/Madhva,[36] and in two chapters the *Saurapurāṇa* bitterly attacks him and describes him "as a cārvāka, a most malignant, disguised promulgator of the defamation of Śiva" and his followers as "wicked creatures... mlecchas, śūdras."[37]

Important evidence of Śaiva intolerance and fanaticism is found in the attitude of the Coḷa ruler Kulottunga II, who removed the statue of Viṣṇu from the courtyard of the Chidambaram temple[38] as also in the story of the twenty Śaiva priests committing suicide to protest the introduction of Vaiṣṇavite symbols in it.[39] This fits in with the story of the persecution of Rāmānuja (1017–1137), who, according to the conventional account, was forced to withdraw from his centre of activity in Srirangam (Tamilnadu) in 1098 to Mysore (Karnataka) for nearly twenty-five years;[40] and there is the story of the bigoted Coḷa king who ordered the eyes of one of his disciples to be put out.[41]

The spiteful attitude of the Śaivas towards Vaiṣṇavas is evident from an epigraph of 1160, which records the decision of the *mahāsabhā* of Tirukkadiyur that the property of a Śaiva who engaged in social intercourse with the other group would be forfeited and made over to the local temple.[42] So great was the enmity that a Vaiṣṇava Nāgā, according to one tradition, took a vow not to eat his meal without killing at least one Śaiva monk, and a Śaiva in turn swore never to take his food unless he had slain one Vaiṣṇava.[43] According to another tradition, two Gosain leaders had taken a vow to slay two Vairāgīs daily before tasting food.[44] The most unambiguous example of religious intolerance is, however, provided by the Vīraśaiva hagiographical text which tells us how a Vedāntist was humiliated by Bāsava at the court of Bijjala and how a Vedic scholar was ridiculed by the Lingāyats, who had the Vedas recited by dogs[45]

The Śaiva-Vaiṣṇava hostility was not confined to the upper echelons of society. It was seen among lower social ranks as well. An eighteenth-century Tamil work, for example, describes how in their quarrel the Śaiva and Vaiṣṇava wives of a low caste man dragged their gods in a most unseemly manner.[46] Similarly, in the nineteenth century, J.A. Dubois refers to "numerous troops of religious mendicants and vagabonds always ready to provoke each other and to hurl gross and obscene abuse at each other's heads."[47] One may not be far from the truth in suggesting that these "mendicants and vagabonds" included members of higher as well as lower castes and that different social segments were involved in the Śaiva-Vaiṣṇava conflicts.

While there are many more examples of mutual hostility between Śaivas and Vaiṣṇavas, sources amply testify also to the conflict between Brāhmaṇism and heterodox sects. Early evidence of brāhmaṇical hostility towards Jainism, for example, comes from its canonical text, the *Āyārāngasuttam*, according to which monks hid themselves in the day and travelled by night lest they be suspected of being spies.[48] Similarly, the *Arthaśāstra* of Kauṭilya contemptuously describes the followers of non-Vedic sects as *vṛṣala* or *pāṣaṇḍa* (e.g., Śākyas, Ājīvikas), assigns them residence at the end of or near the cremation ground (*pāṣaṇḍacandālānām śmasānānte vāsaḥ*) and prescribes a heavy fine for inviting them to dinners in honour of the gods and the manes,[49] though the occurrence of the word *pāṣaṇḍa* in the edict of Aśoka "is not necessarily pejorative" because he appointed *dharmamahāmātras* to look after the affairs not only of the Buddhist Sangha, the brāhmaṇs and the Ājīvikas but also those of "some other religious sects" (*pāṣaṇḍeṣu*).[50]

The toleration of dissenting faiths which was the hallmark of Aśoka's policy is not seen, however, in later times; for the celebrated grammarian Patañjali (second century BC) observed that the śramaṇs and brāhmaṇs are "eternal enemies (*virodhaḥ śāśvatikaḥ*) like the snake and mongoose."[51] The Buddhist work *Divyāvadāna* (third century) describes Puṣyamitra Śunga as a great persecutor of Buddhists who marched out with a four-fold army, destroying stūpas, burning monasteries and killing monks as far as Sākala (Sialkot), where he announced a prize of one hundred *dīnār* for every head of a śramaṇ.[52] Texual evidence indicates that the brāhmaṇical animosity towards Buddhism and Jainism became intense in subsequent times. Uddyotakara (seventh century) is said to have refuted the arguments of the Buddhist logicians Nāgārjuna and Dignāg, and his arguments were reinforced by Vācaspati Miśra (ninth century). Udayana, another anti-Buddhist logician and the founder of the Navya Nyāya school, launched a sharp attack on the atheistic thesis of Buddhism in his *Ātmatattvaviveka*, which is also known as the *Baudhadhikkāragrantha* on account of its outright rejection of the ideas of Buddhists. Several brāhmaṇical thinkers outside the school of Nyāya also attacked Buddhism and Jainism. For example, Kumārila Bhaṭṭa (eighth century), the south Indian dialectician, rejected the views of all unorthodox religious movements, especially Buddhism and Jainism, because, according to him, whatever is contradicted by a Vedic statement has to be rejected: *virodhe tv anapekṣyaṃ syād*.[53] He goes to the extent of saying that "they are like ungrateful and alienated children who refuse to acknowledge what they owe to their parents" because they "use the [Vedic] idea of *ahimsā* as an instrument of their anti-Vedic propaganda."[54] Śaṅkara, Kumārila's younger contemporary, is even more rigid and uncompromising. He categorically rejects all traditions outside the Vedas, including those of the Bhāgavatas and the Pañcarātrins,[55] and accuses the Buddha of "incoherent prattling (*asambaddhapralāpitvā*) or even deliberately and hatefully leading mankind into confusion...."[56] Similarly, Madhusūdana Sarasvatī, the sixteenth-century Bengali commentator on the *Bhagvadgītā*, holding that the teachings of materialists, Buddhists and others are like those of the *mlecchas*, excludes them from his consideration.[57]

The attitude of the orthodox philosophers found an echo in the Purāṇic texts as well. According to the *Viṣṇupurāna* a Buddhist is unclean and any one who dines with him goes to hell and the *Saurapurāṇa* says that the Cārvākas, Buddhists and Jains should not be allowed to settle in a kingdom.[58] Similarly, the early medieval literary texts provide highly pejorative portrayals of the Buddhists and the Jains. The *Mattavilāsa-prahsana*, a farce written by the Pallava ruler Mahendravarman (seventh century), depicts Buddhists as morally depraved, dishonest and the scum of the earth; a corrupt Buddhist monk is made to ask "...why did [the Buddha] not think of sanctioning the possession of women and the drinking of *surā* (*kinnukhalu strīparigrahaḥ surāpānavidhānam ca na dṛṣṭam*)?"[59] The *Prabodhacandrodaya*, a drama written by Kṛṣṇa Miśra (eleventh century), describes both Buddhism and Jainism as *tāmasika* (arising out of darkness), depicts a Buddhist monk as indulging in worldly pleasures[60] and a Jain monk as naked, devoid of manliness (*nivīrya*), the hair of his head plucked out and carrying a peacock feather in his hand.[61]

The heterodox sects did not lag behind in their denunciation of brāhmaṇical beliefs, practices and thought. The Jain logician Akalaṅka (seventh to the eighth centuries) was full of scorn for the Vedic animal sacrifice, and the famous scholar Hemacandra (twelfth century) dubbed Manu's verses supporting ritual violence as part of *hiṃsāśāstra*. In the seventh century the Jain commentator Jinadāsa described Maheśvara (Śiva) as "the son of a nun who had been magically impregnated by a wizard seeking a suitable repository for his powers"[62] and in the sixteenth century the *Pāṇḍavapurāṇas*, which are the Jainised version of the *Mahābhārata*, show Viṣṇu in a negative light and portray Kṛṣṇa as "scheming and selfish."[63] The Jain texts are thus replete with hostile statements about the brāhmaṇical sects,[64] and, not surprisingly, the Jain community is known to have appropriated many brāhmaṇical religious establishments.[65]

Similarly the Buddhist contempt for Brāhmaṇism was never a secret. As is well known, the Buddha himself described the three Vedas as a "foolish talk" and "a waterless desert", and their wisdom as "a pathless jungle" and "a perdition".[66] In early medieval times, the Buddhist hostility towards Brāhmaṇism and other religions like Jainism became sharp. At the theoretical level this is evident from works like the *Tattvasaṃgrah* of Śāntarakṣita (eighth century) who critically reviewed Nyāya, Mīmāṃsā, Śāṅkhya and Jain philosophies from the Buddhist point of view.[67] Hostility of the Buddhists towards Brāhmaṇism manifested itself in various other ways as well. They criticized the brāhmaṇical practice of bathing at *tīrthas* and in the Ganga, and displayed a disdainful attitude to brāhmaṇical deities who were treated as menials and subordinate to Buddhist gods and goddesses.[68] Not surprisingly, they are often portrayed in some early medieval sculptures as being trampled upon by Buddhist gods;[69] and Dharmasvāmin, the Tibetan scholar who visited Bihar in the thirteenth century, tells us that the Buddhists had put an image of Śiva in front of Buddha's image so as to protect it from the wrath of non-Buddhists.[70]

Evidence of Buddhist and Jain antipathy towards Śaivism, however, appears to be less voluminous in comparison to the copious references to the Śaiva hostility towards the heterodox sects. So fierce was the opposition of the Śaivites to them that they possibly destroyed the Buddhist works like the *Kuṇṭalakeci* and the *Vimpicārakatai*, and the Jain texts like the *Vaḷaiyāpati* and the Jain *Rāmāyaṇa;*the intolerant Śaivas willfully destroyed even Tamil Siddha works.[71]

The Śaivite and Vaiṣṇavite invective against Buddhists and Jains was far more than empty words; for their persecution from around the middle of the first millennium is borne out by copious evidence. Hsüan Tsang (seventh century) states that the Gauḍa king Śaśānka, a contemporary of Harṣavardhana, cut down the Bodhi tree at Gaya and removed the statue of the Buddha from the local temple, which has remained a site of religious contestation ever since. He also tells us that the Huṇa ruler Mihirakula, a devotee of Śiva, destroyed 1, 600 Buddhist *stūpas* and monasteries and killed thousands of Buddhist monks and laity.[72] Kalhaṇa (eleventh century) refers to the destruction of a Buddhist monastery by the Śaivite king Jalauka, who ruled over Kashmir after the death of his father Aśoka.[73] An important evidence of the persecution of Buddhists in Kashmir, however, dates from the reign of the king Kṣemagupta (950–8), who destroyed the Buddhist monastery Jayendravihāra at Śrīnagara and used the materials from it in constructing a temple called Kṣemagaurīśvara.[74] Similarly, in Uttar Pradesh, forty-seven deserted sites of fortified towns in Sultanpur district are the ruins of Buddhist cities which were destroyed by fire when Brāhmaṇism won its final victory over Buddhism.[75] A Tibetan tradition has it that the Kalacuri king Karṇa (eleventh century) destroyed many Buddhist temples and monasteries in Magadha; and Tārānātha (seventeenth century) refers to the destruction of eighty-four temples in the region including Nalanda[76]—a statement which receives indirect support from the Tibetan text *pag-sam-jon-zang* according to which some "Hindu fanatics" destroyed the famous library there.[77] An interesting example of antagonism towards Buddhists in south India is provided by a thirteenth century Ālvār text which tells us that the Vaiṣṇava poet-saint Tirumaṅkai stole a large gold image of the Buddha from a *stūpa* at Nagapattinam and had it melted down for reuse in the temple which he was commissioned by the god Viṣṇu himself to build.[78]

While the brāhmaṇical hostility towards Buddhists has

been adequately documented by scholars in recent years[79], there is also substantial evidence of antipathy towards and persecution of Jains, especially from south India, where proponents of devotional Śaivism (Nāyanārs) and Vaiṣṇavism (Ālvārs) consistently portrayed them as hated "others" from the sixth to the seventh centuries onwards. This is evident, among other sources, from the *Tevāram* (tenth century), a collection of hymns attributed to the three early Nāyanār saint-poets. Two of them, Appar (seventh century) and Sambandar (seventh century), denigrated the Jains in abusive language. The former speaks of them as the "shameless Jain monks", "naked Jains who fast by night", "wicked monks who eat in barbaric ways", "the weak and filthy Jains with their yellowing teeth"; the latter refers to them as "mad Jain monks who wear mats, and pluck their hair and eat their food standing".[80] A vivid description of the encounter of these two Nāyanār saints with Jains is available in the twelfth-century hagiographical work, the *Periyapurāṇam* of Sekkilār. The most important and well known part of his narrative relates to how Sambandar defeated the Jains in all contests and succeeded in converting the Pāṇḍyan king of Madura from Jainism to Śaivism, leading eventually to the impalement of eight thousand Jain monks. Although there is no record of such a massacre,[81] Śaiva intolerance of Jains is corroborated by several legends found in the *Sthalapurāṇa* of Madura.[82] Similarly, the conversion of the earliest known Jain cave temple in Tirunelveli district (Tamilnadu) into a Śaiva shrine in the seventh century[83] and the depiction of scenes of violence on the walls of the Kailashnath temple of Kanchipuram[84] and on the *mandapam* of the Golden Lily tank of the Minaksi temple at Madura bear testimony to the persecution suffered by Jains in Tamilnadu.

Evidence of the persecution of Jains also comes from other parts of India. In Rajasthan, for example, a Jain Śvetāmbara temple was taken over by the Śaivites. In Karnataka, they were a perpetual *bête noire* of the militant Śaivite Lingāyat/Vīraśaiva sect, which started in the twelfth century. The hagiographies of its leader Bāsava furnish evidence of the slaughter of Jains,[85] and of the appropriation of their temples at many places by the Vīraśaivas. At Ablur in Haveri district a Jain temple was desecrated in 1160 when the Vīraśaiva Ekāntada Rāmayya defeated the Jains in debate, demolished their temple and built a shrine in honour of Vīra Somanātha, which contains sculptured panels depicting scenes of his encounter with them.[86] In Dharwad district, the Megudi temple at Hallur and the Doddappa temple in Adargunchi village, originally constructed for Jain worship, were taken over by the Vīraśaivas.[87] Leaving aside the specific cases of the appropriation of *basadi*s (Jain monasteries), there is also evidence of their destruction on a large scale by some individual Vīraśaiva fanatics. Devara Dasimayya (eleventh century), for example, is said to have destroyed about seven hundred *basadi*s (Jain monateries)[88] and Ekāntada Rāmayya is believed to have destroyed eight hundred *basadi*s.[89] According to one estimate about half of the total number of *basadi*s were destroyed, and anything between 1800 and 2000 out of 8000 temples were ruined.[90] The victimization of the Jains became so severe that they had to seek the intervention of the Vijayanagara ruling family in the fourteenth century; but the Vīraśaivas continued to persecute them, as is clear from several sixteenth century inscriptions from the Srisailam area of Andhra Pradesh. One of them tells us that a chief named Liṅga took pride in beheading Śvetāmbara Jains.[91] The Jains remained a hated lot until very late, and this is remembered in passages like *hastinā tāḍyamāno pi na gacched jaina-mandiram* (even under the threat of being trampled upon by an elephant, one should not enter a Jain temple).[92] Thus our survey of evidence, though far from exhaustive, shows that the followers of the brāhmaṇical sects did not, as they are said to have done, practise tolerance towards non-brāhmaṇical faiths: on the contrary, they seem to have played a leading role in fomenting religious conflicts and perpetrating sectarian violence during the early medieval period and later.

Our sources indicate that the increasing militancy of the brāhmaṇical sects was accompanied by their gradual militarization. An analysis of the inscriptional data shows that the term *caṭṭa*, which occurs in the epigraphs along with *bhaṭṭa*, indicates that the brāhmaṇs received training in the martial arts. The word *caṭṭa*, found in a record from Parthivapuram (AD 866), has been interpreted to mean that brāhmaṇ students were required not only to study Vedic lore but also to receive military training in the centres called *śālāis* attached to Viṣṇu temples.[93] Several similar temple-supported establishments existed in Kerala during the early medieval period, an important one being the Kāntalūrśālai, which became famous for its military role in the Coḷa-Cera conflict.[94] The counterparts of the *śālāis* were called *ghaṭikās* in the Cālukya and Pallava territories, the most famous being the one at Kanchi. That the *śālāis* and *ghaṭikās* imparted military education to brāhmaṇs is borne out by literary texts from both north and south India[95] —a fact which may not be entirely unrelated to the emergence of militant ascetic orders of the Śaṅkara school.[96] The militarization of brāhmaṇical sects and the growth of temple militias created conditions for violent conflicts between arms-bearing brāhmaṇs and the votaries of non-brāhmaṇical sects.

There is little doubt that Brāhmaṇism was inherently intolerant, as all religions are; and that its intolerance, often expressed through violence, may have received much sustenance from the martial brāhmaṇs. It is thus difficult to swallow the claim that "Hinduism" has "a propensity to assimilate rather than to exclude" or that tolerance is the very essence of "Hinduism qua Hinduism."[97] Equally, to say that Islam brought violence to a land which until then had not known it, is to ignore the mélange of evidence to the contrary. Groups of warrior ascetics and soldier *sādhus* had come into being much before Islam arrived in India, and they fought among themselves.[98]

II

Scholars and politicians who pay glowing tribute to "tolerant Hinduism" also proudly proclaim that it is a non-proselytizing religion with no scope for conversion,[99] their purpose being to distinguish it from Christianity and Islam. Since the brāhmaṇical sects covered by the modern term "Hinduism" did not have a founder, a basic text or an organized monastic establishment, they may not have proselytized in the same manner as Christianity or Islam; but there is evidence that conversion was not unknown in early India. A later Vedic text, the *Tāṇḍya Brāhmaṇa*, also known as the *Pañcaviṃśa Brāhmaṇa*, describes the *vrātyastoma* sacrifice that the *vrātya*s were required to perform in order to become eligible to have social intercourse with the orthodox *ārya*s. The *vrātya*s have been generally taken to mean people living outside the pale of brāhmaṇical religion, and the *vrātyastoma* rite served the purpose of their conversion to it.[100]

Mention may also be made of the *dīkṣā* ceremony, generally understood in the sense of initiation (*upanayana*) or consecration, which "implies death to profane existence, enables man to gain sacred knowledge and wisdom, a higher stage of existence and access to heavenly life."[101] Without expatiating on the meaning and significance of this ceremony in the various ritual contexts, it may be pointed out that its importance in different Indian religions can hardly be exaggerated. In Vaiṣṇavism, for example, the main object of *dīkṣā* is purification, without which an individual cannot be admitted to the religious order or community;[102] and in Kashmir Śaivism, it is "the most important method of attaining integral Śivahood." Similarly it is mandatory for members of the Vīraśaiva community because it alone opens the door of Vīraśaivism to them. Of particular significance here is the fact that this route is available also to outsiders who seek admission to the fold.[103] Thus *dīkṣā* is best thought of as an early and necessary stage in converting to the faiths named; and its very existence speaks of the possibility of conversion.

Even if there are differences of opinion about the nature and significance of this ritual,[104] the practice of religious conversion in Śaivite sects seems to have been common. The chief function of the monastery founded by Bāsava at Kalyana in 1156, as well as that of the other traditional Vīraśaiva monasteries established at other places after the twelfth century, was to convert non-Lingāyats to Vīraśaivism.[105] Tradition has it that in Karnataka the Jains were coerced to convert on a large scale to Vīraśaivism in the wake of Ekāntada Rāmayya's victory over them.[106]

Evidence of conversion also comes from mythology, religious texts as well as the secular literature. Among the early myths, the legend of Dakṣa Prajāpati points implicitly to religious conversion within the fold of Brāhmaṇism. It has many versions, but at its core is "the conflict between the Vedic sacrificial religion and the Rudra-Śiva religion which ... was reconceived into a conflict between Vaiṣṇavism and Śaivism" in the epic and Purāṇic texts.[107] The climax of the story is represented by Śiva's destruction of the sacrifice performed by Dakṣa, followed by the Dakṣa's realization of Śiva's superiority and conversion to him.[108]

There are also textual references to the procedure to be followed during conversion. The *Nāradaparivrājakopaniṣad*, for example, sets out in detail the way in which renouncers are to be converted or admitted to the Daśanāmī orders said to have been established by the earliest disciples of Śaṅkarācārya.[109] The *Somaśambhūpaddhati*,[110] a manual compiled by Somaśambū in the second half of the eleventh century, prescribes a procedure called the *lingoddhāra* (conversion ritual) for converting people from other creeds to Śaivism by the ritual removal of earlier religious affiliation, the purpose of the conversion being the realization that without becoming a Śaiva, salvation is unattainable.[111] Similarly, a Tantric text called the *Kubjikānityāhnikatilaka* (1197) describes the conversion of nine Buddhists to the Kaula religion. According to the tradition recorded in it, when Śrīnātha alias Tūṣnīśa alias Unmanīśanātha, the first of the ancient *gurus* of the Kubjika school of Tantra, went to the land of the *gandharvas* (*gandharvaloka*), he was questioned by some Buddhists living there. He told them that he was a *siddha* (perfect) and possessed the supreme divine instruction (*divyajñānavaralabdhaka*). Upon this the Buddhists laughed at him and challenged him to prove his statement. Śrīnātha, the story goes, uttered the syllable HUM and all the Buddhist monasteries collapsed. The monks acknowledged his authority, and later he converted them.[112] Among the secular works, the *Prabodhacandrodaya* of Kṛṣṇa

Miśra (eleventh century) records how, after an interesting conversation with a Buddhist and a Jain, and after offering them wine and women, a Kāpālika succeeded in converting them to Śaivism.[113]

Religious conversion may have been of central importance to many renouncers who travelled in different parts of the subcontinent, and defeated their philosophical rivals in debate, thus "conquering the quarters", more or less like the kings of yore performing *digvijaya*. The first among them was the Advaita theologian Śaṅkara, who not only defeated his rivals but also established four seats of learning in the four corners of the subcontinent, each of them becoming a centre of pilgrimage and perhaps of conversion to Śaivism; a tradition popular among the Himalyan people has it that he defeated the Buddhists with both *śastra* and *śāstra* (weapons and arguments).[114] Like Śankara, several medieval peripatetic renouncers bitterly opposed to his order and exponents of principal Vaiṣṇava theological traditions undertook long journeys, defeated their opponents in debate, and won them over to their own views. Madhva (thirteenth century), proponent of the Dvaita Vedānta school, Vallabha (fifteenth-sixteenth century), founder of the Puṣṭimārga sect and his younger contemporary Caitanya, the patriarch of the Bengal Vaiṣṇavism were thus among the important religious leaders inspired by a strong missionary zeal. While much evidence of conversion may be available from the hagiographies of medieval saints and *gurus*, an important piece of information recorded in the *Periyapurāṇam* of Sekkilār (twelfth century) may be mentioned here. Its author Sekkilār tells us that the Nāyanār saint Appar was born in an orthodox Śaiva family of the Vellāla community but became a Jain monk at an early age. Agitated, his elder sister sought Śiva's help. Appar was then afflicted with a serious abdominal disorder, which was cured not by the Jain physicians and their mantras but only by the grace and miracle of Śiva. Repentant over his earlier conversion to Jainism, he came back to the fold of his family faith. Enraged at this, the Jains brought charges against him before the Pallava king Mahendravarman, who was a follower of Jainism. Appar, however, succeeded in convincing the king of the truth of Śaivism, whereupon Mahendravarman himself became a Śaiva. Sekkilār also gives an account of the encounter between another Śaiva saint, Sambandar, and the Jains. The queen and the minister of the Pāṇḍyan king, he tells us, invited Sambandar to Madurai to drive out the Jain monks who exercised their hold over the king. The saint went to Madura, proved the superiority of his miracles over those of the Jains and converted the king to Śaivism; and 8,000 Jains are said to have been impaled on the occasion. Sekkilar's narrative, related in the *Periyapurāṇam* five centuries after the events, may be a tall tale with questionable facticity.[115] But the conversion of Appar, Mahendravarman and the Pandyan ruler remains true.

Most of these references to conversion, with the exception of *vrātyastoma*, belong to the early medieval period and subsequent times, when the important Purāṇas were composed. As pointed out earlier, they provide substantial evidence of sectarian rivalries, but it is just as important that they betray a strong brāhmaṇical hostility towards the proselytizing activities of the votaries of the heterodox sects: the *Visṇupurāṇa*, for example, tells us that the Buddha came to the earth in order to indoctrinate the *daityas* against the Vedas.[116] The Purāṇas were used, on the one hand, to resist the conversion of people to non-brāhmaṇical sects and, on the other, as an instrument for the diffusion of brāhmaṇical religious ideas among the various ethnic groups to which they refer.[117]

Like the propagation of Purāṇic lore, the practice of making land grants to brāhmaṇs and their religious establishments also played a significant role in the dissemination of the brāhmaṇical world view among the marginalized people. As a result of donations of land and villages to brāhmaṇs, their settlements came up in different parts of the country during the early medieval period. They became specially important in the economically backward regions where the brāhmaṇs, living as they did at a higher level of material existence, were able to disseminate their own religious beliefs and practices. In many cases the obligations of the recipients of the land charters included not only the teaching of Vedic lore but also the actual performance of brāhmaṇical rites and rituals, which enabled them to make inroads into tribal societies and religions. For instance, an interesting eighth-century inscription from the Raipur district in Chhattisgarh mentions two Śaiva ascetics, Sadyaḥśivācārya and Sadāśivācārya, and records the dedication of a temple to the latter and his spiritual successors along with several plots of black-soil land (*kṛṣṇatalā*) located in different villages. It states that the ascetics, in return for the endowment, were expected to arrange a free feeding house (*annasya sattram*), a sacrificial rite (*yāga*), the exposition of the Śaiva doctrine (*vyākhyāyaḥ samayasya*) and the ceremony of initiation (*dīkśā*) into the Śaiva faith, which was capable of securing salvation (*nirvāṇa-dakṣa*).[118] This record clearly indicates that land gifts to priests in the peripheral areas were an important and effective instrument for spreading religious beliefs and practices among tribal groups and for their conversion to brāhmaṇical sects.

That the idea of conversion was not alien to Brāhmaṇism is also known from an early medieval legal text, the *Devalasmṛti*, which states that if brāhmaṇs and members of other castes are carried off by *mlecchas* and indulge in forbidden acts, they can be purified by performing the prescribed penance (*prāyaścitta*).[119] It also lays down that anyone who has lived with *mlecchas* for between five and twenty years can be purified by undergoing two *cāndrāyaṇas*.[120] The idea of Devala and other early medieval law-givers that anyone who left his religion could be taken back into its fold after purification amounted to reconversion, [121] which in practice could not have been different from conversion. This anticipated the later *śuddhi*[122] movement led by the Arya Samaj founded in 1875 by Dayanand Saraswati (1824–1883) who considered it his primary task to reconvert (purify, *śuddhi*) Muslims and Christians and to bring all people within the fold of the Vedic religion which he considered to be the best of all religions. Though in its initial phase the *śuddhi* movement did not find favour with the Sanātanists who viewed Hinduism as a non-proselytizing religion,[123] Dayananda himself initiated the practice of conversion/reconversion and performed the first *śuddhi* of a Muslim in 1877 at Dehradun and gave him the name Alakhdhari. Another missionary was Swami Vivekananda (1863–1902) who established the Ramakrishna Mission in 1897, organized centres of his order not only in India but also in the West; for he wanted "heroic workers... to go abroad and help to disseminate the great truths of the Vedanta" and convert people of Europe and the US.[124] Proselytization received much support from the Hindu Mahasabha founded in 1905 whose long time supremo V.D. Savarkar (1883–1966) was a fanatic champion of missionary activities; not surprisingly, one of its presidents, N.C. Chatterjee, stated in 1952 that "there is no greater historical truth than that the Hindu religion had been a proselytising religion."[125] The Rashtriya Swayamsevak Sangh and its affiliates like the Vishwa Hindu Parishad with branches world wide under various brand names have been pursuing their plan of organized proselytization in India and abroad. In addition, there are numerous organizations and innumerable jet set glamour gurus and sadhus, with questionable personal track record, who are busy converting people to various forms of Hinduism. Denial of the proselytizing nature of Hinduism, then, is highly misleading and pulls the wool over people's eyes.

III

The Hindutva groups, that have been propagating the myth of a tolerant and non-proselytizing Hinduism, have also been orchestrating the fiction that cow has always been sacred for Hindus and abstention from eating its flesh is a mark of Hindu identity. By contrast they stereotype the Muslims as cow killers who introduced beef eating in India. Accordingly they have been demanding a national ban on cow slaughter denying the bulk of historical evidence which shows that beef eating was not Islam's "baneful bequeathal" to India; nor is abstention from it a mark of Hindu identity.

The flesh of cattle very much suited the palate of the ancient Indians, especially the Vedic Aryans, who were largely pastoral nomads and practiced animal sacrifice.[126] In the *aśvamedha* (horse sacrifice), the most important of their public sacrifices, more than 600 animals (including the wild ones like boars) and birds were killed and its *finale* was marked by the sacrifice of 21 sterile cows.[127] The *gosava* (cow sacrifice) was an important component of the *rājasūya* and *vājapeya* sacrifices[128] and in the latter, the *Śatapatha Brāhmaṇa* tells us, a sterile spotted cow was offered to Maruts.[129] Similarly a sterile cow was sacrificed in the *agniṣṭoma*[130] and immolation of seventeen dwarf heifers under three[131] was an important element in the *pañcaśāradīyasava* (*darśapūrṇamāsa*). That the flesh of the sacrificial victim was meant for human consumption is clear from passages,[132] which discuss the mode of cutting up the immolated animal and the distribution of its various body parts by the *samitāra* who killed the victim by strangulation.

Cow was also killed on festive occasions like marriage[133], and reception of guests *(arghya/madhuparka)*. The *Ṛgveda* refers to a Vedic hero, Atithigva, whose name literally means slaying cows for guests.[134] The *Aitareya Brāhmaṇa*, states that if the ruler of men comes as a guest or any one else deserving of honour comes, people kill a bull or a cow.[135] Several Gṛhyasūtras describe *madhuparka* both independently[136] as well as part of the marriage ceremonies in which cow was slain more than once in honour of guests;[137] Pāṇini uses the term *goghna* for a guest.[138]

On certain occasions cattle were slaughtered for community as well. One of them was the *gavāmayana*, a sessional sacrifice, performed by the brāhmaṇs, culminating in an extravagant bacchanal frolicsome festival, *mahāvrata*. Similarly the *gṛhamedha*[139] was some kind of a lavish communal feast in which an unspecified number of cows were slain. Killing of cows at the time of cremation and during subsequent funerary rites like *śrāddha* performed in honour of the Manes was recommended in the Vedic and early dharmaśāstra texts. Beef eating was so much *de rigeuer* that cow may have been killed even on flimsy grounds. If one were eager, for instance, to have a learned son with a long life he could, according to an Upaniṣadic precept, eat a mess of veal or beef or other flesh with rice and ghee.[140]

Evidently then there is little doubt that the early Aryans slaughtered animals and cattle including the cow whose flesh they ate with great relish. Not surprisingly, beef was the favourite food of the much respected sage from Mithilā, Yājñvalkya, who is said to have made the well-known statement that he would continue to eat the flesh of cows and oxen so long as it was tender (*aṃsala*),[141] though his obdurate position may also imply that already in his time an opinion against beef eating was gaining ground.

It has been argued that the cow was described as *aghnya* (unslayable) in the Vedic texts and was therefore sacred. The term *aghnya/aghnyā* (lit. not to be slain) has been used at four places in the *Ṛgveda* and the *Atharvaveda* as a masculine noun equivalent to bull or ox and 42 times with a feminine ending to mean a cow.[142] Attention has also been drawn to the use of words for cow as epithet or in simile and metaphor with reference to entities of highest religious significance,[143] though these occurrences do not indicate their primary sense with reference to the actual animal. But all this hardly supports the view that the cows were sacred and inviolable. Admittedly certain degree of inviolability may have come to be associated with the cow belonging to the brāhmaṇ for whom it was an ideally preferred form of *dakṣinā* (sacrificial fee);[144] for there are many references to his interest in his *dakṣiṇā* (the good milch cow),[145] and to the dire consequences that will befall one who withholds it or injures or misappropriates it and the corresponding benefit accruing to him who bestows it.[146] The special importance attached to the brāhmaṇ's cow, however, cannot be stretched to mean that the Vedic bovine was divine and unslayable.

In the later Vedic period the Upaniṣads began to question the efficacy of animal sacrifice for achieving self realization[147] and this culminated in the doctrine of *ahimsā* which became the defining trait of Buddhism and Jainism. These two religions, as is well known, forcefully challenged the Vedic sacrificial slaughter of animals including the cattle. But the undermining of brāhmaṇical world of sacrifice did not lead to the total disappearance of the cattle flesh or other meat types from the Indian dietary menu. Gautama Buddha himself is known to have eaten beef and pork. Aśoka, who raised Buddhism to the level of world religion and whose compassion for animals is undeniable, allowed certain specified animals to be killed for his kitchen. But his list of animals exempted from slaughter does not mention the cow; nor does the *Arthaśāstra* of Kauṭilya specifically mention cow as unslayable. Like Buddhism, Jainism also enthusiastically took up cudgels for non-violence but it did not develop the sacred cow concept. The cattle continued to be killed for food throughout the period of the Mauryas.

In the centuries following their rule Manu (200 BC–AD 200), whose law book is the most representative of the legal texts and has much to say on the lawful and forbidden food, does not exclude cow from the list of edible animals. He asserts that killing of animal on ritual occasions is non-killing,[148] and injury (*hiṃsā*) as enjoined by the Veda (*vedavihitahiṃsā*) is known to be non-injury.[149] Manu also recalls the legendary examples of the most virtuous brāhmaṇs of the days of yore who ate ox-meat and dog-meat to escape death from starvation (X.105-9). Since Manu does not mention beef eating as a taboo one can infer that he did not treat cow as sacrosanct—in fact the killing of cow and other cattle on ritual occasions (*madhuparka*, *śrāddha* etc), according to his commentator Medhātithi (ninth century), was in keeping with the Vedic and post-Vedic practice.[150] Another lawgiver, Yājñvalkya (AD 100–300), lays down that a learned brāhmaṇ (*śrotriya*) should be welcomed with a big ox or goat (*mahokṣaṃ vā mahājaṃ vā śrotriyāyopakalpayet*) delicious food and sweet words.[151] The lawgivers generally accept as lawful all those sacrifices, which, according to them, have Vedic sanction.

The dharmasāstric evidence receives corroboration from the epics. The *Mahābhārata* makes a laudatory reference to the king Rantideva in whose kitchen two thousand cows were butchered everyday, their flesh, along with grains, being distributed among the brāhmaṇs (III.208.8-9).[152] The *Rāmāyaṇa* speaks of Sītā as promising to worship the river Yamuna with thousand cows and a hundred jars of wine when Rāma accomplishes his vow[153] (II.55.19-20) and refers to Bhāradvāja as extending generous hospitality to Bharata's troops, regaling them with meat and wine (II.85.17), and welcoming Rāma by slaughtering "the 'fatted calf'."[154] Similarly, the earliest Buddhist Tamil epic, *Maṇimekalai* (sixth century AD) relates the story of one Apputiran (lit. the son of a cow) who tried to rescue a cow from the brāhmaṇs eager to kill it for sacrifice and food.[155]

The continuity of the tradition of eating flesh including that of the cattle is also echoed in early Indian secular literature. In the Gupta period, Kālidāsa alludes to the story of Rantideva mentioned in the *Mahābhārata.*[156] More than two centuries later, Bhavabhūti (AD 700) refers to instances of guest reception, which included the killing of a heifer.[157] Rājaśekhara (tenth century) mentions the practice of killing an ox or a goat in honour of a guest[158] and Somadeva (eleventh century) narrates the story of seven brāhmaṇ boys who ate a cow.[159] In the twelfth century, Śrīharṣa describes a variety of non-vegetarian delicacies served at a dazzling marriage feast and refers to two instances of cow killing[160], though in the same century the Cālukya king Someśvara indicates his preference for pork, which, despite the lawgivers' abhorrence for it, continued to be sacrificed and eaten by non-Muslims in India.[161]

The above evidence indicates that beef was part of *haute cuisine* in ancient India much before the advent of Islam in the subcontinent. Even when the brāhmaṇs began to view cattle killing with disfavour, the medieval authors of exegetical works continued to mention the ancient practice; as recently as the early twentieth century Mahāmahopadhyāya Madana Upadhyāya, a brāhmaṇ from Mithilā, recalled several passages from earlier texts indicating that cows and buffaloes were done to death on ritual occasions in the past and referred to the contemporary Nepalese practice of eating buffalo meat.[162] Significantly the dharmaśāstra texts often treated cow killing as nothing more than a minor behavioural aberration[163] which they increasingly associated with the proliferating number of untouchable castes.[164] The inviolability of the cow is thus a myth; and so is its supposed holiness. Cow is not a deity and there is no cow statue. Once a year on the Gopāsṭami day it is decorated and offered flowers and garlands but it has no temple to it. On the contrary it is often found bumbling between the ordinary automobiles as well as between the luxurious limos, causing traffic hazards and browsing on garbage heaps. Not surprisingly, the holiness of the cow is elusive—as elusive as Hindu identity itself!

ENDNOTES

1. Wilhelm Halbfass, *India and Europe: An Essay in Understanding*, Motilal Banarsidass, Delhi, 1990, p. 407.
2. P.J. Marshall, *The British Discovery of Hinduism in the Eighteenth Century*, Cambridge University Press, Cambridge, 1970, p. 245.
3. *The Gospel of Sri Ramakrishna: Originally recorded in Bengali by M., a disciple of the Master, (Sri Sri Ramakrishna Kathāmrita)*, Translated into English by Swami Nikhilananda, Ramakrishna-Vivekananda Center, New York, 2007, p. 642 cited in Jyotirmaya Sharma, *Cosmic Love and Human Apathy: Swami Vivekananda's Restatement of Religion*, Harper Collins India, New Delhi, 2013, p. 91. Sumit Sarkar may be right in arguing that in the *Kathāmrita* there "is no developed sense of a sharply distinct Hindu identity—let alone any political use of it" (*Writing Social History*, Oxford University Press, Delhi, 1997, 324). But the above statement certainly strikes a discordant note in his overall perception of religions.
4. Jyotirmaya Sharma, op. cit., p. 91.
5. See also Torkel Brekke, *Makers of Modern Indian Religion in the Nineteenth Century*, Oxford University Press, New York, 2002, pp. 40–2.
6. The supposed tolerant nature of Hinduism has been the subject of considerable debate in academic circles in the twentieth century. Paul Hacker, for example, used the word "inclusivism" in his discussion of tolerance/intolerance in Indian religions and considered it exclusively an Indian phenomenon, though according to some (e.g. Zagorin) the modern concepts of religious toleration and freedom are the offspring of European civilization (Paul Hacker, "Religiose Toleranz und Intoleranz in Hinduism", *Saeculum*, vol. 8 (1957), pp. 167–79; Perez Zagorin, *How the Idea of Religious Toleration Come to the West*, Princeton University Press, Princeton, 2003, pp. xii–xiii). Several scholars (e.g. Hauer, Golzio etc.) have, not surprisingly, questioned his views—the latter, in

fact, refers to the statement of the Dvaita philosopher Madhva (1199–1278) according to whom the king should punish those who are against the Vaiśṇavas: J.W. Hauer, *Toleranz und Intoleranz in den nichtchristlichen Religionen*, Stuttgart, 1961, pp. 90ff; Karl-Heinz Golzio, "Das Problem von Toleranz und Intoleranz in Indischen Religionen anhand epigraphischer Quellen" in Helmut Eimer, ed., *Frank Richard Hamm Memorial Volume*, Indica et Tibetica Verlag, Bonn, 1990, pp. 89–102.

7. Nirad C. Chaudhuri, *The Continent of Circe*, Chatto and Windus, London, 1965, p. 39.
8. Amartya Sen, *The Argumentative Indian*, Allen lane, London, 2005, pp. 3-33.
9. R.C. Hazra, *Studies in the Purāṇic Records on Hindu Rites and Customs*, Motilal Banarsidass, Delhi, 1975, pp. 41–2; Wendy Doniger O'Flaherty, *The Origin of Evil in Hindu Mythology*, Motilal Banarsidass, Delhi, 1988, pp. 204–11.
10. *Varāhpurāṇa* 4.2; *Matsyapurāṇa* 285. 6–7; *Agnipurāṇa* 49.8; *Bhāgvatpurāṇa* X.40.22 and I.3 cited in John Clifford Holt (*The Buddhist Viṣṇu: Religious Transformation, Politics, and Culture*, Cambridge University Press, New York, 2004, p. 15). In his interesting study Holt ably demonstrates that while Brāhmaṇism accorded the Buddha the status of an *avatāra* of Viṣṇu in India, Buddhists in Sri Lanka incorporated Viṣṇu in their religious culture.
11. Hazra, *Purāṇic Records*, p. 41; Kunal Chakrabarti, *Religious Process: The Purāṇas and the Making of a Regional Tradition*, Oxford University Press, Delhi, 2001, p. 153.
12. H. Krishna Sastri, *Memoirs of the Archaeological Survey of India*, vol. 26, Central Publication Branch, Government of India, Calcutta, 1946; reprint, Swati Publications, Delhi, 1991, pp. 5ff.
13. *Alberuni's India*, tr. Edward Sachau, Trubner & Co., London, 1910, p. 380.
14. P.S. Jaini, *Collected Papers on Jaina Studies*, Motilal Banarsidass, Delhi, 2000, pp. 325–49.
15. *Varāhapurāṇa*, 48.22 [Panchanan Tarkaratna, ed., Vangavasi Press, Calcutta, B.S.1313]
16. P.S. Jaini, *Collected Papers on Buddhist Studies*, Motilal Banarsidass, Delhi, 2001, p. 90.
17. *Yathā hi coraḥ sa tathā hi buddhastathāgatam nāstikamatra viddhi*, *Rāmāyaṇa*, II.109.34 cited P.V. Kane, *History of Dharmaśāstra*, vol. II, Part 2, Bhandarkar Oriental Research Institute, Poona, 1974, p. 721. For a contrary view see Ram Shankar Bhattacharya,

"Buddha as Depicted in the Purāṇas", *Purāṇa*, vol. 24, no. 2 (1982), pp. 384–404.

18. O'Flaherty, *Origin of Evil*, pp. 208–9; Phyllis Granoff, "Holy Warriors: A Preliminary Study of Some Biographies of Saints and Kings in Classical Indian Tradition", *Journal of Indian Philosophy*, vol. 12 (1984), p. 296.
19. Jaini, *Papers on Jaina Studies*, pp. 343–4.
20. John A Grimes, "Darśana", in Sushil Mittal and Gene Thursby, eds., *The Hindu World*, Routledge, London and New York, 2005, p. 539.
21. A. Danielou, *Hindu Polytheism*, Parthenon, New York, 1964, p. 12.
22. W. Ivanow, "The Sect of Imām Shāh in Gujrat", *Journal of the Bombay Branch of Royal Asiatic Society*, vol. 12 (1936), pp. 19-70.
23. J. Talboys Wheeler, ed., *Early Travels in India (16th and 17th Centuries)*, Calcutta, 1864, reprint Deep Publications, Delhi, 1974, p. 78.
24. E.W. Hopkins, "The Divinity of Kings", *Journal of the American Oriental Society*, vol. 51 (1931), p. 314
25. Sukumari Bhattacharji, *The Indian Theogony*, New Penguin Books, New Delhi, 2000, p. 124; Wendy Doniger O'Flaherty, *Hindu Myths*, Penguin, Baltimore, 1975, p. 118.
26. Access to the river Ganga at a place like Kanakhala, which is spoken of highly in the *Mahābhārata* and in later texts, was given much importance by both the Vaiṣṇavas and the Śaivas. Śaiva ascetics fought for the right to enter the Ganga at the most auspicious times of the Kumbhamela. According to one account the Nāgā sanyāsīs Bhavānanda, Surasurānanda and Kamalānanda "won a decisive victory at Hardwar over Bairagis, the Vaiṣṇava ascetics, in 1266" (G.S. Ghurye, *Indian Sadhus*, Popular Prakashan, Bombay, 1964, p. 103). Śaiva and Vaiṣṇava groups also fought a battle at Hardwar in 1760 in which, according to one estimate, 18, 000 were killed. This battle decided the issue once and for all in favour of the Śaiva ascetics (Klaus Klostermaier, "The Original Dakṣa Saga", in Arvind Sharma, ed., *Essays on the Mahābhārata*, E.J. Brill, Leiden, 1991, p. 112). Another example of sectarian intolerance comes from Ayodhya, where an open confrontation took place between the Śaiva sanyāsīs and the Vaiṣṇava vairāgīs after the death of Aurangzeb in 1707 over control of religious places and the pilgrims' fees and gifts (R.S. Sharma, *Communal History and Rama's Ayodhya*, revised edition, People's Publishing House, Delhi, 2000, pp. 14–5; Hans Bakker, *Ayodhya*, E. Forsten, Groningen, 1986, p. 149).

27. *Viṣṇupurāṇa*, I.9.56 (Panchanan Tarkaratna, ed., Vangavasi Press, Calcutta, B.S.1331).
28. J. Gonda, *Viṣṇuism and Śivaism: A Comparison*, Mushiram Manoharlal, Delhi, 1976, pp. 92–3.
29. Ibid, 92–3, 196 note 55.
30. Ibid, p. 93.
31. Ibid, 196–7.
32. Ibid, 92–3; P.V. Kane, op. cit., vol. II, pt.1, pp. 168–89.
33. Gonda, *Viṣṇuism and Śivaism*, p. 196 note 58.
34. Ibid., p. 196.
35. Ludo Rocher, *The Purāṇas*, Otto Harrassowitz, Wiesbaden, 1986, p. 22.
36. Wendy O'Flaherty, *The Origin of Evil*, p. 209.
37. Rocher, op. cit., p. 22.
38. K.A. Nilakanta Sastri, *The Coḷas*, University of Madras, Madras, 1975, pp. 644–5.
39. Gonda, *Viṣṇuism and Śivaism*, p. 196 note 57.
40. Nilakanta Sastri, *The Coḷas*, p. 644; idem, *A History of South India*, Oxford University Press, Delhi, 1987, p. 437.
41. Gonda, *Viṣṇuism and Śivaism*, p. 196 note 49.
42. Nilakanta Sastri, *The Coḷas*, p. 645.
43. Klaus K. Klostermaier, *A Survey of Hinduism*, Munshiram Manoharlal, Delhi, 1990, p. 335; Ghurye, op. cit., p. 177.
44. W.G. Orr, "Armed Religious Ascetics in Northern India, " *Bulletin of the John Rylands Library*, vol. 24 (1940), p. 86.
45. R.N. Nandi, "Origin of the Vīraśaiva Movement", in D.N. Jha, ed., *The Feudal Order*, Manohar, Delhi, 2000, p. 485 note 47.
46. C. and H. Jesudasan, *A History of Tamil Literature*, Y.M.C.A., Calcutta, 1961, p. 246; Gonda, *Viṣṇuism and Śivaism*, p. 94.
47. Ibid., p. 94.
48. *Āyārangasuttam*, tr. H. Jacobi, Sacred Books of the East, XXII, II.3.1.10.
49. *Arthaśāstra*, II.4.23; III.20.16. (R.P. Kangle, ed. and tr., 3 pts., reprint, Motilal Banarsidass, Delhi, 1990).
50. It has been pointed out that heresy was in the eye of the beholder. "To the Hindus as a whole, Buddhists and Jains and Cārvākas ... are heretics. To many Vaiṣṇavas, Śaivas are heretics, and to many Śaivas, Vaiṣṇavas are heretics ... the Jains regarded the Hindus as heretics": Wendy Doniger O'Flaherty, "The Image of the Heretic in the Gupta Purāñas," in Bardwell L. Smith, op. cit., p. 116.
51. *The Vyākaraṇa Mahābhāṣya of Patañjali*, 2.4.9, ed., F. Kielhorn, third

edition, Bhandarkar Oriental Reserch Institute, Poona, 1962, Vol. I, p. 476.

52. Cowell, E.B. and R.A. Neil, eds., *Divyāvadāna*, Cambridge University Press, Cambridge, 1886, pp. 433–4.
53. Cited in Halbfass, *Tradition and Reflection: Exploration in Indian Thought*, SUNY Press, Albany, 1991, p. 61.
54. Ibid., pp. 61, 95–6.
55. Ibid., p. 59.
56. Ibid., p. 57. For Śaṅkara's refutation of Buddhist philosophical positions see D.H.H. Ingalls, "Śaṁkara's Arguments Against the Buddhists", *Philosophy East and West*, vol. 3, no. 4 (January 1954), pp. 291–306.
57. Halbfass, *India and Europe*, p. 361.
58. *Saurapurāṇa*, 64.44; 38.54, ed., V.G. Apte, Anandasrama Sanskrit Series, Poona, 1924.
59. *Mattavilāsa Prahasana* of Mahendravikramavarman, ed. and tr., N.P. Uni, College Book House, Trivandrum, 1973, p. 49.
60. Sita Nambiar, ed. and tr., *Prabodhacandrodaya of Kṛṣṇa Miśra*, Motilal Banarsidass, Delhi, 1998, Act III, verse 9.
61. Ibid., pp. 44–5.
62. Paul Dundas, *The Jains*, Routledge, London, 1992, p. 201.
63. Jaini, *Papers on Jaina Studies*, p. 353.Cf. Dundas, op. cit., pp. 200–06.
64. The famous Jain teacher Haribhadra (eighth century) critiqued Buddhism as well as Vedānta in his *Yogadṛṣṭisamuccaya* (Christpher Key Chapple and John Casey, *Reconciling Yoga: Haribhadra's Collection of Views on Yoga*, SUNY Press, Albany, 2004). According to Paul Dundas the Jain texts also indicate a persistent tension between Jainism and Buddhism and frequently refer to great Jain teachers defeating Buddhists in debate. He draws attention to a verse in the *Sthānāngasūtram* which satirizes Buddhist monastic life "as involving a soft bed, food and drink, gambling and at the end of it all deliverance" and refers to the Jain narrative texts which record stories of "Buddhists falsely converting to Jainism to contract marriages with pious Jain girls, seeking revenge upon those who have genuinely converted, and generally fomenting trouble against the Jain community." (Dundas, op. cit., p. 207). The Buddhists on their part were not very kind to the Jains whom they "criticized for being uncaring, hypocritical and hurtful"; the *Maṇimekalai* ridicules a Jain as an "unwashed Jain monk who lumbers along the street 'like an elephant in distress'." (Anne E. Monius, *Imagining a Place for*

Buddhism, Oxford University Press, New York, 2001, pp. 75, 194n127)

65. An important example of the Jains taking over the brāhmaṇical religious establishment is available at Khajuraho. See Julia Hegewald, "From Śiva to Pārśvanātha: The Appropriation of a Hindu Temple for Jaina Worship," *South Asian Archaeology*, 2001, pp. 517–23.
66. Bhikhu Jagdish Kassapa ed., Tevijjasutta, *Dīghanikāya*, Nalanda-Devanagari-Pali Series, Government of Bihar, Patna, 1958.
67. *Tattvasaṃgraha of Śāntarakṣita*, ed. Dwarkadas Shastri, Baudha Bharati, Varanasi, 1968; tr. Ganganatha Jha, Gaekwad Oriental Series, Baroda, 1937. The Buddhists are also known to have taken over Jaina establishments like the one at Vatagoali (Paharpur, West Bengal): Asim Kumar Chatterjee, *A Comprehensive History of Jainism*, vol. 1, Munshiram Manoharlal, Delhi, 2000, pp. 92–3.
68. *Sādhanamālā*, XLI.II, nos. 260, 263-4, etc., cited in B.N. Sharma, "Religious Tolerance and Intolerance as Reflected in Indian Sculptures", *Journal of the Ganganath Jha Research Institute*, Umesh Mishra Commemoration Volume, 1970, p. 665.
69. B.N. Sharma, op. cit., pp. 65–6.
70. G. Roerich, *Biography of Dharmasvāmin*, K.P. Jayaswal Research Institute, Patna, 1959, p. 64.
71. Kamil Zvelebil, *Companion Studies to Tamil Literature*, E.J. Brill, Leiden, 1992, pp. 46–7
72. Samuel Beal, *Si-Yu-Ki: Buddhist Records of the Western World*, Munshiram Manoharlal, Delhi, 1969, pp. 171–2.
73. *Rājataraṅgiṇī of Kalhaṇa*, I.140–4 (tr., M.A. Stein, reprint, Motilal Banarsidass, Delhi, 1979–84).
74. Ibid., VI.171–3.
75. A. Führer, Archaeological Survey, Lists, N.W. Provinces and Oudh, p. 325; cited in B.N.S. Yadava, *Society and Culture in Northern India in the Twelfth Century*, Central Book Depot, Allahabad, 1973, p. 346.
76. Debiprasad Chattopadhyaya, ed., *Tārānātha's History of Buddhism in India*, Motilal Banarsidass, Delhi, 1970 (reprinted 1990), pp. 141–2.
77. B.N.S. Yadava, op. cit., p. 346. It has been generally held that Bakhtiyar Khalji destroyed the university at Nalanda. D.R. Patil, however, categorically states that it was destroyed by the Śaivas (*Antiquarian Remains of Bihar*, K.P. Jayaswal Research Institute, Patna, 1963, p. 304). This view has been discussed at some length by R.S. Sharma and K.M. Shrimali (*A Comprehensive History of*

India, vol. IV, pt. 2 [AD 985–1206], Manohar, Delhi, chapter XXV(b): Buddhism, footnotes 79–82).

78. Richard H. Davis, *Lives of Indian Images*, first Indian edition, Motilal Banarsidass, Delhi, 1999, p. 83.
79. Johannes Bronkhorst, *Buddhism in the Shadow of Brāhmaṇism*, Leiden, 2011; Giovanni Verardi, *Hardships and Downfall of Buddhism in India*, Manohar, Delhi, 2011; Tiziana Lorenzetti, "Political and Social Dimensions as Reflected in Medieval Indian Sculpture", Proceedings of International Conference *In the Shadow of the Golden Age: Art and Identity in South Asia from Gandhara to the Modern Age*, University of Bonn, 2011.
80. Indira Viswanathan Peterson, "Sramaṇas Against the Tamil Way", in John Cort, ed., *Open Boundaries: Jain Communities and Cultures in Indian History*, SUNY Press, Albany, 1998, p. 171.
81. For an insightful discussion of the impalement legend, see Paul Dundas, op. cit., pp. 109–10; Richard H. Davis, "The Story of the Disappearing Jains", in John Cort, op. cit., pp. 213–24.
82. P.B. Desai, *Jainism in South India and Some Jaina Epigraphs*, Jaina Samskrit Samrakshaka, Sholapur, 1957, p. 82.
83. Romila Thapar, *Cultural Transaction and Early India*, Oxford University Press, Delhi, 1987, p. 17; K.R. Srinivasan, "South India", in A. Ghosh, ed., *Jaina Art and Architecture*, vol. 2, Bharatiya Jnanpith, Delhi, 1975; R. Champakalakshmi, "Religious Conflict in the Tamil Country," *Journal of the Epigraphical Society of India*, vol. IV (1978), pp. 69–81; John Cort, op. cit., pp. 107–8.
84. R.N. Nandi, *Social Roots of Religion in Ancient India,* K.P. Bagchi, Calcutta, 1986, p. 97.
85. Velcheru Narayana Rao, *Siva's Warriors: the Bāsava Purāṇa* of Palkuriki Somanātha, Princeton University Press, Princeton, 1990, pp. 200–13,
86. *Epigraphia Indica*, V, no. 25, ll.69–80. Cf. P.B. Desai, op. cit., p. 182; David N. Lorenzen, "Warrior Ascetics in Indian History", *Journal of the American Oriental Society*, 98 (1978), pp. 64–5. Shantinath Dibbad, "The Construction, Destruction and Renovation of Jaina Basadis: A Historical Perspective", in Julia B. Hegewald, ed., *The Jain Heritage: Distiction, Decline and Resilience*, Samskriti, New Delhi, 2011,
87. Julia A.B. Hegewald and Subrata K. Mitra "The Past in the Present: Temple Conversions in Karnataka and Appropriation and Reuse in Orissa", in idem, eds., *Re-Use: The Art and Politics of Integration and Anxiety*, Sage Publications, Delhi, 2012, pp. 54–84.
88. Shantinath Dibbad, op. cit., p. 71.

89. Ibid., pp. 69–70.
90. Ibid., pp. 63–76.
91. P.B. Desai, op. cit., p. 23.
92. Dev Raj Chanana, "The Sanskritist and Indian Society", *Enquiry*, Monsoon, 1965, p. 65.
93. Kesavan Veluthat, *Brāhmaṇa Settlements in Kerala*, Sandhya Publications, Calicut, 1978, Appendix II, pp. 102–15.
94. Ibid.; M.G.S. Narayanan, "Kāntallūr śālāi: New Light on the Nature of Aryan Expansion to South India", *Proceedings of the Indian History Congress*, Jabalpur, 1970, pp. 125–36.
95. The Jain work *Kuvalayamālā* of Udyotanasūri (eighth century) describes a maṭha at Vijaya, where students from different parts of India such as Lāṭa, Karnataka, Mālava, Kannauj, Mahārāṣṭra, Saurāṣtra, Śrīkanṭha and Sindha, received instruction in such diverse subjects as archery (*dhanurveda*), manoeuvring with a shield (*phalakakrīḍā*), use of the sword and the bow (*asi dhanu praveśa*), fighting with a spear (*kuntayuddha*), fighting with clubs (*lakuṭiyuddha*) and fighting with arms (*bāhuyuddha*) (Shanta Rani Sharma, *Society and Culture in Rajasthan c.* AD *700–900*, Pragati Prakashan, Delhi, 1996, p. 231). Several *maṇipravāla* texts, especially the *Candrotsavam* (fifteenth century) and the *Keralolapatti* (seventeenth century) show the association of brāhmaṇs with martial arts.
96. Ghurye, op. cit., chapter VI.
97. Arvind Sharma, "Some Misunderstandings of the Hindu Approach to Religious Plurality", *Religion*, vol. 8 (Autumn 1978), p. 145.
98. David N. Lorenzen ("Warrior Ascetics in Indian History", pp. 61–75) has argued that the military orders of ascetics became significant during the period of Muslim rule. Also see William R. Pinch, *Peasants and Monks in British India*, reprint, Oxford University Press, Delhi, 1999.
99. In the early sixties M.S. Golwalkar asserted that "our religious missionaries who reached distant lands in ancient times did not force their religion on other people" (*Bunch of Thoughts*, Sahitya Sindhu Prakashan, Bangalore, 1966, reprint, 1996, p. 189). In a similar vein P. Venugopal in an article published in the *Organiser* (18 may, 2003, p. 9) wrote that "Hindu religion ... does not believe in conversion" or Hindus do not "go to other countries to market their religion."
100. P.V. Kane, op. cit., vol. II, pt. 1, pp. 385–9; Jan Gonda, *The Ritual Sūtras*, Otto Harrassowitz, Wiesbaden, 1977, pp. 539, 641.

101. J. Gonda, *Change and Continuity in Indian Religion*, Mouton, The Hague, 1965, p. 316
102. Ibid., p. 398.
103. Ibid., p. 433; H.M. Sadasivaiah, *A Comparative Study of Two Vīraśaiva Monasteries*, University of Mysore, Mysore, 1967, pp. 104–6.
104. What most scholars have viewed as conversion has been understood as purification by S.N. Biswas ("Über das Vrātyaproblem in der Vedischen Ritualliteratur", ZDMG, vol. 105, 1955, pp. 53 cited in J.C. Heesterman, "Vrātya and Sacrifice", *Indo-Iranian Journal*, vol. 6 (1962–3), p. 2.
105. H.M. Sadasivaiah, op. cit., pp. 88–9, 168ff.
106. P.B. Desai, op. cit., pp. 182–3.
107. Klaus Klostermaier, "The Original Dakṣa Saga", p. 110.
108. Ibid., pp. 125, 128; Sukumari Bhattacharji, op. cit., p. 124.
109. Ghurye, op. cit., p. 93.
110. The earliest manuscript of the text belongs to Vikrama 1130 (AD 1073). It has been edited by several scholars, the last and most authentic edition being by Madame Brunner-Lachaux published in three parts by Inst. Francais Indologie, Pondicherry. For details of the text and the conversion ritual, see Heinrich von Stietencron, "Religious Configurations in Pre-Muslim India and the Modern Concept of Hinduism", in Vasudha Dalmia and Heinrich von Stietencron, eds., *Representing Hinduism: The Construction of Religious Traditions and National Identity*, Sage Publications, Delhi, 1995, pp. 51–81.
111. Ibid, pp. 56–7; Axel Michaels, *Hinduism: Past and Present*, Orient Longman, New Delhi, 2005, pp. 20–1.
112. *Ṣaṭsāhasra Saṃhitā*, ed. and tr. J.A. Schoterman, E.J. Brill, Leiden, 1982, p. 38; Teun Goudriaan and Sanjukta Gupta, *Hindu Tantric and Śākta* Literature, Otto Harrassowitz, Wiesbaden, 1981, p. 149.
113. *Prabodhacandrodaya*, Act III.
114. It has been asserted on the basis of traditional chronologies of the Kancipura monastery that its fourteenth abbott, Ujjvala, died fighting the heretics in Kashmir whereas its sixteenth abbott, Surendra, was actually enthroned for a while after defeating his rivals in debate. (William S. Sax, "Conquering the Quarters: Religion and Politics in Hinduism", *International Journal of Hindu Studies*, vol. 4, no. 1 (April, 2000), p. 47.
115. Richard H. Davis, "The Story of the Disappearing Jains: Retelling the Śaiva–Jain Encounter in Medieval South India", in John E. Cort, op. cit., pp. 213–24.

116. *Viṣṇupurāṇa*, III.18. Cf. Vijay Nath, *Purāṇas and Acculturation: A Historico-Anthropological Perspective*, Manohar, Delhi, 2001, p. 195.
117. The role of the Purāṇas in bringing about religious and cultural change in the peripheral areas has been discussed perceptively at length by Vijay Nath, op. cit., chapter 8. Also see Kunal Chakrabarti, op. cit.
118. Senkapat Stone Slab Inscription of the time of Śivagupta Bālārjuna, Ajay Mitra Shastri, ed., *Inscriptions of the Sarabhapurias, Panduvaṃśins and Somavaṁśins*, Motilal Banarsidass, Delhi, 1995, pt. II, pp. 154–9, verses 15–22.
119. M.L. Wadekar, *Devalasmṛti Reconstruction*, 2 vols., Chowkhamba, Delhi, 1996. The chapter on *mlecchitaśuddhiḥ* contains as many as seventy-one verses dealing with the *śuddhi* (purification) of those who were taken away by *mlecchas* or stayed with them for five to twenty years.
120. P.V. Kane, op. cit., vol. II, pt. 1, pp. 389–91.
121. Ibid., p. 391.
122. P.V. Kane uses the term *parāvartana* for reconversion and even equates it with the ancient *vrātyastoma* (op. cit., vol. IV, p. 118). On the basis of the *Hindukaraṇavidhi* prepared by the Dharmanirnayamandala, Lonavala (Maharashtra), he has also suggested "a model but brief rite for the *parāvartana* for those who were forcibly converted or for those who voluntarily left the Hindu fold" (ibid).
123. Since caste system (*varṇāśramadharma*) has always occupied a central position in the orthodox sanātanist Hindu religion, and since the Arya Samajist ideology preached the necessity to recognize merit-based caste and not the traditional hereditary caste system, questions were raised about how a convert could be looked upon as a Hindu unless he or she was assigned a place in the caste hierarchy. This added a controversial dimension to *śuddhi* (reconversion) but in the early twentieth-century leaders like Madan Mohan Malaviya lent support to this movement (Christophe Jaffrelot, *Hindu Nationalism: A Reader*, Permanent Black, Delhi, 2007, 68–9)
124. *Speeches and Writings of Swami Vivekananda*, vol. 2, Allahabad 1988, 561–2. Torkel Brekke, op. cit., p. 48. Cf. Paul Hacker, "Der religiöse Nationalismus Vivekānandas", in L. Schmithausen, ed., *Kleine Schriften*, Steiner, Wiesbaden, 1978, pp. 565–79. There are many Hindu sects which are actively engaged in converting people, but the discussion of their activities is beyond the scope of this paper.

125. N.C. Chatterjee, *Presidential Address, All-India Hindu Mahasabha*, 30th Session, Bhopal, 28 December 1952, 3.
126. For a detailed history of the cow in India see D.N. Jha, *The Myth of the Holy Cow*, Verso, London, 2002 Indian edition, Navayana, Delhi, 2009.
127. L. Renou, *Vedic India*, Indian reprint, Indological Book House, Varanasi, 1971, p. 109.
128. R.L. Mitra, *Indo-Aryans*, reprint, Indological Book House, Varanasi, 1969, vol. I, p. 361.
129. G.U. Thite, *Sacrifice in the Brāhmaṇa Texts*, University of Poona, Poona, 1975, p. 77.
130. Renou, op. cit., 105; Kane, op. cit., II, pt. 2, p. 1158.
131. Mitra, op. cit. p. 363.
132. *Taittirīya Saṃhitā*, VI.3.10.2-6 (tr., A.B. Keith, reprint, Motilal Banarsidass, Delhi, 1967); *Gopatha Brāhmaṇa* (*Pūrvabhēga*), I.3.18 (ed., R.L. Mitra, reprint, Indological Book House, Delhi, 1972).
133. *aghāsu hanyate gāvo*, *Ṛgveda*, X. 85. 13c (ed., T. Aufecht, Bonn, 1877).
134. Macdonell, A.A. and A.B. Keith, *Vedic Index of Names and Subjects*, Indian reprint, Motilal Banarsidass, Delhi, 1958, vol. II, p. 145.
135. *Aitareya Brāhmaṇa*, III. 4, cited in Kane, op. cit., vol. II, pt. 1, p. 542, note 1254.
136. *Āśvalayana Gṛhyasutra*, I.24. 1–33; *Pāraskara Gṛhyasūtra*, I.3. 1-31; *Khādira Gṛhyasūtra*, IV.4.5-23; *Gobhila Gṛhyasūtra* IV. 10. 26; *Hiraṇyakeśi Gṛhyasūtra*, I. 4. 12-13; *Āpastamba Gṛhyasūtra*, V. 13. Sacred Books of the East, Vols. 29–30. 1-20. Also see S.C. Banerji, *Dharma-Sūtras: A Study in Their Origin and Development*, Punthi Pustak, Calcutta, 1962, p. 157, fn.39); Kane, op. cit., II, pt. 2, p. 542; A.B. Keith, op. cit., p. 374
137. *Āpastamba Gṛhyasūtra*, I.3.5-8; *Śāṅkhyayana Gṛhyasūtra*, I.12.10.
138. *dāsagoghnau sampradāne*, *Aṣṭādhyāyī*, 3.4.73. ed. and tr., S.C. Vasu, Motilal Banarsidass, Delhi, 1967. Cf. V.S.Agrawala, *India as Known to Pāṇini*, Prithvi Prakashan, Varanasi, 2nd edn, 1963, p. 100.
139. J.C. Heesterman, *The Broken World of Sacrifice: An Essay in Ancient Indian Ritual*, University of Chicago Press, Chicago, 1993, pp. 190–3, 200-2.
140. *atha ya icchet putro me paṇḍito vigītaḥ, samitiṃ-gamaḥ, śuśrūṣtāṃ vācaṃ bhāṣitā jāyeta, sarvān vedān anubruvita, sarvam āyur iyād iti, māṃsodanaṃ pācayitvā sarpiṣmantaṃ aśnīyātām; īsvarau janayita vai, aukṣṇena vārṣabheṇa vā*, *Bṛhadāraṇyaka Upaniṣad*, VI. 4. 18, Radhakrishnan, S. *The Principal Upaniṣads*, (with introduction, text and translation), Oxford University Press, Delhi, 1991, p. 326.
141. *tasmāddhenvanaḍuhornāśnīyāt/ tadu hovāca yājñvalkyaḥ/*

aśnāmyevāhaṃ māṃsalam cedbhavatiti/ Śatpatha Brāhmaṇa, III.1.2.21 quoted in Kane, op. cit., vol. II, pt. 2, p. 773.

142. W. Norman Brown, "The Sanctity of the Cow in Hinduism", *Madras University Journal*, vol. XXVIII, no. 2 (1957), p. 33. Kane (op. cit., II, pt. 2, p. 772–3) also cites Vedic passages mentioning the word *aghnyā*. Cf. I. Proudfoot, *(Ahiṃsā and a Mahābhārata Story*, Australian National University, Canberra, 1987, p. 14.
144. A.A. Macdonell (*Vedic Mythology*, Strassburg, 1897, Indian reprint, Indological Book House, Varansi, 1963, pp. 150–1) makes the valid point that the cow entered the conceptions of Vedic mythology—a view repeated by him and Keith in the *Vedic Index*, II, p. 146. But on Macdonell's own admission, this was owing to the great utility of the cow.
144. Etymologically the word *dakṣiṇā* is so called because it imparts power or strength to the receiver (Apte, *The Practical Sanskrit-English Dictionary*, s.v. *dakṣiṇā*). It is used in the sense of a good milch cow or the richly milking one in the Vedic texts because it gave wealth and hence strength to the priest. See Thite, op. cit., pp. 151–61; I. Proudfoot, op. cit., p. 3 and note 22 on p. 185.
145. M. Bloomfield, *Religion of the Veda*, G.P. Putnam's Sons, New York and London, 1908, pp. 69ff
146. Norman Brown, op. cit., p. 43 draws attention to several passages from the *Ṛgveda* and the *Atharvaveda* to prove this point. Also see N.J. Shende, *The Religion and Philosophy of the Atharvaveda*, Poona, 1952 reprinted by the Bhandarkar Oriental Research Institute, Poona, 1985, p. 124; Herman W. Tull, "The Killing That Is Not Killing: Men, Cattle and the Origins of Non-Violence in the Vedic Sacrifice", *Indo-Iranian Journal*, 39 (1996) pp. 236–7.
147. That the Upaniṣadic position on sacrifice was different from that of the Vedic texts is clear from many passages (e.g. *Bṛhadāraṇyaka Upaniṣad*, 1.4.10; 3.9.6; 3.9.21; *Chāndogya Upaniṣad*, 1.10–12; 4.1–3) to which attention has been drawn by several scholars.
148. Ibid., V.39
149. Ibid., V.44.
150. *govyajamāṃsamaprokṣitaṃbhakṣayed...madhupākṛtānāmevāsad-rūpama nūdyate*: Medhātithi on Manu, V.27; *madhuparkovyākhyātaḥ tatra govadhavihitaḥ:* Medhātithi on Manu, V.41; see *Mānava-Dharma-śāstra*, ed., V.N. Mandalik, Ganapat Krishnaji's Press, Bombay, 1886, pp. 604, 613.
151. *Yājñavalkyasmṛti*, I.109. (ed. T. Ganapati Sastri, Munshiram Manoharlal, Delhi, 1982)
152. *Mahābhārata*, III.208.8–9 (Bhandarkar Oriental Research Institute, Poona, 1919-1966). For further references see S. Sorensen, *An Index to the Names in the Mahābhārata*, Motilal Banarsidas, Delhi,

1963, pp. 593–4.

153. *Rāmāyaṇa*, II.55.19–20 (Critical edition, Oriental Institute, Baroda, 1960-1975)
154. R.L. Mitra, op. cit., p. 396
155. *Maṇimekalai*, 13.1–22, 28, 31–34, 35–48, 51–104 cited in Katherine E. Ulrich, "Food Fights: Buddhist, Hindu and Jain Dietary Polemics in South India", *History of Religions*, vol. 46, no. 3(2007), pp. 233–4.
156. *Meghadūta*, with the commentary of Mallinātha, ed. and tr., M. R. Kale, Motilal Banarsidass, Delhi, 1979, I.48.
157. *Mahāvīracarita*, Rampratap Tripathi Shastri, ed. with Hindi tr, Lok Bharati Prakashan, Allahabad, 1973. III.2. *Uttararāmacarita*, with notes and the commentary of Ghanaśyāma, ed. and tr., P.V. Kane and C.N. Joshi, Motilal Banarsidass, Delhi, 1962, Act IV.
158. *Bālarāmāyaṇa*, of Rājaśekhara, Gangasagar Rai, ed., Chowkhamba, Varanasi, 1984, I.38a
159. *Kathāsaritsāgara* of Somadeva, ed. with Hindi tr., Pandit Kedarnath Sharma, Bihar Rashtrabhasha Parishad, Patna, VI, 117–8
160. *Naiṣadhamahākāvyam*, with the commentary of Mallinātha, ed., Haragovind Shastri, Chowkhamba, Varanasi, 1981, XVII.173, 197.
161. Frederick J. Simmons, *Eat Not This Flesh*, University of Wisconsin Press, Madison, 2nd edition, 1994, pp. 51–6; K.T. Achaya, *A Historical Dictionary of Indian Food*, Oxford University Press, Delhi, 1999, p. 187. James Tod, writing in the early nineteenth century, reports the hunting and eating of wild boar among various groups including the Rajputs (*Annals and Antiquities of Rajasthan*, vol. 1, Smith, Elder and Co., London, 1829, 1st Indian reprint, Oriental Books Reprint Corporation, New Delhi, 1983, pp. 451-2). However, the anti-pig sentiment, traceable to pre-Islamic times in West Asia, has been very strong among Indian Muslims, though certain Islamic groups in Mauritania, Morocco, Algeria, Tunisia, Kurdistan and Indonesia permit pork. Interestingly, the two Persian doctors, Avicenna (980–1037) and Haly Abbas (930–94), spoke favarourably of pork as food (Simmons, op. cit., pp. 35, 341, n. 180–82)
162. *Palapiyūṣalatā* by Mahāmahopadhyāya Madana Updhyāya, Gourīśayantrālaya, Darbhanga, Samvat 1951.
163. *Atrismṛti*, verse 314 in *Aṣṭadaśasmṛtyaḥ* (with Hindi tr. by Sundarlal Tripathi, Khemraj Shrikrishnadas, Venkateshwar Steam Press, Bombay, Saka 1846.
164. *Vyāsasmṛti*, I.12. in *Aṣṭadaśasmṛtyaḥ* (with Hindi tr. by Sunderlal Tripathi, Bombay, Saka 1846.

Section II

QUESTIONING THE SYMBOLS

4

Trident Stridency*

K.M. Shrimali

Phagi, near Jaipur, where local Dalits were prevented by the upper-caste Hindus from bathing in the village pond.

Asind (Bhilwara district), where a sixteenth century "Masjid Sawai Bhoj" (in use till 1956) was destroyed by a mob in July 2001 and an instant temple of Hanuman was created at the site of the demolished mosque.

Gangapur in Sawai Madhopur, where three people were killed in police firing when a mob tried to block the Moharram procession in Godhara's aftermath.

All these places in Rajasthan witnessed mass distribution of *triśūla*s (tridents) with a great fanfare in recent months by the Bajrang Dal and the Vishwa Hindu Parishad (VHP). These performances are christened as "*triśūla dīkṣā*" and the programme has been going on for the last several years in different states of India. The ideologues of the programme have projected it as a venture of "glorious cultural resurgence" to invigorate "Hindu" ethos. Flaying "*triśūla dīkṣā*", Swami Agnivesh, a prominent social activist and Arya Samaj leader, said recently at Jaipur, that in the Hindu tradition there was no such practice. "*Triśūla*" distributed by VHP were weapons and they had no religious sanctity. How old is the history of

---

* Reprinted from the *Frontline*, Vol. 20, No. 11 (May 24-June 06, 2003).

triśūla as a "religious symbol" and/or a weapon? What does *triśūla* symbolize? What has been the real meaning of *dīkṣā* in the multifarious Indian cultural traditions?

Any claim about the hoary antiquity of the word *triśūla* would remain suspect. Its allusions as Śiva's weapon are rather rare even in the Epics (*Mahābhārata* and *Rāmāyaṇa*). A diminutive 'trident' (*triśūlikā*) occurs only once in a seventh century work (*Kādamabarī*). *Triśūlinī* as the name of Durgā is impossible to locate in texts prior to the ninth century. Some lexicons datable between ninth and fifteenth centuries acquaint us with *triśīrṣaka* (not *triśūla*), three-headed thing (possibly, but not necessarily, a 'trident').

In contrast, the antiquity of '*śūla*' is much older. However, its meanings and connotations are extremely varied and very often they do not have any religious ring around them, far less any specific sectarian linkage. The earliest occurrence of *śūla* is in the *Ṛgveda* (*c.*1500–1000 BC) but in the sense of a sharp pin or stake on which meat was roasted. *Śūlakṛta* (roasted on a pit) occurs in a post-sixth-century work of Sanskrit fiction. In the later Vedic ritual literature (*c.*1000–500 BC) *śūlagava* was an 'ox fit for spit' presented as an offering to Rudra. In the Epics, *śūla* occurs in the sense of a sharp instrument or pointed dart, may be as a lance or a spear. In the Law Book of Manu it became a stake for impaling criminals. While medical treatises mention *śūla* in the sense of acute pain, in the erotic works (not before AD fourth century) it acquires the meaning of a harlot or prostitute.

Śiva or Durgā as wielders of *śūla* in their hands are not mentioned in any pre-sixth-century literary work. In inscriptions, too, *śūladhara*, *śūlapāṇi*, and *śūlin* as epithets of Śiva figure only after the mid-sixth century. In the early medieval lexicons, there is even an allusion to *śūla* as 'a bow'. Incidentally, these lexicons also speak of *śūlika* as the illegitimate son of a brāhmaṇ and a śūdra woman or as the son of a kṣatriya and an unmarried śūdra woman

Though not much work has been done on archaeology of early Indian weapons, yet the broad contours of advances in metal technologies are fairly clear. Be it the prehistoric rock paintings depicting numerous hunting scenes, or the exquisite glyptic art of thousands of seals and sealing of the Harappan civilization, or even the actual remains of several metal artifacts, *triśūla* is conspicuous by its complete absence in them.

Finished metal objects were important symbols of wealth and power in the Indus cities. A large copper/bronze 'cooking pot covered with a bronze plate' was found buried in Harappa. It contained several copper weapons and tools. The repertoire included 22 axes of differently shaped edges and blades, 10 daggers, 13 spear heads, one arrowhead, one lance head, one marble mace head, ten chisels, two saws, etc. These included both used and unused artifacts. Scholars who have, following the lead of John Marshall, persistently and obstinately argued for the presence of 'proto-Śiva' (claim was contested by Mackay, Marshall's colleague, and has been repeatedly questioned by many others since then) and 'Hinduism' in the Harappan pantheon, have failed to produce any evidence of *triśūla* in any form—not even in more than 400 signs identified in the Harappan script.

Apart from the aforesaid marble mace-head, stone mace-heads with an hour-glass type perforation bored from both ends for shaft insertion, and copper mace-head have also been known from Mohenjo-daro and Harappa. Stone mace-heads have been noticed in other varying cultural contexts as well, namely, mesolithic Langhnaj (Gujarat), neolithic Burzahom (Jammu & Kashmir), chalcolithic Ahar (Rajasthan), Navdatoli (Madhya Pradesh), and Chandoli (Maharashtra) spanning between second-first millennia BC.

The Epics make distinctive allusions to clubs and maces. The famous mace-dual between the two cousins (Bhīma and Duryodhana), providing a gruesome *finale* to a long-drawn family feud over property, brought down the final curtain on the *Mahābhārata* war. Indeed, multifarious uses of *gadā* by hunters, and merchants and traders traversing inhospitable tracks passing through forests, have been worked out. Some have even seen a prototype of this weapon of crushing power in its use as a primary tool (digging stick) of the early farmer.[1] However, as a weapon of offence and defense, its popularity gradually declined when iron weapons became more frequent. If the classical accounts of Diodorus Siculus, Curtius Rufus, and Arrian (c. first century BC to first century AD) are to be believed, the Śibis lost against Alexander (late fourth century BC) because they fought with clubs. Its retention in the iconography of Viṣṇu was perhaps reduced to a stylized attribute.

Even a casual study of the *Rāmāyaṇa* and the *Mahābhārata* reveals that there were many levels of warfare. While some tribes and many heroes fight with branches or trunks of trees, with rocks and boulders and sometimes even with their teeth, nails and fists; there are also allusions to some mechanical contrivances. However, if one were to undertake a statistical count of number and types of weapons in Indian literary tradition, it would become obvious that the supreme weapon in the Epics as well as in the Vedic literature is the bow and arrow. More than thirty different types of arrows, each with a unique identity and name of its own, are mentioned in the epics.

Spears/lances and javelins vie in popularity with bows and arrows. The Epics also mention explicitly swords and daggers of different shapes and sizes. Spears and harpoons figure in prehistoric rock paintings, Harappan seals and in the vast repertory of 'Copper Hoards' from different parts of north India. Spear and arrowheads made of bones, copper and iron are attested from all over India. The efflorescence of iron arrow and spear-heads is particularly seen during the period between *circa* 500 BC and AD 300. From Kaushambi (near Allahabad) alone, nearly 400 arrowheads of as many as 11 types were unearthed in the 1950s. Archaeologists have been able to document antennae-hilted copper swords from about the second millennium BC and from such geographically scattered regions as Bactria (Bactria Margiana Archaeological Culture in northern Afghanistan, which is fast emerging as one of the most probable matrix representing archaeological counterpart of Ṛgvedic culture), Ganga-Yamuna *doab* and chalcolithic Karnataka (at Kallur, for instance).

In the early historic context, especially in the post-Mauryan centuries (*c.*200 BC to *c.* AD 300), varied weaponry is seen in sculptural depictions of mostly non-religious significance in north India and the Deccan. These include graphic presentation of war scenes in the stūpas at Sanchi and Bharhut, as well as sculptures from Mathura, Bhaja (near Pune) and Gandhāra. Six types of lances, six types of swords, five types of daggers, four types of shields, varieties of bow and arrow along with occasional depiction of mace, spear, thunderbolt, battle-axe, and *cakra* have been identified in these art remains. The representation of *triśūla* in these remains, as in the Epic allusions, is very rare. That bows and arrows retained their importance amidst this growing diversification of weapons is evident in the phenomenal specialization achieved in this genre. Thus, a Buddhist text (*Milindapañha*) of these centuries makes separate mention of bow manufacturers, bowstring makers and arrow fletchers. This compares favourably with the two Epics (composition between c. 400 BC and c. AD 400)—in the *Rāmāyaṇa* for instance, three types of bowstrings are mentioned, of which *jyā* occurs 38 times.

The earliest iconographic delineation of *triśūla* in the specific context of Śiva does not go beyond the first century BC and is usually seen in the coins of Śaka-Parthian and Kuṣāṇa rulers (up to circa AD third century), the so-called 'foreigners.' In the case of Kuṣaṇa depictions, *triśūla* is sometimes combined with battle-axe (*paraśu*).

It may be recalled that all these dynasties began their careers in the Indian subcontinent from the regions in the northwest which had witnessed considerable penetration of Greek influence from at least the fourth century BC. It should be incisive to recall that barring sculptural representations of popular gods, goddesses, demi-gods, vegetative, and fertility divinities such as *yakṣa*s and *yakṣī*s, the genesis of anthropomorphic representations of major Indian deities—both brāhmaṇical and non-brāhmaṇical, is invariably traceable to Greek and Roman influences located in that region. To illustrate, phenomenal numismatic treasures were found at Ai Khanoum in Afghanistan during excavations at the site between 1965 and 1978 (thanks to the barbaric rampage of the Taliban, the site has been completely destroyed and the treasure of antiques has most probably reached predatory antique markets of Europe and the United States). Amongst these treasures were six unique coins of an Indo-Greek king Agathocles (180–170 BC) depicting, for the first time, two popular deities of Viṣṇuite pantheon, namely, Vasudeva Kṛṣṇa and his elder brother Samkarśana Balarāma with their characteristic identifiers, that is *cakra* and *hala* (plough) respectively. Similarly, delineation of Indra has been identified in the coins of some other Indo-Greek kings of comparable vintage. That Gandhāra was the matrix of the earliest Buddha images (Buddha also figures on coins of the Indo-Greeks from about the second century BC), is fairly well-known.

The antiquity of specific "religious symbols" and their association with specific religious cults and creeds is a complex phenomenon. Sketching the history of "Sacred Prostitution", Penzer noted: "The principal deities of the dancing-girls are those to whom the temples, in which they are employed, are dedicated... Minor deities, such as Bhadrakali, Yaksi and Gandharva are worshipped by the figure of a trident or sword being drawn on the wall of the house, to which food and sweetmeats are offered on Fridays."[2] The Greek God Poseidon and "Trident" are inseparable. There are several other Graeco-Roman divinities who are intimately identified as wielders of trident. It is also well-known that many of the cultural traits/symbols of the 'civilized' Mediterranean world came from much older civilizations located in the valleys of the Nile, and Tigris-Euphrates. In early Mesopotamian religion, Ishtar was the goddess of war as well as of love, of prostitutes as well as of mothers. Iconographically, she is symbolized by her great tripartite sceptre (trident).

Indian religio-philosophic traditions have phenomenal connotations of *dīkṣā* which is loosely translated as consecration or initiation. There is hardly any religious strand which has not provided space for some or the other kind of *dīkṣā*. *Dīkṣā*s are described in brāhmaṇical and non-brāhmaṇical, Vedic and non-Vedic, Sanskritic and non-Sanskritic traditions. At one level, we get to read in Vedic texts about the *dīkṣā* of sacrificer performing various public sacrifices such as the *aśvamedha*.

•*Dīkṣā*, in these contexts, involved purification of sacrificers by the officiating priests. In the expansive Vedic literature on domestic rituals, *dīkṣā* became integral mechanism of entering into the privileged social strata—the *upanayana* (the Sacred Thread ceremony, in which a brāhmaṇ 'teacher' receives a boy as a pupil) providing the occasion for it.

Widespread ideas and customs in connection with initiation were gradually embedded in Viṣṇuite and Śivaite traditions. Though release from the bondages of worldly mire, happiness, prosperity, a long life, etc. are among the ideals to be realized through *dīkṣā*, yet the Viṣṇuite pattern was clearly aiming at a more sectarian and theistic orientation of this institution. It underlined its character as an initiation to a life of devotion and as an entry point through which closer and intimate rapport with the God was feasible.

Śivaism urges the absolute necessity of *Śaivī dīkṣā*, that is initiation into a Śaiva 'order'. All Śaiva schools are agreed that the one who has the authority to initiate others is the qualified *guru* (the preceptor)—indeed there was almost a deification of the *guru*. One major definition of *dīkṣā* obtainable in a Śaiva Āgama text lays down that it paves the way for eradicating impurities of mind and body, and destroys 'animality' (*pasutva*).

In the hands of Tantricists, who are recognized as an important constituent of non-Vedic traditions, *dīkṣā* acquired new heights. As many as 25 kinds of *dīkṣās* are outlined in the *Jayadratha-Yāmamala*. As in the Śaiva Āgamas, Tantras, too, underline the supreme importance of the preceptor (*acārya* or *guru*), who has the mastery over the scriptures, who understands the real significance of rites, and who is disciplined physically and mentally. *Guru* is the pivot of the Tantrik *sādhanā*, who purifies the *sādhaka* (aspirant, practitioner) and dispels his darkness (ignorance). Tantrik *dīkṣā* is particularly marked by its relative egalitarianism cutting across not only class divides but also the gender divide. It was accessible to the śūdras as well as to women. Many of the preceptors of Tantrik Buddhism were renowned women who hailed from the downtrodden sections of the society.

Where does '*triśūla dīkṣā*' of the Bajrang Dal and VHP stand? Evidently nowhere. Epic-Puranic mythology is replete with examples of Śiva giving his favourite weapons to divinities, devotees, and more often to *rākṣasas*. Thus, Ravana, Madhu, Arjuna, Paraśurāma, and even Viṣṇu were recipients of Śiva's various weapons. Significantly, none of these allusions mention *triṣūla* as Śiva's weapons. In the classic myth of the creation of Durgā to kill the demon Mahiṣa (narrated in the *Devī Māhātmya* of the *Markaṇḍeya Purāṇa*), for which more than a dozen divinities gave their treasured weapons, Śiva gave his *śūḷa* (not *triśūla*) which is invariably translated as spear/lance rather than trident.[3]

Gods bestowing weapons as boons or favours to their devotees do not fall within the purview of scores of connotations of *dīkṣā*. The long and varied traditions of *dīkṣā*, forming part of our rich heritage are, therefore, being distorted beyond recognition. How prophetic was the assertion of the author of the *Dharmasindhu*, namely, in the Kali age (to which we are supposed to be belonging) there is no *dīkṣā* but only *upadeśa* (sermon/discourse)!

The VHP has often claimed that its programme of '*Triśūla Dīkṣā*' aims at consolidation of the 'Hindu' society. This attempt of the VHP to equate 'Hindu' identity with '*triśūla*' raises several questions. Out of the phenomenal variety of symbols that it could choose from, it was the *triśūla* that the VHP found the most suitable. Why *triśūla* alone? That the appropriation of this symbol is directly related to the VHP's hate campaign against the three Ms (minorities in general and Muslims in particular, Marxists/Communists and Macaulays, that is, the English-educated liberal democrats) is as clear as daylight. Is *triśūla* only a symbol of violence and intimidation? What kind of 'Hindu' society is being sought to be consolidated through this newly created ritual?

Notwithstanding the resurgence of the OBCs and Dalits in the last fifteen years, the new leadership of the VHP vested in the hands of such OBCs as Uma Bharati, Vinay Katiyar and, of course, Praveen Togadia, is refraining from making any frontal attacks on 'brāhmaṇical' moorings of the so-called

'Hindu' society. We read in later Vedic texts about entrenched ruling elite (read brāhmaṇs and kṣatriyas) devising new sacrifices that were performed publicly to incorporate such tribal communities that stood at the periphery of the 'Aryan' society. Effectively, however, these marginal communities remained outside the charmed circles of politically, socially and ritually privileged higher varṇas. Invariably, the absorption of the marginals was within the ranks of the śūdras. Entitlement to being a *'dwij'* ('twice-born') by undergoing *upanayana* and donning the 'sacred thread' was clearly denied to them. Why doesn't Mr Togadia distribute *'janeu' (yagyopavīta)*? Wouldn't that be a cheaper proposition and a greater signal of peaceful transition to upward social mobility within 'Hindu' society?

The Hindu Mahasabha had stood for "Hinduising India and militarizing Hinduism". The VHP is clearly its lineal descendant. Even in this context, the rationale of invoking the symbol of *triśūla* is somewhat sinister. Singhals and Uma Bharatis swear by the name of Lord Rāma. Shouldn't bow and arrow have been their natural choice then? Again, why hasn't the VHP chosen the *'sudarśana cakra'*, that great weapon of Lord Kṛṣṇa/Viṣṇu? It would not only have been faster than *'triṣūla'* but also more effective from greater distances—perhaps it could also have been used more clandestinely! Long history of Viṣṇuism is a narrative of 'brāhmaṇical' entrenchment. Is this the reason for Togadia's reluctance to appropriate 'brāhmaṇical' symbols?

In Indian mythology, specially that of Sanskrit texts, Viṣṇu is rarely shown as bestower of weapons—not even to his devotees, from whom he expects complete surrender. A painting in a nineteenth century manuscript of the *Devi-Māhātmya* depicts aforesaid narrative of gods bestowing their weapons and attributes on the Devī. Śiva, the ascetic, is most prominently shown handing over his trident. The *cakradhara* and *gadādhara* (Viṣṇu, the wielder of *cakra* and club) is conspicuous by his absence in this depiction.

In contrast, Śiva and his family members and constituents of his entourage are great givers of boons and weapons to their devotees. Often they are also made to perform dirty tricks. So,

Ṛgvedic Rudra is the punisher of his incestuous father Prājapati; in the famous narrative of the Churning of the Ocean for *Amṛt* (Nectar), Śiva drank poison to help *suras* (gods led by Viṣṇu) against *asuras* (demons); and in the sacrifice conducted by Dakṣa (devotee of Viṣṇu), partly to mark his opposition to his daughter's resolve to marry Mahādeva [read gender insensitivity of Viṣṇuites], Śiva's *ganas* did their master's bidding and destroyed the sacrifice completely. The narrative of Dakṣa's sacrifice is also symbolic of the reluctance of the brāhmaṇical order to make space for non-brāhmaṇical (Rudra-Śiva's "non-Aryan" and even "pre-Aryan" origins have been in the field of historical writings for a very long time) forces.

From the Ṛgvedic period, Rudra is a dreaded god whose darts are sought to be warded off. He was a cruel hunter and raider, who with the bow, his characteristic weapon, shoots arrows at cattle and people. Later, in the *Yajurveda (Śatarudriya* hymn) he is evil, positively malevolent and abhorrent, and his associations are obnoxious. Taste the sample of this 'dismal litany' (the *Śatarudriya*): "Homage to the cheater, the swindler, to the lord of the burglars ..., the lord of cut-purses... the lord of the pluckers..." Is it a mere coincidence that many of these appellations are associated with Śiva and his son Skanda as well?

That Viṣṇu uses dubious stratagems to preserve brāhamaṇical social order and often requisitions help from non-brāhmaṇical quarters, almost in a villainous manner, can be seen in the *Kāśīkhaṇḍa* (of the *Skanda Purāṇa*) narrative of the manner in which Kāśi (ancient Varanasi) became the city of many gods. It tells us about a king named Ripunjaya (Divodāsa) who agreed to the divine creator Brahmā's request to restore social order only on the condition that "all the gods would retire from the earth and return to their proper places in heaven" (read the message: the gods were the troublemakers). Even Śiva had to retire to the Mt. Mandāra. Having banished all gods from the earth, Divodāsa was able to establish a Righteous kingdom like a true *dharmarāja*. Kāśī became a city of flawless social harmony. Seeing this as a threat to their own power, the gods plotted to bring about his downfall. After the failure of numerous divinities, Viṣṇu was sent. He transformed himself into a Buddhist monk and Śrī (Viṣṇu's consort) took the form of a Buddhist nun. Garuḍa, Viṣṇu's mount (*vāhana*), became monk's student. The three of them preached throughout the city and its suburbs, spreading the Buddhist message which was contrary to brāhmaṇical *dharma* of castes. The citizens began to go astray, Divodāsa's power began to fade and ultimately he had to yield to the wishes of gods and retire in order to make space for numerous divinities.

The VHP's programme of "*triśūla dīkṣā*" conceals its real character—collaboration in the maintenance of brāhmaṇical patriarchal social order. No wonder, the Rashtriya Svayam Sevak Samgh, which has always stood for such an order, blesses this programme. Bhanwar Lal Sharma, President of the Rajasthan Brahman Mahasabha, is seeking to unify the 182 brāhmaṇ sub-castes in the state in the name of Lord Paraśurāma (one of the incarnations of Viṣṇu) and with his *farsā* symbol.

Recently (on 30 April 2003) VHP conducted an "idol installation ceremony" at the "Ayyappa temple" within the area of the Idukki Dam (Kerala). The claims of tribal priests to perform "*poojas*" were set aside and the rituals of "idol installation" were performed by Kerala Namboodiri brāhmaṇs. This new turn of events came closely on the heels of VHP supremo Ashok Singhal's visit to the state and launching the *Triśūla Dīkṣā* ceremony at Alwaye on 26 April. Singhal threatened to "eliminate" all minorities, communists and secularists.[4]

Would the new *triśūladhārīs* (Dalits and OBCs) fight Bhanwar Lal Sharma's brigade of the wielders of *paraśu* or even those who are consolidating themselves by brandishing their swords? Notwithstanding mythological allusions to brāhmaṇ Paraśurāma's wrath against kṣatriyas, there are numerous realistic assertions of their collaborative efforts to lord over the real productive forces of the society. The use of the new *triśūladhārīs* in Gujarat is an indicator of their machinations to once again exploit them and make them do their dirty tricks. Forces of economic liberalization and globalization working for fast track upward mobility of the haves find in the *'triśūla dīkṣā'* programme a convenient subterfuge. *Triśūla* is a symbol of intimidation only against the three Ms, but in the larger context of the so-called "Hindu" society, it would remain blunted, without sharp cutting edges and piercing points. It does not show the will of the new *ācaryas* (Togadias and Singhals) to make any progressive thrust towards creation of a more broad-based egalitarian social order that would really challenge the iniquitous status quoist forces.

ENDNOTES

1. It is not improbable that artifacts that are commonly understood as "war weapons", may have served multiple purposes or may have evolved from "tools" meant for productive purposes. D.D. Kosambi (*An Introduction to the Study of Indian History*, 1975 edition, p. 68) had suggested: "the Indus people did not have the plough...but only a toothed harrow which may be recognized as one of the Indus script ideograms." Could "trident" evolve from such a "toothed harrow" and serve similar purpose? Incidentally, the axe called *paraśu* or *kuliṣa* in the *Ṛgveda* served as both a wood-cutting implement and a weapon of war.
2. *The Ocean of Story*, being C.H. Tawney's translation of Somadeva's *Kathāsaritsāgara*, vol. I, 1923, p. 262.
3. Is the VHP rethinking about the nomenclature of their programme? Banner on the Dias at the 'Triśūla Dīkṣā' at Delhi on 4 May, 2003 simply read 'Shakti Diksa'.
4. For similarities between VHP's *'triśūla dīkṣā'* and hate campaigns against the Blacks, other minorities and Communists conducted by notoriously racist Ku Klux Klan of the United States of America through symbolism of "cross burning", see Amar Farooqui, "Trishul Dikhsa, Cross-burning and the Politics of Hate", *Mainstream*, 3 May 2003, pp. 19–21.

5

The Swastika*: Insignia with an Identity Crisis

Mahima Singh

I

In the month commemorating the 60th anniversary of the liberation of Auschwitz, a debate opened in the European Union on whether a ban should be implemented on the use of Nazi symbols such as the swastika across the continent.[1] The proposal for the ban was tabled fairly soon not only because some nations felt that such an act would have treaded on the freedom of expression, but also because it provoked a wave of passionate protesting by the Hindu community in Europe, particularly in Great Britain, where members of several Hindu organizations and their friends urged for the symbol to be seen as "the second most sacred symbol in the Hindu tradition which has been used for 5,000 years to ward off evil."[2] However, the proposition resurfaced during Germany's presidency of the European Union in early 2007 where the ban was intended to make it unlawful to deny the Holocaust and

* The spelling employed is the generic one, i.e. swastika, rather than the Sanskritic *svastika*, for the symbol in its origin and use can be contained in no one human language or culture. Though the damage of attributing to this universal symbol an exclusively Sanskritic nomenclature has already been done, one can do one's part by indulging in a spot of academic political correctness.

genocide and to display any symbol of Nazi power. The justification for the proposal was summed up by *The Guardian* in the following words:"The European Commission says that in a time of growing Islamophobia, racism, and hostility to foreigners across Europe, a decision to criminalise hate-speech and praise of Nazi crimes would send a strong signal."[3] This time, Hindu forces across various countries of the Union joined in a more intensified effort to resist the ban. Awareness building through workshops and petitioning was carried out with increased gusto by Hindus not only in Great Britain, but also in Belgium, France, Italy, and the Netherlands, to garner support to resist the ban.[4] One popular petition on the Internet, among others, was the "Stop the abuse against the Swastika and the distortion of the term "Aryan",[5] addressed to Franco Frattini, the European Commissioner for Justice, Freedom and Security, which received nearly seven hundred signatures from supporters (including a small fraction of non-Hindus) the world over. It would be worth quoting snippets of the petition here:

> We support all worldwide Hindu efforts to reclaim this ancient and sacred symbol. ... we do not reclaim the Nazi swastika and, if democratically elected governments wish to ban the grotesque parody of this most Hindu symbol, whilst leaving the Hindu Swastika intact and available for public use by Hindus, we see no reason to oppose such a ban. However, if this course is followed, then it seems logical to us that the term "Aryan" as a racial connotation should also be universally disowned. It should be recognised that Hindus have always known Sanskrit "Arya" to mean a person of noble quality. The idea of an "Aryan race", a European Imperialist invention, is yet another example of how racist and Nazi ideology has stolen symbolism and meaning from the most ancient surviving culture in the world, warped it, and manufactured it for nefarious purposes. ... we are launching this petition to call for the rejection of the Nazi swastika and the rejection of the "Aryan Race" term. Also, we call on the European Parliament to fund the re-education of the public about the true Hindu meanings of the symbols along with the understanding of Hinduism as a whole.[6]

With the above in mind, my attempt in this paper is to survey evidence of the presence of the swastika in various ancient and surviving cultures and to examine, against this background, how Hindu is the swastika? Further, was a Nazi "Aryan race" connotation around the swastika—implying fascism, extreme Right-wing ideology and racism—exalted in Hindutva discourse to fuel communal, if not racist, sentiment in the 1930s-40s in India, contemporary to its use in Germany? Also, since the debate in the European Union regarding the proposed ban of the swastika is quite strictly limited to the symbol's ominous link to the Holocaust,[7] leading to a sentimental response and blanket claims by parts of the Hindu community, my attempt in the present paper has been to make the symbol historical.

II

The symbolism of the swastika was discussed by many scholars in the late nineteenth and early twentieth century in the Indian and world contexts. While Goblet d'Alviella[8] (1894) and Thomas Wilson[9] (1896) were among the earliest to provide fairly exhaustive accounts of the swastika or swastika-like delineations in ancient art and trace the origin and the course of the migration of the symbol across the world, several scholars discussed both its geographical dispersal as well as its symbolism and significance in ancient art. As early as 1876, the French Indologist Èmile Burnouf asserted that the swastika denoted the invention of fire and its sacred remembrance:

> the [svastika and sauvastika] represent the two pieces of wood which were laid down crosswise upon one another before the sacrificial altars, in order to produce the sacred fire (*agni*), and the ends of-which were bent round at right angles, and fastened by means of four nails [that, when drawn, represent the dots under the four arms of the swastika], so that this wooden scaffolding might not be moved. At the point where the two pieces of wood were joined, there was a small hole, in which a third piece of wood, in the form of a lance (called *pramantha*), was rotated by means of a cord made of cow-hair and hemp, till the fire was generated by friction. Then the fire (*agni*) was put on the altar close by, where the priest poured the holy Soma, the juice of the tree of life, and made, by means of purified butter, wood and straw, a large fire.[10]

In 1880, the numismatist E. Thomas propounded the view that the swastika is a solar symbol, and stated that its depiction took the place of the sun on some of the coins from Andhra, such as when the swastika was inserted within circles on coins, representative of the four-suns on the Ujjain pattern of coins, implying that the symbol's very positioning hinted at its meaning.[11] Rev. S. Beal (1880) built further on the symbol's association with the sun to say that it connoted the idea of circumambulation in correspondence with the observed movement of the sun from left to right or right to left, depending upon the individual's positioning in either hemisphere, thus accounting for both the right-oriented and left-oriented swastikas.[12] Thus, the swastika as a sign of luck was recognized only as a result of facing "sunways", while turning the other way, it was considered unlucky.[13] Further, Thomas also attributed to the swastika the symbolism of the sun on the basis of his analysis of the signs of the Jain *tīrthankaras*. Struck by the absence of solar symbolism in the *cinhas* of the *tīrthankaras*, he stated that since the sign of the eighth *tīrthankara* was the half-moon, the sign of the swastika, attributed to the seventh *tīrthankara*, Supārśva, must depict the sun.[14] Attempts were also made to interpret the significance of the swastika outside the Indian subcontinent. Notable among them is the one by Prince John Loewenstein (1941)[15] who explained its significance on the basis of its depictions in Samarra (where four female figures composed a swastika on sepulchral pottery, or in association with such animals as the fish which, owing to its reproductive power is recognized as a symbol of fecundity), or in Troy (swastika depictions on female face-urns, mostly on the vulva), and viewed it as a fecundity symbol. He also drew attention to the swastika's occurrence in Susa (4000 BC) on the head of a dog which is regarded as a lunar symbol in ancient folklore and in Boeotia (700 BC) where "it appears as one of the attributes of a fecundity-goddess together with that well-known lunar symbol, the bull's head." Thus, on the basis of the swastika's possible association with deities and animals having lunar associations, he argued for its lunar symbolism.[16] (p. 53).

Despite different interpretations of the symbolic meaning of the swastika the scholarly opinion has generally weighed in favour of its being a sign of good luck.

III

The provenance of swastika in different parts of the world assumed a new significance in the first half of the twentieth century; for it undermined the exclusive Germanic claims to its origins, and presented a significant academic counterpoint to its Nazification by Hitler who used it as a symbol of racial genocide of unprecedented magnitude. Not surprisingly anti-Nazi scholars like Norman Brown were happy to note the discovery of the "exceedingly common" occurrence of swastika bearing seals at Harappa and Mohenjodaro, and to assert that "it existed in India before the arrival of the Aryans" who took it from their "non-Aryan predecesors" and "gave it the Sanskrit name Swastika".[17] His view received support from the work of E.J. Mackay, a member of John Marshall's team conducting archaeological activities at the Harappan sites, who was of the view that perhaps the symbol first originated in Elam,[18] from where it made its way to the Shahi Tump Grey Ware culture of Baluchistan, which pre-dates the Harappan culture and is perhaps related to south Iran,[19] eventually making its way into the Indus valley.[20] The swastika bearing stamps in the Harappan culture are dated to 2300–2000 BC,[21] after which the symbol remained unknown for a millennium or so. The Vedic texts do not mention swastika at all, though they occasionally mention the word *svasti*.[22] However, it resurfaced around 800 BC as a decorative motif in the Painted Grey Ware used for domestic purposes and identified with later Vedic culture.[23] It would thus appear that in the Indian subcontinental context the symbol is not only pre-Vedic but also pre-Harappan[24] and has nothing to do with the Vedic Aryans who, according to the Hindu Right, were the original inhabitants of India and were the authors of the Harappan civilization.

The earliest epigraphic evidence of the swastika in India is found in the Jaugada version of the two separate edicts of Aśoka with both clockwise and counter-clockwise delineations.[25] In the post-Aśokan period from the time of Khāravela (second century BC) onwards the symbol appears on inscriptions at several places like Mathura, Peshawar, Udayagiri-Khandagiri hills and Amaravati but it is found oftener on cave inscriptions in western India at such places as Bhaja, Junnar, Kanheri, Karle, Kuda, and Nasik. The swastika does not appear on epigraphs in any definite pattern and is depicted diversely, at their beginning or end or at both.[26] It generally appears as a mark of auspiciousness as is clear from the Nasik inscription of Uṣavadāta (No. 10), where the symbol precedes the word *'siddham'*.[27] As an auspicious mark, the swastika seems to have been quite common in western India, especially in the Buddhist and Jain centres, during the early centuries of the Christian era, when it frequently appears also as a coin-device "in copper cast coins, and in different issues which are collectively known as tribal coins including the local varieties."[28]

IV

The basal form of the swastika is the cross which has a universal appeal and is inextricably linked with the physical aesthetics and symbolic insinuation of the number four, especially in terms of the number's abstraction in the sense of, say, directionality in space and time.[29] As an *axis mundi* that simultaneously connects and divides (marking the concurrence of two lines at the centre, yet opening the centre to the outside, dividing into four equals), the cross has unmistakeable cosmological associations with the number four—four *Veda*s, four *varṇa*s, four *āśrama*s, among others. In the *Puruṣasūkta*, "all creatures are one-fourth of him [the primodial man], three-fourths [have] eternal life in heaven"[30] and according to the *Chāndogya Upaniṣad* (*Ch. Up.*), the self has "four feet" or four quarters—speech, breath, eyes and ears.[31] That the cross has a divinity regarding directionality is evident from the *Ch. Up.* 3.18.2.[32] This directionality and its further division into quarters is evident from another passage of the *Ch. Up.* where Satyakāma acquires knowledge about the four feet of Brahman from a bull.[33] A similar directionality is clearly visualized in

Buddhist architecture at Stupa II at Sanchi where the four entrances and the pattern produced are aligned to the cardinal directions. According to Adrian Snodgrass, the swastika in Buddhist art is also homologous with the wheel.[34] He states:

> if the svastika is compared with the figure of the cross inscribed within a circle, the basic equivalence of the two symbols is apparent, the rotation of the wheel being indicated in the first case by the circumference of the circle and in the svastika by the lines which are to be thought of in the manner of ribbons streaming in the wind. Like the wheel, the svastika represents movement about a fixed and unmoving axis and, like the wheel, it is a symbol of the generation of universal cycles from forever-Present Centre. It represents the generation of currents of energy, and is a symbol of the action immutable Principle, the "unmoved mover", with manifestation.[35]

The Jain connotation of symbol may be gleaned from a study of twenty-eight *āyāgpaṭa*s (votive slabs decorated with objects of Jain veneration) from Mathura, dated to the first century BC-AD by Sonya Rhei Quintanilla.[36] She classifies the *āyāgpaṭas* into two categories—diagrammatic (twenty-one in number) and pictorial (seven in number)—where the first is characteristically marked by a small central circle in which a sacred object such as a *stūpa* or a *cakra* or a lotus is depicted, which is surrounded by a symmetrical arrangement of symbols, one of which is often the swastika.[37] According to her the large curved swastika found in some of the *āyāgpaṭa*s, coming out directly from the central circle or from the second concentric circle of *nandyāvarta*s (an elaborated swastika), "may depict that the realm outside of the circle is within the world of birth, death and rebirth."[38] She further states that "in the Jaina context the svastika can be symbolic of *saṃsāra* or cyclical existence, the four arms denoting the four possible types of rebirth within *saṃsāra*. Thus in a diagrammatic *āyāgpaṭa* ... only the central circle [may] represent the immortal region of liberated beings, while the remainder of the diagrams refer to the universe, the realm of the *saṃsāra*."[39]

A sphere of human activity where the cross logically figures is that of weaving which requires the crossing of two threads at the centre.[40] The process of weaving is representative of its key elements: a vertical line, a horizontal line and the coinciding centre. Within such a framework lies the cosmic symbolism of the weaving of space and time to which a reference can be found in the *Bṛhadāraṇyakopaniṣad* in a dialogue between Yājñavalkya and Gārgī, where the former demonstrates his superiority in the assembly convened by Janaka.[41] That the thread also conveys a symbolic meaning in literary texts is clear from the word *sūtra*[42] which implies the chapter of a book.

The multivalence of the swastika and the diversity of its meaning and significance can also be seen from the semiological point of view [43] according to which only the act of interpretation renders the sign meaningful, and without interpretation the sign does not exist as a sign at all. This boils down to the fact that every artist who used the swastika in the ancient world for artistic depiction was confined by his own understanding of the sign, producing newer meanings bound by the context of his/her own experience, and we as present day interpreters are also similarly limited by our own understanding of the swastika as a symbol of blessing and luck, by the manner in which we see it being used around us today, and by the understanding of the very meaning and derivation of the word 'svastika'. Such an understanding not only enables us to appreciate the sectarian—brāhmaṇical, Buddhist, and Jain—contexts in which the swastika may have been used but also to comprehend the process of its Aryanization and the manner in which its racist connotation has promoted the use and interpretation of the symbol as a language of hate.

V

The chief architect of the "Aryan swastika" may be said to be Heinrich Schliemann (1822–1890) who excavated Homer's "Troy".[44] In the philological discourse of his times, links between certain languages that came to be part of the "Indo-European" language family[45] led Aryanists to look for an original, proto-Indo-European language, or proto-Aryan, the speakers of which were thought to have had a material culture that was the root of the material culture of all Indo-European speakers. In looking for a material trace of the Aryans then, Schliemann claimed the swastika and swastika-like delineations on pottery fragments at Hissarlik (in present day Turkey, identified by Schliemann as Troy) to be proof of the Aryan race.[46] For Schliemann, finding a swastika on a piece of pottery at Hissarlik enabled him to forge immediate links between Assyrians, Vedic Aryans, and the Greeks—the ancient cultures all of which possessed this symbology in text and/or material culture. "...The alchemy at work at Hissarlik", it has been rightly pointed out, "transformed mundane material excavation into the substance of a myth, and Aryanism was the modern myth within which this change could be accomplished, with the swastika functioning as both Aryan sign and Aryan archaeological evidence."[47] Thus, both philology and-prehistory facilitated the construction of the myth of Aryanism, established a "tradition of the symbol" in the Aryan swastika, and "fulfilled the conditions for an automatic continuity with the past."[48] The repetition of the symbol of the swastika helped recreate a community based essentially on a racial identity, and the swastika became a symbol that had to be *reconstructed and preserved*[49], thereby undergoing a fresh construction altogether.

The appropriation of the swastika as the insignia of the Aryan man in the nineteenth and twentieth centuries has impregnated the symbol's pragmatics with ominousness and odiousness. Though the symbol today is a generic ideogram of hate, its Nazi semantic was, to all intents and purposes, racist. Malcolm Quinn, who has made a comprehensive and insightful analysis of its modern semantic, places the symbol against the background of the discourse of nationalism in the nineteenth century, which subsequently found a bolder voice in Hitlerian racism in the twentieth.[50] For him, the swastika as used in the nineteenth and twentieth centuries was not only produced by a cultural context, but itself produced the context that facilitated its own interpretation. With its "original", archaic meaning lost and redundant, it became an identity giver in terms of both nation and race, the former identity articulated through the latter, that is the symbol gave meaning without itself being meaningful. In the context of the swastika being appropriated as an identity-giver to race and eventually getting recognized as a potent symbol of racism, he states: "[T]he swastika 'stood for' the Nazi party; but the party also facilitated the 'mission' of the swastika, which was to unite racist (anti-Semitic) image with an Aryan racial identity. The concentration camps are the monuments to this attempt to produce a race from the sign of racism, the phantom Aryan from the murder of the living Jew."[51] This is evident from the construction of the swastika in Hitler's own words as laden with an essentially racist semantic: "the swastika signified the mission allotted to us—the struggle for the victory of Aryan mankind and at the same time the triumph of the ideal of creative work which is in itself and always will be anti-Semitic."[52] In this context, Quinn asserts that "Nazism was not fascism in extremis, it was the institution of racist extremism in the form of a fascist political programme. In other words, Nazism was fascism plus the swastika."[53] But while he appeals for the swastika to be "desymbolized" to make it "historical"[54] perhaps it would do us best to acknowledge that the nineteenth-century discourse around "Aryanism" and Hitler's own employment of the symbol in political theatrics has become an inextricable part of the symbol's character and content, for though the symbol has left behind inerasable footprints in human history of aesthetics and religiosity, its presence, as it were, has truly only been felt in a global context through the fairly recent and sinister semantic that has been attributed to it.

The Aryan semantic of the swastika also found its way into Hindutva discourse in the 1930s and '40s in India which stood not as much for racial purity as for religious purity for an Indian/Hindu nation. The theory of "indigenous Aryanism" in India helped legitimize Hindu nationalism, and got a morale boost from an echo of similar "revivalism" in Germany. But the nature of Aryan discourse in India was different from that in Germany, even though the latter drew on the former to better articulate its implication. The former stood for racial hygiene fuelling anti-Semitism leading to the annihilation of Jews, the latter for religious hygiene resulting in Islamophobia and elimination of Muslims. This difference, however, need not be overemphasized. As Marzia Casolari[55] has irrefutably shown, Hitler's anti-Semitic ideology shaped and sharpened the anti-Muslim rhetoric of the Hindu nationalist forces in the 1930s when the 'Aryanized' swastika used in contemporary Germany found its way into their understanding of the Hindu nation building. Inspired by the youth movement of Germany and Balilla and other fascist organisations of Italy, they began to organize themselves on fascist, militaristic lines to combat the internal enemy—the Muslim. One among the several centres for physical education and paramilitary training was the Swastik League, founded in March, 1929, whose aim was "to improve the physique of the Hindu society."[56] The emphasis on the need for the Hindu community to acquire a militaristic character "to remove the present defects [in society]" was made clear by B.S. Moonje's address to the members of the Swastik League in August, 1935, where he was quoted in the Swastik Herald as saying:

> with a population of seven crores, Muslims in India would be able to supply a crore of able-bodied soldiers, excluding children and old men. There being no castes among the Muslims, every man can become a soldier, unlike the Hindoos, among whom the system of dividing the society into castes and sub-castes still prevails. ... it is in order to make it possible to supply that number of soldiers that the Hindoo youths must be trained properly.[57]

It is, however, noteworthy that despite the fact that the swastika was the official symbol of the Swastik League, appearing on all of the official paperwork as letterhead and on the institute's flag, there is no explicit mention of an Aryan connotation associated with the Hinduness of the institute that might hint at how deliberate the reason was for naming their League as such. For the League, "the sign of the Swastika stands for unity, peace and goodwill amongst the people, and Swastik League's justification for existence is to strive for the creation and maintenance of such unity, peace and goodwill."[58] However, the League needed to clear its name in the face of contemporary Nazism's synonymy with the symbol of the swastika which it did by proclaiming that Hitler was "the enemy of humanity" but the League "a saviour of humanity."[59]

Like the Swastik League, the signatories to the above mentioned internet petition seem to distance themselves from the "grotesque parody of this *most Hindu symbol*"(emphasis added) by the Nazis but enthusiastically support the world wide Hindu efforts to "reclaim" this "*most ancient and Hindu symbol*"(emphasis added). Their condemnation of the Nazification of the swastika is hypocritical; for it does not cover up the sympathy for and exaltation of Nazism eloquently expressed by many Hindu nationalists, notably M.S. Golwalkar.[60] Similarly their effort to reclaim the symbol is vain; for it flies in the face of evidence. Found in many parts of the globe, the swastika can hardly be claimed as exclusively Indian, let alone Hindu. Considering the temporal and spatial spread of the swastika in the pre-Nazi context, the sign, in all the infinite possibility of meanings it holds in its aesthetic form, exemplifies simply the infinite possibility of the human mind. And its symbolism in the art, religions and aesthetics of ancient India is merely one such possibility.

ENDNOTES

1. "60th anniversary of the liberation of Auschwitz: Debate on anti-Semitism", from the Daily Notebook of the European Union, 26 January 2005. http://europa.eu/rapidpressReleasesAction.do?reference=DN/05/52&format=HTML&aged=0&language=EN&guiLanguage=en The proposition for the ban was inspired by, if was not wholly in response to, Prince Harry's surprising choice of outfit at a fancy dress party at which he wore a German Afrika Corps uniform and Nazi-style swastika armband, a gesture that stirred considerable uproar in the European media and political arena.
2. Ramesh Kallidai, Secretary General, Hindu Forum of Britain, quoted in "Hindus want to 'reclaim' swastika", BBC News, 19 January 2005. http://news.bbc.co.uk/2/hi/uk_news/4188141.stm.
3. Ian Traynor, "Germany bids to outlaw denial of Holocaust across continent", *The Guardian*, 15 January 2007. That this issue was

re-raised to illustrate Germany's repentance of the Holocaust is clear from the then German Minister for Justice, Brigitte Zyrpies's statement, "[the] historical experience [of the horrors of Nazism] puts Germany under a permanent obligation to combat systematically every form of racism, anti-Semitism and xenophobia", quoted from Timothy Garton Ash, "A blanket ban on holocaust denial would be a serious mistake", *The Guardian*, 18 January 2007.

4. Paul Majendie, "European Hindus oppose German call for swastika ban", *Reuters*, 16 January 2007.
5. http://www.petitiononline.com/sa108hhr/petition.html
6. Ibid. For a succinct comment on the hypocrisy and calculatedness of a primarily upper-caste NRI response to the proposed ban, see D. Parthasarthy, "The NRI Becomes Aggressive: Swastika Controversy and Beyond", *Economic and Political Weekly*, vol. 40, no. 11, 12-18 March (2005), pp. 1018–9.
7. The Nazification of the swastika has widened its pragmatic gamut, and in varying contexts, it implies not only fascism, extreme right-wing ideology and racism, but also anti-communism, anarchy and alternate culture in music and fashion. The Jewish community itself acknowledges that today the symbol of the swastika when found as part of graffiti related to hate-crimes is a contextually malleable symbol of hate and aggression. In this flow, the Jewish Anti-Defamation League, a pan-American non-governmental agency for the protection of civil rights, conceded that the swastika is no longer considered synonymous with anti-Semitism. In July 2010, *The New York Times* quoted the League's national director as saying, "The swastika has morphed into a universal symbol of hate. Today it's used as an epithet against African-Americans, Hispanics and gays, as well as Jews, because it is a symbol which frightens." Laurie Goodstein, "The Swastika Is Deemed 'Universal' Hate Symbol", *The New York Times*, 28 July 2010.
8. Goblet d'Alviella, *The Migration of Symbols*, Archibald Constable and Co., Westminster, 1894.
9. Thomas Wilson's *The Swastika: The Earliest Known Symbol, and its Migrations*, Smithsonian Institution, Washington, 1896,
10. Émile Burnouf, *La Science des Religions*, 1876, p. 256, cited in Heinrich Schliemann, *Ilios: The City and the Country of the Trojans*, Harper and Brothers, New York, 1881, p. 351.
11. E. Thomas, "The Swastika", *The Indian Antiquary*, vol. 9, 1880, pp. 65–6. This has also been conceded by Max Müller in his letter

to Heinrich Schliemann on the swastika (Schliemann, op. cit., p. 348). Max Müller states that Thomas' conjecture lends itself to understanding the left and right oriented swastikas, where the right facing one, i.e. the *svastika*, was perhaps a symbol of the vernal sun, and the left-facing one, i.e. the *sauvastika*, represented the autumnal sun. (Ibid., p. 348)

12. Rev. S. Beal. "The Swastika", *The Indian Antiquary*, vol. 9, 1880, pp. 67–8. According to Beal, "The *crampons* at the ends of the arms of the cross are, in Buddhist symbolism, mostly, though not always, drawn to the *right* – denoting, as we argue, the sun's movement round the earth from left to right. Now it is plain that this is always the apparent movement of the sun in *Northern latitudes*, that is, in latitudes to the north of the Tropic of Cancer. In Northern countries ... therefore we find the *crampons* of the + drawn to the right. ... The shadow of the sun, or, in other words, his apparent movement, is not always from left to right, but sometimes in intertropical countries, apparently from right to left, and this has generally attracted attention. Thus the Phoenicians who were in the fleet dispatched by Pharaoh Necho were surprised to find the sun in the north instead of the south —and so the ambassadors sent from North India to the Emperor Claudius expressed the same astonishment—and the first Portuguese navigators, who voyaged south along the coast of Africa, noticed the same fact—so that wherever sun worship prevailed in such tropical countries, his path would be represented from both *left to right*, and from *right to left*. Hence the double form of the Swastika, the *crampons* being found on either side of the arms of the cross, apparently without distinction ..." p. 68.
13. Beal, op. cit.
14. E. Thomas, op. cit., pp. 65–6.
15. Prince John Loewenstein, "The Swastika: Its History and Meaning", *Man*, vol. 41, May-Jun., 1941, pp. 49–55
16. Ibid., p. 53
17. William Norman Brown, *The Swastika: A Study of the Nazi Claims of its Aryan Origin*, Emerson Books, New York, 1933, pp. 19–22, http://www.archive.org/stream/swastikastudyofn00brow#page/n5/mode/2up. Other similar academic attempts to undermine Nazi claims to swastika include John Prince Loewenstein, op. cit., pp. 49–55. Basing his analysis on the swastika-bearing sepulchral pottery found at Samarra and Susa, and Heinrich Schliemann's Trojan swastika-bearing spinning

whorls, among other evidence, Loewenstein insightfully conjectures that trade and migration facilitated the dispersal of the swastika and that in the Near east and Europe "the movement took place from the south to the north-west [towards Moravia and Bohemia]..." thus, implicitly ruling out Germanic claims to the origin of the symbol (op. cit., p. 52).

18. E.J. Mackay, *Early Indus Civilisations*, first published as *The Indus Civilization*, Clay and Sons Ltd., London, 1935, 2nd enlarged and revised edn, edited by Dorothy Mackay, Luzac, London, 1948 and reprinted, Indological Book House, Delhi, 1976, pp. 71–2.
19. Aurel Stein, "An Archaeological Tour in Gedrosia", *Memoirs of the Archaeological Survey of India*, no. 43, 1931, cited in H.D. Sankalia, *Prehistory and Protohistory of India and Pakistan*, Deccan College Postgraduate and Research Institute, Pune, 1974, pp. 323–4.
20. Ram Sharan Sharma, *Advent of the Aryans in India*, Manohar, New Delhi, 1999, pp. 27-8.
21. Ibid., p. 27.
22. M. Monier Williams, *Sanskrit-English Dictionary, sv svasti.*
23. Chap IV of Sharma, *Material Culture and Social Formations in Ancient India*, Macmillan, Delhi, 1997. Sharma speaks of the complete unrelatedness of Harappan pottery and Painted Grey Ware, claiming that the latter could not have had Harappan ancestry.
24. Sharma, *Advent of the Aryans*, p. 28. Susan Huntington has suggested that the Indo-Europeans in the Indian subcontinent borrowed the swastika from the Harappan usage and hence contact between them and the Harappans may have taken place (*The Art of Ancient India: Buddhist, Hindu and Jain*, Weatherhill, New York, 1993, p. 23.). But the Harappan ancestry of the Painted Grew Ware has been effectively rejected by many scholars though they recognize the occasional "interlocking" of the former with the latter at several places in the Panjab and Haryana (R.S. Sharma, *Material Culture*, pp. 82, 157; idem, *The Advent of Aryans*, pp. 47–8).
25. Sarkar, H. and B.M. Pande, *Symbols and Graphic Representations in Indian Inscriptions*, Aryan Books, New Delhi, 1999, p. 23.
26. Ibid., p. 25.
27. Y.S. Vavikar, "Some Remarks on the swastika", *Indian Antiquary*, vol. 27, 1898, p. 196.
28. Sarkar and Pande, op. cit., pp. 23–5.
29. Julian Ries,, tr. By Kristine Anderson, 'Cross', in Mircea Eliade,

ed., *Encyclopedia of Religion*, vol. 3, Macmillan, New York, 1987, pp. 123–7.

30. *Ṛgveda*, 10.90.3, tr. Ralph T.H., Griffith, *The Hymns of the Rigveda*, London, 1896, reprint Kessinger Publishing LLC, Whitefish, Montana, 2007.
31. Chandogya Upaniṣad (hereafter *Ch. Up.*), 3.18.2: "This Brahmana has four feet; the speech is one foot, the breath one foot, the eyes one foot, the ears one foot. That is in regard to the self." Translation from Paul Deussen, *Sixty Upaniṣads of the Veda*, part 1, tr. V.M. Bedekar and G.B. Palsole, Delhi, 1980, p. 116., first printed in 1897.
32. *Ch. Up.* 3.18.2: "... Now in regard to the godhead; the fire is one foot, the wind is one foot, sun one foot, *the directions one foot.*", Paul Deussen, op. cit., p. 116.
33. *Ch. Up.* 4.5.2: "I will also proclaim to you a foot of Brahman."—"You, venerable Sir, proclaim it to me."—And he (the bull) said to him: "One sixteenth is the easterly region, one sixteenth the westerly region, one sixteenth the southerly direction, and one sixteenth the northerly. This, my child, consists of the four sixteenth feet (the fourth (quarter) part) of Brahman, which therefore is called the expansive one.", Paul Deussen, op. cit., p. 123–4.
34. Adrian Snodgrass, *The Symbolism of the Stupa*, Motilal Banarsidass, Delhi, 1992, p. 78. Huntington, op. cit., p. 62.
35. Snodgrass, op. cit., pp. 82–3. Snodgrass also explains the depiction of left- and right-oriented swastikas by correlating their symbolism to that of the spirals in Buddhist art:

    The two spirals represent the forces emanating from the two poles [*puruṣa* and *prakṛti*] of the World Egg, one unrolling upwards and the other downwards, produced by the Egg's rotation around the axis that joins the two poles. The actions and reactions produced by the upward and downward flowing currents of forces actualize the innumerable modifications of the virtualities contained within the Egg. The same significance inheres within the double svastika, whose counter-posed arms represent the contrary movements of the upward flowing influences of Earth and the downward flowing influences of Heaven. (p. 296)
36. Sonya Rhei Quintanilla, "Āyāgpaṭas: Characteristics, Symbolism, and Chronology", *Artibus Asiae*, vol. 60, no. 1, 2000, pp. 79–137.
37. Ibid., p. 83.
38. Ibid., p. 94.

39. Ibid., p. 94. According to Y.S. Vavikar, the swastika is the symbol of the Siddha, he who is free from *sāmsāric* existence in the next life, i.e. is above the four *sāmsāri*c destinies of being born as god (*deva*), human (*manuṣya*), hell being (*narkī*) or animal or plant (*tīryañca*)—"The point or bindu in the centre from which the four paths branch out is *jīva* or life, and the four paths symbolize the four conditions of life. But as a Siddha is free from all these, the end of each line is turned to show that the four states are closed for him:", Y. S. Vavikar, op. cit., p. 196.
40. Dagobert Runes and H.G. Schricket, eds., *Encyclopedia of the Arts*, Peter Owen Ltd., London, 1965, p. 803.
41. *Bṛhadāraṇyakopaniṣad*, 3.8.7—'That which is above the heavens, O Gargī, and that which is below the earth and that which is between both—the heavens and the earth, that which they call the past, the present and the future—all that is interwoven lengthwise and crosswise in space." Paul Deussen, op. cit., p. 463.
42. From "*siv* which means to sew or to string or to put together, Monier-Williams, *Sanskrit-English Dictionary*, sv. *siv*.
43. Semiotics, a discipline which emerged with the work of Swiss linguist Ferdenand de Saussure (1857–1913), is the study of signs, where a sign could imply any unit that affects communication, be it a word, a sentence, a drawing, or a facial gesture. It was further developed, among others, by the American philosopher Charles Sanders Peirce (1839–1914), according to whom the semiotic process of producing the sign and giving it meaning happens through the relationship between the form of the sign, i.e. the "representamen", the mental image that makes sense of the sign, i.e. the "interpretant", and the thing to which the sign is referring, i.e. the "object" or "referent". Charles Sanders Peirce, "Logic as Semiotic: The Theory of Signs" in Justus Buchler, ed., *Philosophical Writings of Peirce*, Dover Publications, New York, 1955, pp. 98–119. Also see Meike Bal and Norman Bryson, "Semiotics and Art History", *The Art Bulletin*, vol. 73, no. 2, June, 1991, pp. 174–208.
44. Malcolm Quinn, *The Swastika: Constructing the Symbol*, Routledge, London, 1994.
45. William Jones' oft quoted "Third anniversary discourse" published in the *Asiatik Researches*, vol. 1, 1788, pp. 413–31, contributed significantly in this direction, where he inferred that languages such as Sanskrit, Greek, Latin, Celtic, Gothic and Old Persian shared grammatical similarity, and are perhaps the descendents of a common ancestral language, what linguists

today call Proto-Indo-European.

46. "All that can be said of the first settlers [of Hissarlik] is that they belonged to the Aryan race, as is sufficiently proved by the Aryan religious symbols met with in the strata of their ruins (among which we find the [image of swastika]) both upon the pieces of pottery and upon the small curious terracottas with a hole in the centre, which have the form of the crater of a volcano or of a *carrousel*", Heinrich Schliemann, *Troy and its Remains: A Narrative of Researches and Discoveries made on the Site of Ilium and in the Trojan Plain*, 1875, Phillip Smith (ed.), John Murray, London, 1976, p. 16, quoted in Quinn, op. cit., p. 35.
47. Ibid., pp. 33–4. It is interesting that in a letter to Schliemann Max Müller explicitly cautioned him regarding the hazards of transposing culturally laden nomenclatures across different societies:

    > I do not like the use of the word *Svastika* of India. It is a word of Indian origin, and has its history and definite meaning in India. I know the temptation is great to transfer names, with which we are familiar, to some objects that come before us in the course of our researches. But it is a temptation which the true student ought to resist, except, it may be, for the sake of illustration. The mischief arising from the promiscuous use of technical terms is very great. ...The occurrence of such [left bending and right bending] crosses in different parts of the world may or may not point to a common origin. But if they are once called *Svastika*, the *vulgus profanum* will at once jump to the conclusion that they all come from India, and it will take some time to weed out such prejudice. (cited in Schliemann, *Ilios: The City and the Country of the Trojans*, p. 346).

    He goes on to state: "That signs identically the same as the Svastika and the Sauvastika occur elsewhere, in China, in Asia Minor, in Etruria, and among the Teutonic nations, is perfectly true. Comparative archaeology may point out this fact, but there it must rest for the present. Identity of form does as little prove identity of origin in archaeology as identity of sound proves identity of origin in etymology." (p. 348).
48. Quinn, op. cit., p. 35.
49. Ibid., p. 8., emphasis in original.
50. Ibid.
51. Ibid., p. 5.
52. Adolf Hitler, *Mein Kampf*, Jaico Publishing House, Twelfth Impression, 2001, p. 411.

53. Quinn, op. cit., pp. 138–9.
54. Ibid., p. 19.
55. Casolari, Marzia, 'Hindutva's Foreign Tie-up in the 1930s—Archival Evidence', *Economic and Political Weekly*, vol. 35, no. 4, 22 January 2000, pp. 218–28.
56. National Archives of India (NAI), Jayakar papers, microfilm, rn 13, document entitled "The Second Anniversary Celebration, 1931" of the Swastik League, p. 2. A definitive sway towards fascist ideology is clear from the League's president M.R. Jayakar's own praises of Mussolini's Avant Guardista, an organization that gave military training to boys between the ages 14 and 18 years, announcing the League's own attempt to organize a cadet corps on similar lines, NAI, ibid., *Swastik Herald*, 7 November 1934.
57. NAI, ibid., article entitled 'Dr. Moonje at the Swastik Mandir' in *Swastik Herald*, 1 September 1935.
58. NAI, ibid., "First Annual Report of the Swastik League", 1930, p. 1.
59. "Hitler discriminates between Aryans and non-Aryans, between Germans and Jews. The League, though it is a purely Hindu organisation, does not make a difference between the Hindus and the non-Hindus. ... The League stands for construction. [Hitler] is the enemy of humanity. The League is a saviour of humanity." NAI, ibid., Article entitled "Hitler and the Swastik League", in *Swastik Herald*, July-August 1940.
60. The most eloquent expression of the Hindu nationalist admiration of Hitler's racist policies came from M.S. Golwalkar:

    German national pride has now become the topic of the day. To keep up the purity of the nation and its culture, Germany shocked the world by purging the country of the Semitic races—the Jews. National pride at its highest has been manifested here. Germany has also shown how well—neigh impossible it is for races and cultures, having difference going to the root, to be assimilated into one united whole, a good lesson for us in Hinduism to learn and profit by ... [the Muslims] must either adopt the Hindu culture and language, must learn to respect and revere Hindu religion, must entertain no idea but the glorification of the Hindu nation ... in one word they must cease to be foreigners or may stay in the country wholly subordinated to the Hindu nation claiming nothing, deserving no privileges, far less any preferential treatment, not even citizen's rights." (*We or Our Nationhood Defined* cited in Casolari, op. cit., p. 224.)

Section III

DIVERSITY OF EPIC TRADITIONS

6

Historical Evolution of the Rāma Legend

Suvira Jaiswal

The evolution of the concept of Rāma begins with the tales of a legendary hero and culminates in its becoming a general designation for God at least in a large part of northern India. The outlines of this historical development are now fairly clear but may be quite at variance with the believer's faith which has the capacity to gloss over inconsistencies and has not much use for historical principles.

The ancient Indian tradition has preserved at least three main versions of the Rāma story, the brāhmaṇical, the Buddhist and the Jain. Although the beautiful poem of Vālmīki, who is known as the *ādikavi*, "the first author of ornate poetry", played a role in stereotryping the framework of the Rāma narrative, traces of earlier divergent versions may be found in non-brāhmaṇical, that is, Buddhist and Jain sources. That there were many versions of the Rāma story is tellingly acknowledged through Sītā in the *Adhyātma Rāmāyaṇa*[1] where she remarks: "I have heard many *Rāmāyaṇas* from many *dvijas* (twiceborns), but tell me, did anywhere Rāma go to the forest without Sītā?" Sītā is inseparable from the Rāma story.

Nevertheless, Sītā figures both as the sister and wife of Rāma in the *Daśaratha Jātaka* which is the earliest documentation of the Rāma legend and retains some very primitive features.[2] Here Rāma is a Bodhisattva, and is the eldest son of Daśaratha by his first queen. Daśaratha is the king of Vārānasi and not of Ayodhya, and has two other children from his first queen, Lakhana Kumāra and Sītā Devī. To avoid the evil machinations of their stepmother, who wishes to install her son Bharat Kumāra as heir-apparent in place of Rāma, Daśaratha sends Rāma and Lakhana to exile for twelve years and Sītā accompanies her brothers. Daśaratha dies after nine years and Lakhana and Sītā return to the kingdom, but Rāma comes back only after the completion of twelve years, marries Sītā and is crowned king. He rules for a long time as a wise and benevolent ruler.

It is sometimes argued that by making Sītā both the sister and wife of Rāma the narrator of the Jātaka story has either confused or deliberately perverted the brāhmaṇical version and in the process has given it a different locale. But the theme of brother-sister marriage forms a part of the original myth of several prestigious kṣatriya clans, such as the Śākyas and the Lichchhavis in early Pāli texts and is meant to emphasize the purity of the lineage. Thus, in the *Dīgha Nikāya,* one of the earliest Pāli canonical texts, the Buddha informs the brāhmaṇ Ambattha that king Okkaka (Ikshavaku) wanted to give succession to the son of his favourite queen and hence banished his elder children, who took up their dwelling on the slopes of the Himalayas and out of fear of injuring the purity of their line of descent, married their own (*sakahi*) sisters. Their descendants came to be known as Sākyas as they lived at a spot where a mighty Śāka tree grew.[3] The descent of the Lichchhavis too is traced from a miraculously born twin brother and sister who married each other.[4] Interpreting these myths in terms of "incestuous" relationship is an anachronistic imposition of social norms of a later period on myths meant to convey a different meaning. It is worth noting that the Buddha himself belonged to the Śākya lineage which was highly respected by the Buddhists.

In fact, purity of descent was of vital concern to the ruling class of the *gaṇa-rājyas* of the sixth century BC, as access to political power depended on it. Buddhist sources contrast the insistence of the kṣatriyas on the purity of descent on both sides with the practice of contemporary brāhmaṇs who admitted within their *varṇa* persons of partial non-brāhmaṇ origin.[5] In any case there is no attempt to denigrate the personality of Rāma in the *Daśaratha Jātaka* where Rāmạ is explicitly described as the Great Being, *mahāsatto,* the Buddha in one of his former births, and the model of Buddhist virtue, who remains unruffled even on hearing the news of his father's death and explains to other grieving persons the impermanence of things.

The legend of Sītā being both the younger sister (*kaniṭṭha-bhaginī*) as well as the chief-queen (*agga-mahesī*) of Rāma and famous for her devotion to her husband is incidentally mentioned in the *Vessantara Jātaka.*[6] But the Buddhist texts of the later period hardly make any use of the story of Rāma, perhaps because once Rāma came to be accepted as an incarnation of Viṣṇu, the Buddhists in India preferred to ignore him. He figures as a Boddhisattva in the *Anāmaka Jātaka* which was translated into Chinese in 251 AD and which refers to the abduction of Sītā and the help received from the monkey-king. But the *Daśaratha Kathānam* which was translated into Chinese in 472 AD speaks of Rāma as having the valour and prowess of God Nārāyaṇa (Viṣṇu). It mentions king Kaniṣka; hence the original Indian text could not have been written earlier than the second century AD.[7] Later Buddhist works do not mention Rāma. Textual analysis has clearly established that Books I and VII of Vālmīki's *Rāmāyaṇaa,* where Rāma is described as an incarnation of Viṣṇu, are later additions,[8] perhaps made around first-second centuries AD. Books II-VI, with the exception of a few interpolated passages, depict him simply as an ideal man, the epic hero who is often likened and sometimes equated with the Vedic god Indra.

It is not without significance that the character of Sītā is fashioned out of the concept of a Vedic goddess of the same name who is to be invoked at the start of ploughing operations. In the *Gṛhyasūtras* she is described as possessed of radiant beauty and black eyes and is sometimes mentioned as the wife of Indra and Parjanya. Her name signifies 'furrow' and she is the goddess of agriculture. Vālmīki calls her *ayonija*, 'not born from the womb', and she does not die but goes underground into the receiving arms of Mother Earth. Her foster-father

Janaka is plough-bannered. The *Daśaratha* and *Vessantara Jātakas* add *devī* to her name which may not have been simply an honorofic. Her association with Rāma and Lakhana as their sister suggests a parallel to the worship of Goddess Ekanamaśā along with her brothers Baladeva and Kṛṣṇa, testified by a number of Kuṣāṇa sculptures and the *Bṛhatsaṃhitā* of Varāhamihira.[9] Later, in early medieval times, Ekanamaśā was regarded as identical with Bhadrā or Subhadrā and worshipped along with Baladeva and Kṛṣṇa (= Jagannātha) at the Puri temple of Orissa. Interestingly, the Utkala Khaṇḍa of the *Skanda Purāṇa* speaks of the goddess flanked by Baladeva and his younger brother Vāsudeva in the Puri temple as both the sister and wife of Vāsudeva, embodying his energy.[10] Later, the Oriya poet Balarāma Dās, who composed the Oriya *Rāmāyaṇa*, identified Rāma, Lakṣmaṇa and Sītā with Jagannātha, Balabhadra and Subhadrā, in utter disregard of the implications of transforming a sister into a devoted wife!

Divine symbolisms are not exact replicas of accepted societal norms and in fact may be the result of a long process of development. No doubt, Vālmīki's epic gave final shape to the character of Sītā as the faithful, devoted and long-suffering wife of Rāma, but the process of euphemerization of this goddess seems to have begun long before Vālmīki and there are multiple versions of her origin. In a number of Jain and brāhmaṇical texts Sītā is described as the daughter of Rāvaṇa and Mandodarī: for example, the *Vasudeva-hiṇḍī*, of Sanghadāsa (c. AD 609), the *Uttara Purāṇa* of Guṇabhadra (c. ninth century) and the *Mahābhāgavata* (*Devi*) *Purāṇa*. In the *Adbhuta Rāmāyaṇa* written in Kashmir she is born of the blood of ascetics collected in a pot by Rāvaṇa. Mandodarī drank it and gave birth to Sītā. In these versions Rāvaṇa has her buried in a casket on account of a prophecy that her husband would kill him but Janaka finds her while ploughing in a field and adopts her, whereas Rāvaṇa falls in love with his own daughter. Some other narratives, such as the *Paumacariya* of Vimalasūri and the *Padmapurāṇa* of Raviṣeṇa (both are Jain *Rāmāyaṇas*), follow Vālmīki more closely and make Janaka the real father of Sītā but transfer the incestuous motif in connection with Sītā to her long-lost twin brother Bhāmaṇḍala, who at the instigation of Nārada turns up at her *swayamvara* as a suitor! The mystery surrounding the birth of Sītā and the introduction of the 'incest' motif in various forms reflects her original divine character.

It is possible to see embedded in the conceptions of Rāma, Sītā and Lakṣmaṇa, or Baladeva, Subhadrā (or Ekanamśā) and Kṛṣṇa, an archaic concept of a female deity flanked by two associate male gods originally her brothers assisting her in her cosmic roles. But later, the goddess is subordinated to them and one of her associates rises to the status of her husband, whom she follows in utter devotion in accordance with the patriarchal norms. This hypothesis may explain the overlap of her dual relationship, both as wife and sister, for some time. The contradiction is removed in course of time and she becomes the model of the faithful, obedient wife. In any case, the eulogy of the great mother-goddess called Āryā Devī in the *Harivaṃśa Purāṇa* describing her as the sister of Mahendra and Viṣṇu[11] is again reflective of a matriarchal form of worship, faint traces of which may be discerned only by reading against the grain.

It has been said that Vālmīki wrote in the context of the rising tide of Buddhism, which preached moral values and stressed the ideals of celibacy and monkhood. As opposed to this Vālmīki presented through his poem the brāhmaṇical ideal of virtue exalting the housholder's stage of life, and he provided a role model for all kinds of relationships; father, son, mother, wife, friend, and so on. Weaving together the legendary tales centering around Ayodhya, Kiskindhā and Lankā, his epic created a fascinating saga in which the norms of a patriarchal *varṇa*-based society are upheld by various characters at the cost of a great deal of personal and dramatic appeal. Henceforth, the basic plot of the Rāma story becomes fixed but variations were still possible and have been made down to the present century both in literature and folklore.

The original poem of Vālmīki, leaving out the first and the last books, is supposed to have been composed between the third century BC and the second century AD. By the end of the second century it had already become so popular that the

Kalpanāmaṇḍaṭikā, a text written towards the close of the second century, speaks of its public recital.[12] It is significant that the other great epic, *Mahābhārata,* was also being refashioned about the same time.[13] V.S. Sukthankar,[14] the celebrated editor of the major portion of the critical edition of the *Mahābhārata,* was firmly of the view that the *Mahābhārata* was not an odd conglomerate of amorphous literature patched together but a harmonious work having an organic unity and a conscious design. He gives the credit of transforming a heroic poem of 24,000 verses dealing with the Kaurava-Pāṇḍava war into a *dharmaśāstra* consisting of nearly one lakh verses to a band of inspired Bhargava poets who were partial to the cult of Nārāyaṇa-Viṣṇu and sought to teach and propagate brāhmaṇical social ethics through a popular medium. Sukthankar regards the *Bhagavadgītā* as the keystone of this remodelled version embodying its central message. In our opinion this laid the foundation of what later came to be regarded as 'classical Hinduism'.

The composition of two major epics presenting the ideal of brāhmaṇical social ethics and piety about the same time was not a fortuitous phenomenon but the response of brāhmaṇical intellectuals to a situation of crisis. We have argued elsewhere[15] that in the centuries immediately preceding and succeeding the Christian era Vedic Brāhmaṇism faced a major threat, as animal sacrifices were no longer popular and in demand and the onslaught of Buddhism and other heterodox sects had undermined the prestige and authority of the brāhmaṇs and *varṇa* hierarcy. The earlier close link of the *brāhma* and the *kṣātra,* the priestly and the ruling powers, so typical of later Vedic polity, is not in evidence in post-Vedic times and the capture of political power by the Greeks, Scythians, Kuṣāṇas and other foreign invaders, who came in large numbers and adopted Buddhism and the cults of popular divinities, meant further loss of patronage to Vedic priests. Vedic ritual and intellectual tradition had by now become too rigid and inflexible to accommodate well-known foreign communities who had both political power as well as wealth owing to their participation in the growing nexus of trade and the processes of urbanization, which factors also brought about an improvement in the condition of artisans and craftsmen traditionally ranked as low in the brāhmaṇical social hierarchy and neglected in the Vedic religious tradition. Brāhmaṇical thinkers and social reformers met these challenges by shifting the emphasis from the Vedic ritual of sacrifice to devotional image-worship of popular deities identified as forms of Vedic gods and goddesses and made their brahmaṇized worship accessible to all irrespective of caste, community and gender.

The framework of classical Hinduism which shows utter "tolerance" or flexibility in matters of belief and symbols of devotion but enjoins rigid adherence to the traditional functions and customs of one's caste while upholding the hierarchy of brāhmaṇical and patriarchal social norms evolved in the circumstances described above. Both the epics played a major role in the formation and dissemination of this ideological pattern. However, it is generally believed that the identification of Rāma as incarnation of Viṣṇu and the introduction of Vaiṣṇavite elements in the *Rāmāyaṇa* is a later development. Apparently this happened after the identification of the popular god Vāsudeva-Kṛṣṇa with the Vedic deity Nārāyaṇa-Viṣṇu and the resultant evolution of the doctrines of incarnation in Bhāgavatism, which was the earlier form of Vaiṣṇavism. Although traditionally the Rāma incarnation is supposed to have preceded Kṛṣṇa incarnation, inscriptional evidence proves the identification of Kṛṣṇa with Viṣṇu in the second and first centuries BC, while the identification of Rāma with Viṣṇu seems to have taken place only around or after second century AD with the growing popularity of Vālmīki's epic and emergence of the synthetic brāhmaṇized cult of Kṛṣṇa-Viṣṇu. The *Mahābhārata* gives the story of Rāma following largely the *Rāmāyaṇa* of Vālmīki but differs in certain details. However, this only shows that the remodelled *Bhārata* epic continued to receive additions and interpolations of episodes, anecdotes and individual passages even after its initial promulgation. Differences could be accounted for by presuming that the composer of the *Rāmopākhyāna* of the *Mahabharata* relied on a variant text of Vālmīki's epic. Or, he may have felt free to invent certain alterations in the genealogy of Rāma and make Vibhīṣaṇa the stepbrother of Rāvaṇa rather than depicting him as his real brother as mentioned by Vālmīki.

More intriguing is the brief narrative in the *Bhāgavata-purāṇa,* which in contradiction to Vālmīki's version of the episode, describes Rāma himself as cutting off the nose of Śūrpaṇakhā in two passages.[16] Vālmīki attributes this act of brutality to Lakṣmaṇa, albeit on the orders of Rāma. Apparently the audience which heard the Purāṇic stories regarded mutilation as just punishment for a bold, shameless woman, so the author of the *Bhāgavata Purāṇa* saw nothing wrong in foisting this exploit on Rāma himself. Most other brāhmaṇical versions of the Rāma story, including Tulsi's *Rāmacharitmānas,* credit this act to Lakṣmaṇa acting on the advice of Rāma and use this incident to expatiate on the frailty and evil nature of woman.

The brāhmaṇical orientation of the Rāma saga created strong reactions in non-brāhmaṇical circles, and whereas the Buddhists stopped making use of the Rāma legend after second century AD in India, the Jains composed their own *Rāmāyaṇas* contesting the brāhmaṇical characterization of key characters and using the story to propagate their own value-system. In the Jain *Rāmāyaṇa*s Rāma is a non-violent follower of the teachings of Mahāvīra Jain and it is Lakṣmaṇa who kills Rāvaṇa. Again, unlike in the brāhmaṇical versions, Rāvaṇa is not evil incarnate, but a great, noble and learned person. His only weakness is his passion for Sītā. He is one of sixty-three great men described by Hemacandra in his *Triṣaṣṭi-śalākā-puruṣa-carita.* Similarly, Śūrpaṇakhā is called Candranakhā in the Jain accounts which do not speak of her disfigurement. Her son Śambūka is killed by Lakṣmaṇa in the Daṇḍaka forests, so she accosts the two brothers, becomes infatuated and is insulted by them. She complains to her brother Rāvaṇa who decides to avenge the insult. The Jain works were composed and recited in constant competition and confrontation with brāhmaṇical works, and an element of counter-culture is conspicuous among them. Several of their works are known as *prati-purāṇas* or counter-Purāṇas and they have mocked and parodied Purāṇic stories. Nevertheless, the Rāma story occupies an important place in their religious tradition and the Jain *Rāmāyaṇa* written by the poet Raviṣeṇa and titled as the *Padmapurāṇa* or *Padma-Carita* is esteemed by the Jains in the same fashion as the Hindus esteem the *Rāmacharitmānas* of Tulsi. A copy of its Hindi translation is to be found in all the Jain temples.[17]

The available Jain versions of the Rāma story are certainly later than the *Rāmāyaṇa* of Vālmīki, and, broadly speaking, follow the same plot but some of these may be said to have access to some independent versions too. Thus the *Uttara Purāṇa* of Guṇabhadra seems to sythesize the Buddhist and brāhmaṇical versions of the Rāma story by making Daśaratha a king of Vārānasī, who later changes his capital to Ayodhya. After the marriage of Rāma to Sītā, Daśaratha makes Rāma his crown prince and sends him to Varanasi to look after his subjects there. Sītā and Lakṣmaṇa accompany Rāma. We have already mentiond that in this work Sītā is the daughter of Rāvaṇa and Mandodarī, and Janaka is her foster-father.

Some other variations in the legend of Rāma are linked with the growth of the concept of *bhakti*, particularly of Rāma *bhakti*. Thus initially Vālmīki speaks of Rāma as a partial incarnation of Viṣṇu representing one-fourth of his potency. Each of the three other sons of Daśaratha too have one-fourth of Viṣṇu's essence in them.

However, in the Vālmīki *Rāmāyaṇa* itself there are passages identifying Rāma as the complete, total incarnation of Viṣṇu. The development has its parallel in the Kṛṣṇa cult. Initially Kṛṣṇa is said to incarnate one black hair of Nārāyaṇa and Baladeva one grey hair. But later, Kṛṣṇavatāra is regarded as the absolute incarnation of Viṣṇu in all his potency.[18]

The exaltation of Rāma as the complete incarnation of Viṣṇu had significant theological and philosophical implications and contributed to the multiplicity of the Rāma symbolism. Thus at one level he was a perfect human being acting as an exemplar, at another level he was God both transcendent as well as immanent, the highest self without beginning. The concept of Sītā, too, undergoes corresponding evolution and at the higher level she is conceived as the creative energy, the *śakti* or power, of comsic Rāma. In the *Adbhut Rāmāyaṇa* written in Kashmir under Tantric influence, she even dominates over Rāma. The work claims to be the eighth *kāṇḍa* (book) of Vālmīki's *Rāmāyaṇa*.

Later the *Adhyātma Rāmāyaṇa*, which deeply influenced Tulsī, integrated the Vedantic, Purāṇic and Tantric concepts of absolute reality in its conception of Rāma and Sītā and while sticking by and large to the structure of Vālmīki's narrative imbued it with new meanings. The *Adhyātma Rāmāyaṇa* became the 'scripture' of the Rāmanandī sect in North India and may have influenced Kabir in choosing the name of Rāma as the general designation of God.[19] However, although his God was merciful and loving, he was formless and not a son of Daśaratha or an *avatāra* of Viṣṇu. Kabir was fighting against the inequalities of the contemporary social system. Hence, his Rāma could not been the Rāma of Vālmīki who was great champion of brāhmaṇical orthodoxy and could behead a sūdra ascetic for committing the sin of transcending his *varṇa* rights. However, the BJP's attempt to transform Rāma into a unitary symbol of 'Hindu nationalism' have political rather than social or religious aims in view.

ENDNOTES

1. *Adhyātma Rāmāyaṇa*, II. 4. 76, quoted by Frank Whaling, *The Rise of the Religious Significance of Rāma*, Motilal Banarasidass, Delhi, 1980, p. 121m f.n. 7.
2. V. Fauböll (ed.), *Jātaka*, 6 vols, Trübner and Co., London, 1877-97, no. 461; Suvira Jaiswal, *The Origin and Development of Vaiṣṇavism*, 1st edn., 1967, 2nd enlarged edn, Munshiram Manoharlal, Delhi, 1981, pp. 140–3; H.B. Sarkar in *The Rāmāyaṇa Tradition in Asia*, ed. V. Raghavan, Sahitya Akademi, New Delhi, 1980, pp. 162–3; Suniti Kumar Chatterjee, ibid. Also see A.L. Basham, *The Wonder that Was India*, Fontana, 1967, p. 41; M.A. Mehendale in *The Age of Imperial Unity: The History and Culture of the Indian People*, vol. II, edited by R.C. Majumdar and A.D. Paluskar, Bharatiya Vidya Bhavan, Bombay, 1951, p. 254.
3. Rhys Davids, *Dialogues of the Buddha*, Pali Text Society (PTS), London, 1889, vol. I, p. 115; *Dīgha Nikāya, edited* by T.W. Rhys Davids and S.E. Carpenter, PTS, 3 vols., London, (1890–1911),

vol. II, pp. 92–3. Also see *Sumangalavilāsinī* (Buddhaghoṣa's commentary on the *Dīgha Nikāya* (ed. by T.W. Rhys Davids, London, PTS, 1886), pt. I, pp. 258–60.

4. Buddhaghoṣa's *Paramattha-Jotikā commentary to Khuddakapāṭha*, ed. by H. Smith, PTS, London, 1915, pt. I, pp. 158–60.
5. Narendra Wagle, *Society at the time of the Buddha*, Popular Prakashan, Bombay, 1966, p. 102.
6. Fausboll, op. cit., vol. VI, p. 558.
7. For references see Suvira Jaiswal, op. cit., p. 140.
8. M.A. Mehendale, op. cit.
9. Suvira Jaiswal, op. cit., pp. 68–70.
10. *Skandapurāṇa, Utkala-Khaṇḍa*, XIX.177, Parashu Rama Chaturvedi, *Dharma*, 2nd edition, Delhi, n.d., pp. 123–4.
11. *Harivaṃśa*, Pandit Ramachandrashastri Kinjawadekar, ed., Shri Venkateswara Press, Poona, 1936, II. 120.6.
12. V. Raghavan, *The Ramayana Tradition in Asia*, p. 5, H.B. Sarkar, ibid., p. 163.
13. Suvira Jaiswal, op. cit., pp. 9f, 232.
14. V.S. Sukthankar, *On the Meaning of the Mahābhārata*, Asiatic Society of Bombay, Bombay, 1957.
15. S. Jaiswal, op. cit., pp. 77f., 232.
16. *Bhāgavatapurāṇa*, Gita Press, Gorakhpur, X. 10.4 and X.10.9.
17. Rama Kant Shukla, *Jainācārya Ravishena Krita Padma-Purana aur Tulsikrit Rāmacharit-Mānas*, Vani Parishad, Delhi, 1974, p. 32.
18. Suvira Jaiswal, op. cit., p.
19. Frank Whaling, op. cit., p. 112.

7

Rāmāyaṇa in the Counterculture: Folk Retellings by Women, Śūdras and the Tribal People*

Nabaneeta Dev Sen

Forever being built and rebuilt, used and abused, the *Rāmāyaṇa* is the most popular epic in South Asia. Unlike the Homeric and Virgilian epics, it is part of a living, vibrant cultural tradition. Its variants have spread far beyond the region, not merely to Southeast Asia but also towards Central Asia, where we find Khotanese, Tibetan, Chinese and Turkistani versions. And even within our subcontinent, the diversity of the Rāma legend is amazing. Let me recount a story I had heard from my friend A.K. Ramanujan. Rāma had lost a ring, which had fallen through a hole in the ground. Since Hanumān can shrink to any size, he followed the ring into the hole and fell straight into the netherworld. Everyone, including the king of Pātālapurī, wondered where this minute monkey had come from, and why. When the king learned why Hanumān had come, he ordered his servants to bring the ring. A big tray was brought which contained a heap of identical rings. The king said, there have been as many Rāmas in the universe as there are rings on this tray, so which one is yours? Hanumān learnt his lesson and returned to our world.

---

* Reprinted from *The Little Magazine*, Vol. VII, Issues 5 & 6.

This is a lesson that we, too, have to learn. Our *Rāmāyaṇa* tradition goes far beyond the classical Sanskrit brāhmaṇical tradition of Vālmīki into the regional language variations of Kamban, Krittibās, Tulsīdās, Saraladās, Ranganātha, Mollā, Chandrābatī and Bhānubhakta, a few names that are generally known. But there are numerous lesser known texts in the regional languages, which move from Vālmīki in various directions in pursuit of the *bhakti* tradition. Apart from these, we have the alternative Buddhist and Jain *Rāmāyaṇa*s, the Islamic interpretations of the Rāma legend in Indonesia and Malaysia, and the enormous wealth of the folk legends of Rāma, including tribal and women's songs, in various parts of South Asia. The range of expression goes beyond the written word to *Rāma kathās,* work songs, women's songs, performed texts like dance dramas, *jātrā*s and plays, only some of which are religious.

We have witnessed the historic TV rendering by Ramanand Sagar, which was supposed to be secular entertainment and drew huge audiences across religious lines, but which did lead some households to hang marigold garlands on the TV and to burn incense in the room while it was on air. To crown it all, we have witnessed a political party's exploitation of the Rāma legend to the hilt. We have watched the institutional abuse of an epic, turning an epic hero into a culture hero, using him to represent the Hindutva ideology, in order to politically exploit the great power that the name of Rāma exerts among the rural as well as the urban population in India. To serve political purposes, Rāma was generously promoted to the status of a national hero in BJP white papers, as if a legendary figure could be turned into a historical personality just by campaigning for it.

This was not the first time, though, that Rāma was brought into the political scene, even if we except Mahatma Gandhi's *Rāmdhun, 'Raghupati Rāghava Rājā Rām'*. In the South, E.V. Ramasami Naicker, or Periyar, had done his fiery bit, presenting Rāma as the brāhmaṇical culture-hero, the oppressor from the North, persecuting the Southern culture hero, the large hearted non brāhmaṇical warrior Rāvaṇa. He even wanted to get in touch with Jinnah to demand a Tamil Nadu as a third nation when India was divided.

The variations of the *Rāmāyaṇa* texts in the regional languages reveal how each region adds its own special spice to the legend. In Hindi, Tulsidās describes Rāma and Sītā falling in love before the *swayamvara* and stops after establishing *Rāmarājya,* whereas in Bengali, Krittibās, who also hints at a love episode, goes on to Sītā's banishment. Kamban's Tamil Rāvaṇa is altogether different, Bhānubhakta uses the *Adbhuta Rāmāyaṇa,* rather than Vālmīki, as the base for his Nepaḷi text, and Saraladās's Oriya *Bilanka Rāmāyaṇa* is a story in which Sītā is the hero, as in the *Śatakaṇṭha Rāvaṇa* or *Sahasrakaṇṭha Rāvaṇa* stories. The 16th century woman poet Mollā followed Vālmīki in Telugu, enjoyed describing the battle scenes and also stopped with *Rāmarājya,* whereas her near contemporary Chandrābatī, writing in Bengali, was in some ways closer to the Jain *Rāmāyaṇa.* However, She took no interest in the epic battle and wrote mostly about the *Uttara Kāṇḍa,* the last chapter of the *Rāmāyaṇa.*

The Buddhist and Jain *Rāmāyaṇas* differ enormously from Vālmīki. Their legends seem to be older and perhaps derive from a more ancient social order, where marriage between brother and sister was allowed, and Sītā is presented as Rāma's sister. In some versions, Sītā is Rāvaṇa's daughter, banished at birth. The narrative details vary a great deal from text to text.

Particularly interesting is the non Sanskrit-folk tradition in Indian literature whose oral renderings of the epics quietly challenge the classical tradition, telling the brāhmaṇical stories in their own fashion, from a slightly different angle. The language is typically a rural dialect and the singer may be a woman, a śūdra, or a tribal. Their songs are composed and transmitted orally. They do not have a fixed form but change a little every time they are sung. Wonderful examples of this tradition are found in the women's orature—the work songs, ritual songs and lullabies that women compose on the fly. They hold up an alternative point of view of the *Rāmāyaṇa* epic, focusing on Sītā's life rather than Rāma's. The mainstream heroic brāhmaṇical values have nothing to do with their lives, but they can identify with the downtrodden, which is how they see Sītā in the epic.

The brāhmaṇical values are rejected by the śūdra and the tribal as well, who are also excluded from mainstream society. And so we hear a collective voice when we listen to oral renderings of the epic tales by the unlettered. It is amazing how close the women's songs are to the śūdra men's songs in emotion, perception, expression, choice of events and responses to the brāhmaṇical text.

A close reading of the text shows that the *Rāmāyaṇa* was a manifesto of the feudal brāhmaṇical social system, one that excluded the disempowered from the public sphere—women, śūdras and tribals. There was no space allotted to them in the warrior-priest power nexus between the king and the sages. So the women sing of their sorrows within their private spaces, among themselves, in their allocated voice. They sing of the most dangerous moments of their lives—child marriage, domestic abuse, childbirth in difficult circumstances, abandonment. If one listens carefully, a hidden critique of the system can be heard.

Perhaps the Little Tradition is stronger in many ways than the Great Tradition, because it springs from life and deals with existential realities. The Rāma legend has been quietly serving an important social purpose in the subcontinent, away from political platforms, religious fanfare and scholarly projects. One of the strands that hold the subcontinent together is the secular and unheard *Rāmāyaṇa* tradition, not the mainstream discourse. It is a unified tradition of *Rāmāyaṇa*s composed in different languages in different parts of the subcontinent, yet astoundingly similar.

Just as the Rāma myth has been exploited by the patriarchal brāhmaṇical system to construct an ideal Hindu male, Sītā too has been built up as an ideal Hindu female to help serve the system. Through Sītā, patriarchal values may be spread far and wide, and women may be taught to forebear all injustice silently.

But there are always alternative ways of using a myth. If patriarchy has used the Sītā myth to silence women, the village women have picked it up to give themselves a voice. These work songs and ritual songs have opened up a rich world of women's *Rāmāyaṇas*. While weeding or sowing in the field or husking or grinding in the courtyard, women across the subcontinent sing these songs. These are connected with the rites of passage of a woman's life. Sītā is the name of the universal woman who attains puberty, gets married, gets pregnant, is abandoned, and gives birth. They call it the *Rāmāyaṇa*, but it is of Sītā that they sing.

In the women's retellings the Rāma myth is blasted automatically, though probably unwittingly. Rāma comes through as a harsh, uncaring and weak willed husband, a far cry from the *maryādā puruṣottama*. The women reprimand him, point out his mistakes, say, 'Rāma you've lost your mind!' This is possible because the women's songs are outside the canon. But even here, Sītā is no rebel. She is still the yielding, suffering wife. But she has a voice. She speaks of her sufferings, of injustice, of loneliness and sorrow.

Across the country, village women identify very closely with Sītā. Mindful of the fundamental insecurity underlining their lives, their songs—whether in Maithili, Bengali, Marathi or Telugu—see the universal woman as an essential orphan, as a being without identity, an ever alienated self in exile. Though village women do have affection for Rāma the child or Rāma the lover, in their folk songs he comes through as a less than perfect man, and a far cry from a hero.

But these songs are not about heroes and villains. It's about everyday life. In the women's retellings, Rāma and Sītā are just ordinary folk, with very ordinary desires, anxieties and problems. They mirror the simple village life and the common concerns of villagers. Through it all, they present a gendered picture of social customs and values.

For example, in this Maithili song, young Sītā is cleaning the courtyard. She comes across a hefty bow, lifts it with her left hand while sweeping with her right. Janaka faints in shock as he had never been able to move the bow himself. Then he bursts into loud laments: "*Ab Sita rahali kumari, yo!* (Now Sita will remain unmarried, oh!)" Since a woman needs a husband stronger than her and Sita has such extraordinary strength, could she ever meet her match?

The wedding songs reflect not just the joy of the union, but also the concerns of child marriage, and the physical dangers it poses for underage girls. In a Telugu song, Sītā's father Janaka takes Rāma's father Daśaratha to the wedding hall and anxiously points to little Sītā, a small child fast asleep on the huge wedding bed: "Look how helpless she looks in that floral bed, she is still an innocent child."

If the wedding songs reflect the anxiety of the parents, the *sasurbas* songs often speak of the suffering Indian bride. In Marathi, these songs reflect the eternal *saas bahu* saga, where the bride is tormented by the mother-in-law: "Rāma gave Sītā his love/On a tiny tamarind leaf/Kaikeyi poured poison in Rāma's ears/So he chews his *pān* all alone/All by himself/ While Kaikeyi waits behind the door/Like a scorpion." Tamarind leaves are tiny—according to women's lore, Rāma clearly didn't have much to offer. And chewing *pān* all by himself symbolized not sharing even his leisure hours with his wife.

Happily, women singers pay a great deal of attention to Sītā's desires during her pregnancy. What does Sītā wish for? In this Telugu song, Sītā is three months pregnant. "What does Sītammā's heart desire?" She desires cottage cheese made from tiger's milk, no less. And Lakṣmaṇa, her dear brother-in-law, gets tiger's milk for her from the forest to make the cheese with.

"But, brother Lakṣmaṇa, I have one more desire in my heart."

"What is it now?"

"In the middle of the blue ocean lies a distant sandbank/ In the middle of the sandbank/stands a single teakwood tree/ From that teakwood tree hangs a special honeycomb/With that honey I wish to eat *sādā dosās*!"

Sītā's exotic taste doesn't please her mother-in-law. She grumbles: "Huh! I, too, was pregnant once, and delivered Rāma and Laksmana alright/But did I ever ask for such outlandish stuff? All I ever craved for was green mangoes and coconut." Thus the women laugh at themselves, asking for the unattainable and settling for the ordinary.

But then Sītā is exiled. In Marathi songs, her chariot has to wait as she fusses over her wifely duties before leaving forever. As we increasingly get exasperated with the detailed instructions of the finicky housewife, the singer changes her tune and confides in her women companions: "Sītā is going to the forest/She is pouring out her heart/only to you and me (saying):/Rama has no compassion/I am five months pregnant" Behind the screen of wifely duties, we can hear the voice of disenchantment and criticism which only women can share among themselves.

In Bangladesh, too, the exile songs are heart-rending, but not necessarily softly worded. Bengali women freely use very harsh words for Rāma. An example: "Five months pregnant, Sītā was in the royal palace, a heartless Rāma sent her off to the forest!" Another song says, "Sītā takes a few steps and looks back a few times/But oh! the palace of that sinner Rāma still rises high." It takes a great deal of accumulated anger to call someone commonly known as the ocean of Mercy (*karuṇasindhu*) ruthless (*paṣanda*). But to brand the *Patitapāban,* one who redeems all sinners, as a sinner (*pāpiṣṭhi*) himself, goes that unbelievable step further.

It reflects the anger of the powerless towards the blatant injustice of the powerful. The women express their anger towards a husband who has banished his pregnant, loyal and loving wife to the jungles for no fault of hers. Sita's giving birth in the forest brings into focus the plight of village women who still give birth under terribly difficult circumstances in a country where maternal mortality and infant mortality rates are very high and postpartum care poor. Even today, most women in India go through childbirth by themselves, without the help of a doctor or nurse.

Take this Marathi song: "Sītābāi has given birth/Where will Sītā find nourishment?/There is no one to cook her a meal.../Sītā is in exile, there is no cradle for her babies/Sītā made a bed of flowers/And placed her twins in it/Sītābai has given birth/The hills and the forests are rejoicing/She has no one else to call her own./Sītā says, 'I have lived a life of rejection.'/All her life she has been neglected by Rāma,/Yes, all her life."

Thus, village women across the subcontinent use the cover of the Rāma legend to sing about the pain and fear of a lonely childbirth, the lack of nourishment of the mother, domestic violence, child marriage, the vulnerability and basic insecurities of a woman who is disposable in a patriarchal society; Sītā is their voice. For they, Like Sītā, have been programmed not to rebel.

The tribal *Rāmāyaṇa*s are countercultural too. The tribals identify with the disempowered and they often choose to speak through Sītā, the foundling, to express their condition. Some even claim their descent from Rāvaṇa, the vanquished hero, while others regard Hanumān as a foreparent. Very few have a complete *Rāmāyaṇa*, but a Rāma tale may be derived from their fragmented versions. When they do have complete poem, like the Karbis of the Northeast, they quite unabashedly call it *Sabin Alum* or *Sita Kengri Alum*—the *Song of Sita*. Like women of the mainstream culture, tribals and śūdras all over India share their sympathies with Sītā, from the Mundas of Chhotanagpur to the Gonds of Madhya Pradesh and the Karbis of the Northeast.

In his essay, "There Hundred Ramayanas" A.K. Ramanujan talks of a śūdra *Rāmāyaṇa* in Kannada, and how the śūdra singer, a man, could not wait to come back to Sītā and her life-experiences from her birth and wedding to her pregnancy and abondonment, her childbirth in the forest, and her moral victory over Rāma. It is not surprising that women and śūdras dwell on the same episodes to tell their tale. Scarcely accidental, it reveals a clear pattern in the manner in which the powerless respond to a brāhmaṇical text.

The tribal songs too look upon Sītā as the essential orphan and see Rāma as the oppressor. No matter if he is a king or a god, Rāma remains distant, inaccessible and unaccountable for his acts. He is the representative of the brāhmaṇical feudal system while Sītā is a child of nature, like the tribals themselves. "According to them, Rāma was not the embodiment of righteousness, an ideal person or an *avatāra*, as projected by Goswami Tulsidas, but an ordinary man with human weakness," writes K.S. Singh on the tribal *Rāmāyaṇas*. In the Munda tales, "Rāvaṇa is described as a noble hero who belonged to one of the clans of the Munda tribe, Timling. Rāma's treatment of Sītā draws adverse comments, she arouses sympathy and remains the symbol of suffering in Munda poetry." Just as the brāhmanical tradition has Hinduized the tribals in its mythology, they too have tribalised the *Rāmāyaṇa* to some extent, and the outcome is amusing as well as enlightening for us.

The Mundas are not alone in claming Rāvaṇa as their clansman. Many other groups identify with Rāma's enemy. A group of Gonds call themselves *Rāvaṇavamśī*—of the House of Rāvaṇa. The Korkus consider Rāvaṇa and Meghnāda to be sacred deities who guard them against disease and disaster. At least two tribes consider the lazy sleeping demon Kumbhakarṇa as a great sage practising deep penance over a long period. The Kuskos and the Bhuiyans both have this myth of Rishi Kumbhakarṇa's *tapasyā*, a most interesting way of using the brāhmaṇical tradition itself to subvert the classical text. And in the *Bhilodi Rāmakathā*, Ādikavi Vālmīki himself is appropriated. He appears in the beginning of the tale as Valio, a Bhil.

But there are other, livelier versions of the Rāma tale among the tribes. For example, the Pardhans have songs describing a physical intimacy between Lakṣmaṇa and Sītā which is far from the innocent relationship between a young man and his sister-in-law that we are used to. This is actually not so shocking, as among many central Indian tribes like the Gonds, the Murians, the Parajas, the Bhataras and the Paharias, an intimate relationship between the younger brother and the elder brother's wife is often permitted. Of course, this is not true of all tribes.

In another tale, the Baigas a sub-tribe of the Gonds (whose origins lie in the Dravidian culture), turn the mainsteam narrative on its head. Here, poor Lakṣmana has to go through fire ordeals—not just one but two—to prove his chastity when Rāma wrongly suspects him of having an illicit relationship with Sītā. After passing the two fire tests a desperate Lakṣmaṇa prays to Mother Earth for shelter and she receives him into her heart. In this most unconventional tribal story, the roles of Sītā and Lakṣmaṇa are reversed.

In these tellings by the excluded, the epic characters are humanised. The golden deer episode, for example, has been explained in different ways in three tribal texts. In a Gond version, Sītā wants to eat venison. Tired of serving fruits and roots to the brothers, she wishes to cook some venison for a change and sends Rāma after the deer. In a tale of the Dubas of Gujarat, Sītā has been tending a beautiful *damro* plant like her baby, but a deer comes and munches it up day after day. An irritated Sītā wants it killed. And in a Telugu women's version, Sītā wants a golden *cholī* made out of the deerskin. In all these tellings, there is a practical reason for wanting the deer hunted down, not merely a princess's whim for gold.

In a Munda song, Sītā is an abandoned tribal girl who is found in a village in a drought year. And Janaka is a peasant. Sītā is abducted by Rāvaṇa when she is grazing goats. The Mundas claim that Riṣyaśringa was a tribal priest who fathered Rāma and his brothers, and the three queens return to him at the end of the epic. He is compared to the bison-horned Murias.

It is intersting to note how the concept of power is freely altered in these tribal versions. In the Mizo Rāma stories, where Lakṣmaṇa and Hanumān play more important roles than Rāma, the epic heroes threaten each other with guns—bows and arrows are outdated. In the Dubla tales, we encounter another modern tool of power. Rāma is a nine-year-old schoolboy when he marries Sītā. He goes to school with a slate and an inkpot (though the two do not go together). And to prepare for the wedding, all the village folk go out into the forests to collect timber and they bring it back in bullock carts. Timber is still the main source of income and livelihood for the tribals in that part of Gujarat. And education, of course, is the modern source of power. Therefore Rāma the tribal boy is sent to school. The Dublas, incidentally, are a nomadic tribe and do not educate their children. This story gives us a ray of hope. The are thinking differently.

The Agarias, an ironsmith tribe in Madhya Pradesh, have the story of *Sahasrakanṭha Rāvaṇa,* who is killed by Sītā. The story is very similar to the Tamil story of *Satakanṭha Rāvaṇa,* and perhaps the Oriya tale of *Sahasrakanṭha Rāvaṇa* is also reflected here.

The Karbi Rāmāyaṇa, which is called the *Song of Sītā,* is regarded as the very first song of the Karbis—their Ādi Kāvya, preceding their music. It has several versions in different parts of the Northeast, with alternative stories about the births of Sītā and Rāma. Rāvaṇa is a great hero and a pious king. The minor gods are jealous of him and conspire to destroy him. A story of Mandodarī giving birth to a large egg follows. A publicly embarrassed and angry Rāvaṇa throws the egg away, and commits his great sin. Now the gods get what they want, the Almighty has to appear as Rāma to punish Rāvaṇa. In this version, the minor gods are the real culprits, who bring about the fall of Rāvaṇa out of jealousy.

In another version, during the epic battle, Rāma has to perform a certain *pūjā,* and only two priests on earth are capable of performing the ritual, Bāli and Rāvaṇa. Rāma has already killed Bāli, and Rāvaṇa is the only priest left. So Rāma invites him with all the due honour to do the *pūjā* and Rāvaṇa accepts. Rāma prostrates himself before Rāvaṇa and Lakṣmaṇa is extremely annoyed at the gesture. But Rāma explains that it was not to his enemy but to his priest that he was paying his respects. Rāvaṇa blesses Rāma, saying that victory will be his. Here is another instance of using the brāhmaṇical value system itself to subvert the classical relationship between Rāma and Rāvaṇa in order to make Rāma bow to the generosity of Rāvaṇa. This is a rather sophisticated story which distinguishes between the concepts of enemy, priest and individual.

Incidentally, the bow that the Karbi Rāma breaks is not the divine *Haradhanu,* but an exceptionally strong weapon made by skilled blacksmiths who worked for twelve days and twelve nights at a stretch. Sītā could lift it with her left hand. At the *swayamvara,* Rāvaṇa was invited first to string it but failed.

In another Karbi version, after marrying Sītā, Rāma stays on in king Janaka's palace, because in the matriarchal social system of the Karbis, the son-in-law is expected to move into his father-in-law's house. But Daśaratha pleads with Janaka to let Rāma return after a year, because he is heir to his throne. So Prince Rāma stays on for a year as a *gharjamāi* to assist Janaka in his agricultural work, and keeps Lakṣmaṇa with him too. Together, they practice *jhum* cultivation in the manner of the Karbis. There is a beautiful dream sequence right at the end of the *Song of Sītā*. After Sītā's descent into the earth, Lava and Kuśa visit their father. That night, Rāma dreams that he is with Sītā. So he wakes up in the morning, walks down to the sea and asks it to give way, so that he can unite with Sītā. The sea obliges and, the loyal Lakṣmaṇa keeping him company, the two enter the netherworld to meet Sītā. So finally, it is Sītā's song.

Let me close with a Mech *Rāma kathā*, which was collected in 1958 in the Northeast. In this rather unusual telling the tribal people have traced the Hindu-Muslim communal conflict back to the *Rāmāyaṇa*. In their version, Lakṣmaṇa had eaten beef, which made him a Muslim. He had two sons, Hassan and Hussein, whom Rāma's two sons Lava and Kuṣa fought and killed. Now, this is indeed an alternative Rāmāyaṇa! Fratricide was not the theme of this epic (unlike the *Mahābhārata)* but it becomes a theme in the counterculture.

Such retellings of the Rāma tale show how, in the hands of the excluded, even as commanding an epic as the *Rāmāyaṇa* can become a tool to critique the very values it projects. And how the disempowered—whether women, the low caste or the tribals—mould Rāma and his story to fit their own space, reflect their realities and give them a voice.

ENDNOTES

This essay draws partly on the Radhakrishan Memorial Lecture delivered at Oxford University in 1996–7. I have examined in greater detail different aspects discussed here in various papers earlier, including "Lady Sings the Blues", "Sisters in Sorrow", "Chandrabati *Rāmāyaṇa*: *Feminising the Rāma Tale*", "The Essential Orphan" and "The *Rāmāyan* from Below".

8

The Plurality of the Sanskrit *Mahābhārata** and of the Mahābhārata Story

James Hegarty

This paper will explore the form and content of the Sanskrit *Mahābhārata*. It will also consider other versions of the *Mahābhārata* story, or parts of it. Amongst these versions, it will focus in particular on the Doordarśan televisual version of the *Mahābhārata*, which was broadcast in the early nineteen nineties in India. It is my intention to demonstrate that, from its inception, the Sanskrit *Mahābhārata* was a text that anticipated, and sought to foster, plurality. By "plurality", in this instance, I refer to multiple views of what is considered to be most important in the conduct and organization of human social life. I will also show that while the inherent plurality of the Sanskrit *Mahābhārata* is capitalized upon by a variety of versions of the tale, it is suppressed to an unprecedented degree in its, relatively recent, Hindi televisual adaptation.

It is, of course, possible to object to any characterization of the agenda of the Sanskrit *Mahābhārata* on formal grounds by suggesting that it was composed over centuries and that its 'plurality' is merely a by-product of its piecemeal and *ad hoc*

---

* Citations from the Sanskrit *Mahābhārata* (*Mbh*) in the endnotes give number of *parva*, sub-*parva* and *śloka* in the *Mahābhārata*, ed., V.S. Sukthankar, et al., Bhandarkar Oriental Research Institute, Poona, 1933-72.

composition.[1] While it is important to bear in mind the capacity for the *Mahābhārata* to be added to, and edited, by subsequent users of the text, this will not do as a theory of authorship. There is a European fairy story that speaks of a stone soup. In this tale a miserly old lady is tricked into opening her larder to a young lad by his proclamation that he is able to make soup from a stone. The story proceeds as follows: The young lad places his stone in a pan of water and tastes his 'soup'. He immediately suggests that, while the soup is coming on well, it would be much improved with a carrot and a stick of celery. Of course, this process of addition continues until the soup is replete with vegetables, meat and stock. This makes for a fine tale of the psychology of greed and has much to tell us even today, but it will not do as a means of characterizing the composition of one of the great works of world literature.[2]

The Sanskrit *Mahābhārata* is a text that exhibits both a design and a complex set of themes.[3] Both the structure and the thematics of the text make it amenable to expansion and to the re-positioning and repetition of materials, but this does not make of it a "stone soup". I will show that this is the case by taking up the relationship between the form and the content of the Sanskrit *Mahābhārata* below. Subsequent to this demonstration of the inherent plurality of the Sanskrit text, I will take up some different versions of the *Mahābhārata* story that reflect this "plurality" (specifically a Sanskrit literary adaptation and a nineteenth-century theatrical adaptation of the *Mahābhārata*). I will then move on to the Doordarśan televisual version, which, I will suggest, reflects a new consciousness of both Hinduism and India that takes us a long way from the flexibility and responsiveness of the *Mahābhārata* story both in Sanskrit and vernacular tradition.

Structure and Theme in the Sanskrit *Mahābhārata*

All too often, accounts of the structure of the *Mahābhārata* are abstruse, technical and difficult to read. To avoid extended discussion in the abstract of the structure of the Sanskrit text, I have elected to take up the analysis of one particular portion of the *Mahābhārata* as a means of introducing both the text as a whole and my contentions concerning its inherent plurality.

The Case of the Contrary Mongoose

The tale I wish to focus upon appears towards the end of the *Mahābhārata*, after the great and destructive battle at its heart, and subsequent to the victorious King Yudhiṣṭhira's consolation by his dying grandfather Bhīṣma. The *Mahābhārata* itself describes the events surrounding the activities of the mongoose as *āścarya*, which is an adjective that carries connotations of both the wonderful and the strange.[4] At this point in the *Mahābhārata*, King Yudhiṣṭhira has been encouraged to perform a grand sacrifice as a means of expiating the sins of battle and of underscoring his rule over the known world. This sacrifice is known as the *aśvamedha* or horse sacrifice (which gives its name to the book in which we find this tale, the *Aśvamedhikaparva*, the Book of the Horse Sacrifice, the fourteenth book of eighteen in the *Mahābhārata*). The *aśvamedha* is in two stages. The first stage involves the release of a horse that, accompanied by an armed band of men, roams over neighbouring territories exacting tribute. The second stage involves the sacrifice of the horse as part of a three-day ritual consecration of the king. We will pick up the tale during the second stage of Yudhiṣṭhira's *aśvamedha*, when the three-day rite is drawing to a close. Yudhiṣṭhira is surrounded by princes, brāhmaṇs, and his entire family. There has already been a vast giving of alms to the poor and King Yudhiṣṭhira stands supreme before the assembled dignitaries with his head showered with flowers (*patatsu puṣpavarṣeṣu dharmarājasya mūrdhani*).[5] It is at this point that our mongoose appears. The mongoose is described as having a 'golden flank' (*rukma-pārśva*).[6] He wastes no time in addressing King Yudhiṣṭhira in a voice that is like 'thunder and lightening' (*vajra-aśani-samam*).[7] His words are challenging indeed:

> O lords of men, this your sacrifice is not equal (*na tulya*) to a handful of barley (*saktu-prastha*) given by a liberal inhabitant of the field of Kuru who practices the discipline of gleaning (*uñcha-vṛtti*)!
>
> *saktuprasthena vo nāyaṃyajñas tulyo narādhipāḥ/*
> *uñchavṛtter vadānyasya kurukṣetranivāsinaḥ //*

The mongoose calls into question the value of the *aśvamedha* by means of comparing it to the practice of gleaning (living by gathering leftover food-stuffs). He asserts that gleaners are more meritorious than those who engage in costly and harmful sacrifices. He provides further evidence for his case by narrating how he came to have a golden flank. The mongoose states that his miraculous transformation occurred when he ate a few leftover grains of barley. These grains had fallen to the floor as a brāhmaṇ, despite the fact that it meant death by starvation for himself and his family, gave barley to a voracious guest. The guest, pleased with the selflessness of the brāhmaṇ, reveals himself to be the god Dharma (the god of duty or religious law). He congratulates the brāhmaṇ and emphasizes the power of the giving of gifts. He also lists kings of the past who have prospered as a consequence of selfless gift giving and who have foundered as a result of showy public sacrifices. After this account, the brāhmaṇ, his wife, his sons, and their wives all depart for heaven as a consequence of their actions. Having completed his narration, the mongoose then points out that, given that his other flank has not turned to gold during the *aśvamedha* of king Yudhiṣṭhira, the rite is something of a failure.

What are we to make of this bold intervention? Given where we are in the *Mahābhārata*, at the critical point of King Yudhiṣṭhira's acceptance of his role as king and of his part in the horrific battle that stands at the heart of the *Mahābhārata* and which cost the lives of most of his extended family and, indeed, his own sons, the mongoose's words are potentially devastating. All the more so for their emphasis on the inhabitants of *kuru-kṣetra* or the field of Kuru, for it is precisely here that the great battle was fought and won at such a terrible cost. As well as this rather negative association, the emphasis on the inhabitants of the field of Kuru (who are, in the mongoose's tale of the voracious guest, very clearly brāhmaṇs) allows for the story to underscore the importance and merit of the brāhmaṇs of that area and not of other areas. There is thus a certain amount of inter-brāhmaṇ rivalry written into our tale.[8] The mongoose calls into question the grand Vedic rites and their value. He emphasizes the importance of intention, of simplicity and of the avoidance of harm to all living creatures (*ahiṃsā*). In so doing, he calls into question not just Vedic sacrifice but the act of war. The idea of non-harm sits at the heart of not just certain forms of Hindu tradition (it is the first restraint named in Patañjali's *Yogasūtra*, for example) but is also central to Buddhist and Jain ideologies. We should also keep in mind that the *aśvamedha* is a rite of royal consecration. This means that the mongoose is questioning not just the religious but also the political establishment and that he is doing so in terms that recall a wide variety of challenging new strains of thought in early South Asia.

We must also remember that this is a story about the past even for its audiences of the immediately pre-common era and after. This allows us to see that certain radical religious ideologies are here being brought into direct conflict with the Vedic religio-political establishment. We have no evidence for ideas of non-harm or vows of poverty until the time of the Upaniṣads (from approximately the seventh century BCE) and the early Buddhists and Jains (two centuries or so later). This is a long time after the events told of in the *Mahābhārata*. The authors of the *Mahābhārata* are guilty here, then, of a certain degree of deliberate anachronism. The story of the defiant and critical mongoose allows for the staging of a religious debate by narrative means. The drama of the mongoose's intervention is combined with a story in which, as we heard, the god of religious law himself offers a historical narrative in which great kings of the past prosper as a consequence of their acceptance of radical new religious values. In this way, new religious ideologies are naturalized, and indeed emphasized as superior, by means of their insertion in the significant past. In our story, this encompasses both the time of the unfolding of the main plot of the *Mahābhārata* (in the aftermath of the war) and the times before this (the remote past of former kings). All of this as a consequence of the interruption of one boldly critical mongoose!

The debate is more complex even than this, however, for a number of reasons. The first of these is that it is not just the mongoose that advocates the superiority of the selfless gift and the absence of harm. The lesson is reinforced by one of the narrators of the *Mahābhārata* itself, Vaiśampāyana, who is a pupil of the putative author of the *Mahābhārata* (at least as the story itself would have it), Kṛṣṇa Dvaipāyana Vyāsa. Vaiśampāyana is narrating the *Mahābhārata* to the grand-nephew of King Yudhiṣṭhira, one King Janamejaya. Having told the strange and wonderful (*aścarya*) tale of the mongoose Vaiśampāyana states:

> O conqueror of distant fortresses, I have told you all about the strange and extraordinary incident at that great sacrifice, the horse sacrifice. Do not somehow retain any pride, O king, at what is achieved by sacrifice, for millions and millions of sages have gone to heaven by means of gleaning alone. The freedom from malice to all creatures, satisfaction with one's lot and one's moral rectitude, self-restraint, truthfulness, and the giving of gifts, all are thought to be equal (to the sacrifice).[9]

> *etat te sarvam ākhyātaṃ mayā parapuraṃjaya /*
> *yad āścaryam abhūt tasmin vājimedhe mahākratau //*
> *na vismayas te nṛpate yajñe kāryaḥ kathaṃ cana /*
> *ṛṣikoṭisahasrāṇi tapobhir ye divaṃ gatāḥ //*
> *adrohaḥ sarvabhūteṣu saṃtoṣaḥ śīlam ārjavam /*
> *tapo damaś ca satyaṃ ca dānaṃ ceti samaṃ matam //*[10]

In this way, as well as integrating the way of gleaning and non-harm in the main plot of the *Mahābhārata* and the remote past of great former kings, the text also allows these ideologies and practices to be reinforced, and as we shall see subtly altered, by one of the internal narrators of the text. This context of narration also stands somewhat nearer to the present of the *Mahābhārata's* various audiences (both ancient and modern) in that it comes, of course, after the events of the *Mahābhārata* and, indeed, after the rule of Yudhiṣṭhira's nephew and successor, King Parīkṣit, the father of King Janamejaya. In fact, in a subsequent genre of religious text that shares the *Mahābhārata's* emphasis on the significant past, the *Purāṇas* (which tend to provide sectarian accounts of the nature and development of the universe and the beings within it), we find that, on occasion, it is Janamejaya and his father who are the first kings of the Kaliyuga, the present and most debased, age of humankind.[11] We should also note that the message is somewhat changed in Vaiśampāyana's summary. Firstly, the list of activities that are said to be productive of heaven is extended to include a wider variety of activities and states of mind. We now find contentment (*saṃtoṣa*) with one's way of life (*śīla*) and one's sense of fair play (*ārjava*) amongst them.[12] This is perhaps a more socially conservative message as what is really being discussed is contentment in a life of scavenging or perhaps even poverty (two ways of interpreting the force of *tapas* here). Even if this mode of life is being made productive of heaven, it is hardly an equitable social philosophy. Secondly, Vaiśampāyana finishes his final exhortation to Janamejaya by stating that these practices are the equal (*samam*) of sacrificial activity. This is a subtly different message to that of our rather more truculent mongoose who emphasized the inferiority of Yudhiṣṭhira's *aśvamedha*. In this way, Vaiśampāyana reinforces, but also mildly subverts, the teaching of the mongoose. He does this as he narrates to no less a figure than King Janamejaya who is a direct descedent of Yudhiṣṭhira and who, at this moment in the text, is engaged in a vast and bloody sacrifice of the snakes of the world (in Sanskrit, a *sarpa sattra*). This is a king who, as we have already heard, also, at least in the view of later traditions, shares our common predicament of 'kaliyugic' modernity. Thus the tale speaks to both Janemajaya's own preference for bloody sacrifice and to the religious possibilities of the present. All of this is made possible by the text's complex range of story telling, and hearing, activities.

The matter does not end even here, however. King Janamejaya does not immediately accept the exhortation of Vaiśampāyana. He demurs and Vaiśampāyana has to tell a further tale of the paramount Vedic god Indra and his discussion with the *ṛtviks* (Vedic ritual specialists). In this tale, a dispute arises at a sacrifice being performed by Indra as to the value of animal offerings. The assembled beings look to King Vasu of Cedi to resolve the matter.[13] He fails to do so and is, as a result, cast into a subterranean hell (*atala*).[14] This story thus pushes the debate back into the mouth of one of the leading Vedic deities, Indra, the divine king. It further shows the dangers to a king (from the neighbouring region of Cedi) who fails to resolve such an issue with due care. In this way, the tale connects a contemporary debate to a Vedic notable and in turn connects him to a relatively local king. This may have also had an attendant regionalist agenda of denigrating the Cedis even as the tale of the mongoose valorised the residents of the land of Kuru.[15] In fact, Vaiśampāyana makes the matter absolutely clear after the tale of Indra, the *ṛtviks* and King Vasu of Cedi when he asserts:

> O Bhārata, Brāhmaṇs, Kṣatriyas, Vaiśyas and Śūdras who turn to the way of gleaning (*tapas*) and who are purified in the fire of the obligatory gift go to heaven (*svargam yānti*).
>
> *brāhmaṇāḥ kṣatriyā vaiśyāḥ śūdrā ye cāśritās tapaḥ /*
> *dānadharmāgninā śuddhās te svargaṃyānti Bhārata //*[16]

It is important to note that even by including all classes of human beings in this way (even the śūdra, who is traditionally forbidden to participate in Vedic sacrificial activity), the social conservatism of the message is in no way lessened. It is only altered. Vaiśampāyana is merely offering a life of noble poverty to all classes.

In this way, within the *Mahābhārata*, we see debates unfold as stories are told. We also see the sheer reach of the text in clustering narratives, all of which take up related themes, that span from the distant past to a king who shares with his audience, then and now, at least in the view of later tradition, the unenviable lot of modernity.[17]

There is a further twist in the tale, however. Subsequent to the arrival of our cast of divine notables, regional kings and impoverished brāhmaṇs, and the questions of King Janamejaya, who can't quite believe that sacrifice is entirely pointless, we find that our mongoose is not entirely what he seems, nor is he acting entirely of his own volition. We are told that our mongoose is, in fact, also the god Dharma (the god of religious law) who had, in former times, deliberately spoilt the milk being used by a brāhmaṇ sage by the name of Jamadagni in order to complete an offering to his ancestors (*śrāddha*). He does this by entering the milk 'in the form of anger' (*krodhaḥ svarūpeṇa*). Dharma's motivation is somewhat playful (as well as risky) as he wishes to see if he will be cursed by the famously irascible Jamadagni who is of the famous brāhmaṇ lineage of the Bhārgavas (named after another Vedic sage, Bhṛgu).[18] In fact, it is the illustrious ancestors of Jamadagni who do the cursing. They condemn Krodha to the form of a mongoose. The condition of release from the curse is rather odd: Krodha will only be restored to his divine form when he insults dharma (*yadā dharmaṃ kṣepsyase mokṣyase tadā*).[19] This is affected by the following means:

> Having derided the son of Dharma with the accusation of the handful of barley, Anger was realeased from his curse because Dharma was Yudhiṣṭhira (*dharmo hy āsīd Yudhiṣṭhiraḥ*).
>
> *dharmaputram athākṣipya saktuprasthena tena saḥ /*
> *muktaḥ śāpāt tataḥ krodho dharmo hy āsīd Yudhiṣṭhiraḥ //*[20]

By means of the *deus ex machina* of the curse, the mongoose's challenge to Yudhiṣṭhira's *aśvamedha* is neutralized. This is achieved in two ways. Firstly, the mongoose is *obliged* to insult the sacrifice. Secondly, the *aśvamedha* and by extension perhaps sacrifical activity in general is founded upon Yudhiṣṭhira's semi-divine identity as the son of Dharma (the god fathered him in circumstances that shall not detain us here). This is expressed in the Sanskrit by means of a total identification of father and son. Yudhiṣṭhira *is* Dharma. Yudhiṣṭhira is the law. Despite the fact that subsequent kings cannot claim such an illustrious father, this must be a comforting sentiment for his descendants.[21] It is also worth noting that with the restitution of the sacrifice comes an implicit defence of the act of war, which is an act conceived of in sacrificial terms throughout the *Mahābhārata*.[22] We should also bear in mind that Jamadagni is the ancestor of another of the hearers of the *Mahābhārata* within the text: As well as Vaiśampāyana's narration to King Janamejaya, we are told in the *Mahābhārata* that a bard by the name of Ugraśravas, who attended Vaiśampāyana's narration, repeated it to a group of brāhmaṇs headed by one Śaunaka, a descendant of Jamadagni and thus also a Bhārgava. The story of the curse of the mongoose, brings together, then, the power of this particular descent group of brāhmaṇs (for it is the ancestors of Jamadagni who do the cursing) and the divine identity of King Yudhiṣṭhira as the son of Dharma (who is the great-uncle of King Janamejaya) in order to rescue the Vedic sacrifice from the religiously, and perhaps socially, revolutionary sentiments of the mongoose.

The story of the mongoose is universally attested amongst the manuscripts of the *Aśvamedhikaparva* that survive to us. It is mentioned in the list of books in the first book of the *Mahābhārata* (known as the *parvasaṃgrahaparva*, which mentions the *nakula-ākhyāna*, 'the tale of the mongoose').[23] The eleventh century epitome of the *Mahābhārata*, the *Bhāratamañjarī* of Kṣemendra, also provides an account of this tale (listing it as the *Nakula-upākhyāna* – "the sub-tale of the Mongoose").[24] The story of the mongoose is also one of the very clear points of agreement between the *Mahābhārata's Aśvamedhikaparva* and a competing version of this text. This is known as the *Jaimini Aśvamedhikaparva*. Jaimini is, in the *Mahābhārata*, like Vaiśampāyana, a pupil of Kṛṣṇa Dvaipāyana Vyāsa. The *Jaiminīya Aśvamedhikaparva* is dated to around the twelfth century.[25] While these two works differ widely in their content they are close to one another in their treatment of our contrary Mongoose. However, there are certain important differences. Where the *Mahābhārata's Aśvamedhikaparva* requires that the mongoose insult Dharma, the Jaimini text states that the mongoose must insult Dharma in the presence of Kṛṣṇa.[26] If we move from this seemingly minor detail to the close of this tale, we find that it has some considerable ripple effects:

> Lord Kṛṣṇa, Hari, Lord of the universe, wielder of the conch shell, the discus and the mace, protected the sacrifice (*yajña*) till the end.
>
> After guarding the sacrifice, the strong-armed one was always worshipped by the Pāṇḍavas. He stayed at the city for many days, enjoying himself.[27]

Jaimini transforms the tale from one that underscores the authoritative status of King Yudhiṣṭhira as Dharma to one that depicts Kṛṣṇa as the defender of the Vedic sacrifice and as the 'Lord of the Universe'. This is not an idea that is alien to the *Mahābhārata*, but it is not one that is brought to the fore at this juncture of the text. The ongoing adaptation of the *Mahābhārata* beyond the text itself is something that we find considerable evidence of on the early South Asian textual record. I will take up a few of these adaptations below.

We are now in a position to see quite how competing ideologies are approached and "managed" in the tales of the *Mahābhārata*. These narratives allow old and new ideas to enter into a form of debate that hangs much more on narrative detail than explicit argument. We can already see that such stories, with their range of internal audiences, also provide all sorts of prompts to readers and hearers outside of the *Mahābhārata*. The capacity to prompt readers and hearers of the text and the desire to integrate new religious ideologies is a recurrent feature of the Sanskrit *Mahābhārata* and a key indicator of its plural agenda. I will take up the prompting activities of the text first of all.

The Trial of Prahlāda and the *Mahābhārata*

In order to understand the role of 'prompting activities' in the Sanskrit *Mahābhārata*, it is necessary to examine a particular example: The second book of the *Mahābhārata*, the *Sabhāparvan*, "the book of the assembly hall", contains the well-known narrative of the dice match between the Kauravas and Pāṇḍavas. In it, the Pāṇḍava king Yudhiṣṭhira is challenged to a rigged dice match at the Kaurava court. The king gambles away all he owns, and even his brothers, himself and finally their common wife, Draupadī. She is dragged into the *sabhā* and is humiliated before the assembled males. As all this occurs, Draupadī questions the legality of her having being staked by someone who had already lost himself and calls for the assembled elders to rule on her plight. This question, combined with the unthinkable events of the dicing, and the humiliation of a noble woman before the court, leads to a very heated debate on the topic of the nature of *dharma*, which may be translated as "law" or "duty" here. The debate fails to resolve either Draupadī's question or to halt the disastrous proceedings.

In the middle of this dramatic tale, we find a small but very significant embedded story. This seemingly rather minor tale is that of the trial of Prahlāda.[28] The tale, narrated by Dhṛtarāṣṭra's wise adviser Vidura, recounts the dilemma of a King Prahlāda, who is required to pronounce on the relative worth of his own son, Virocana, and another young man, Sudhanvan, in a life or death contest. Prahlāda is never in any doubt of Sudhanvan's superiority, and yet he seeks the advice of a sage named Kaśyapa as to the fate of a man who fails to resolve a question of *dharma*. He is told that one who explains *dharma* falsely will kill their offerings and oblations for seven generations upward and downward. Prahlāda holds to what he knows to be *dharmic* and pronounces Sudhanvan to be the better man. Sudhanvan, impressed with the integrity of Prahlāda, lets Virocana live.

The trial of Prahlāda is of central importance in the dice game narrative. It underscores to its principal actors the dangers of the failure to resolve an issue of *dharma*, while it offers the audience comparative material with which to judge events as they progress. It thus unites protagonists and audience in parallel acts of questioning and commentary.[29] The impact of the embedded tale does not help to resolve Draupadī's question, but rather helps to develop further the events of the dicing match as highly ambiguous. Prahlāda is never in any doubt as to the answer of his *dharmic* dilemma; he fears only the consequences of his answer for his son. Draupadī's question, as to whether she had been dharmically staked, however, remains unresolved. In this way, the introduction of the story of the trial of Prahlāda, after a series of conflicting and competing opinions, does not serve to clarify the issues raised thus far, but rather emphasizes the failure of the elders of the assembly to settle the matter. The embedded story, in underscoring the ambiguity at the heart of the dice game, invites response on the part of the audiences both within and beyond the text. The text, even as it emphasizes the irresolvability of an issue, implicitly models debate. Philip

Lutgendorf, in his study of the *Rāmcaritmānas* of Tulsīdās, a medieval Hindi reworking of the story of Rāma and Sītā, draws on this text's organizing conceit of a pool set below a series of descending steps (*'ghat'*),[30] as a fitting description of the above process:

> These metaphorical images suggest the poet's strategy in periodically shifting his focus: to call their attention to contextual material in light of which he desires them to interpret it... (he) thus weaves a series of "commentaries" into the very fabric of the text. Another frame is implied as well...his listeners...in turn may become tellers of and commentators on his story...[31]

The tale of Prahlāda is told again in the *Mahābhārata*, in the *Udyogaparvan*, the fifth book of the *Mahābhārata*, "the book of the effort (for peace)".[32] Here, however, the message is unequivocal: it is a condemnation of Dhṛtarāṣṭra's failure to condemn his villainous son, and arch-enemy of the Pāṇḍavas, Duryodhana. The tale, then, has quite different implications in the two different contexts. This in itself implicitly shows audience members how the very same narrative of the events of the past may be interpreted differently in different contexts. This is precisely because the Kaurava/Pāṇḍava context, at that point in the *Udyogaparvan*, is rather more straightforward in its focus on the condemnation of the villainous prince Duryodhana.

There is, in fact, a narrative in the *Mahābhārata* that makes the role of the audience in the making of meaning explicit: the tale is one in which the snakes, gods, sages and anti-gods all go to Prajāpati, the lord of creatures, for instruction. Prajāpati offers only one brief lesson, the syllable OM. Each class of being interprets the syllable differently, hearing it as an exhortation, respectively, to biting, giving, self-restraint and pride. The text concludes:

Having approached one teacher and been refined (*saṃśkṛtāḥ*) by means of a single sound the snakes, gods, sages and anti-gods were all disposed differently.[33]

> *ekaṃ śāstāram āsādya śabdenaikena saṃskṛtāḥ* /
> *nānā vyavasitāḥ sarve sarpadevarṣidānavāḥ* //

In this way, a relatively minor embedded narrative can have tremendous ramifications. The Sanskrit *Mahābhārata* thus uses embedded stories to weave commentaries into itself. It furthermore exhibits a consciousness with regard to the plurality of interpretations that a given teaching, especially a moral one, is likely to receive.

Vedish not Vedic

Embedded stories also play a more direct role in reflecting and stimulating ideological change in the *Mahābhārata*. There is a pronounced tendency for characters drawn from the Vedic corpus to suddenly find themselves starring in embedded stories in the *Mahābhārata* and often with distinctly non-Vedic co-stars. These stories tend to depart from, re-work, or extend and develop the Vedic past and often, in so doing, expound novel religious teachings. They do not claim that they are part of the Vedic corpus, nor do we find close approximations of the material within that corpus. I have termed these materials, in a somewhat tongue-in-cheek fashion, "Vedish" rather than Vedic. Such material is extraordinarily common in the *Mahābhārata* and can help to reinforce the foregoing analyses of the way in which the structure of the *Mahābhārata* stimulates and reflects plurality as a feature of its very design (certainly in so far as we have the text on the basis of its critical edition).

It is important to give due emphasis to the extent to which the *Mahābhārata* departs from and even subverts Vedic practice and its descriptions of the past. Thus while it is salutary to look for direct engagements with, or retellings of Vedic myths, as Feller and others have done, it is in the way in which the *Mahābhārata* presents innovation as hoary antiquity that we gain some of the more important insights into its particular ideological agendas.

The process of placing stories and teachings in the mouths of Vedic characters extends throughout the *Mahābhārata* and indeed, to an extent, characterizes the text (it is after all the work of "Veda" Vyāsa, the arranger of the Vedic corpus). It is, of course, in those books that contain the most in the way of supplementary material (chiefly, but not only, the *Āraṇyaka*-

, *Śānti-* and *Anuśāsanaparvas*) that we find the majority of these tales.

In the *Āraṇyakaparva* we find a short and relatively simple example of this type of quasi-Vedic dialogue. At this point in the story of the *Mahābhārata,* Dhṛtarāṣṭra is lamenting the events of the dicing but also is reiterating his deep devotion to his problematic son, Duryodhana. Vyāsa responds with a dialogue between the king of the gods and the divine cow, Surabhī. Surabhī cries out in heaven. Indra asks her what upsets her so. She replies:

Look at this ploughman who is maltreating my poor, weak son with his plough while lashing him with his whip.

> *paśyainaṃ karṣakaṃ raudraṃ durbalaṃ mama putrakam /*
> *pratodenābhinighnantaṃ lāṅgalena nipīḍitam //*[34]

Indra, seeing the great attachment of Surabhī for her child, sends a shower of such ferocity down upon the ploughman that he is forced to cease his labours (and, one assumes, his abuses). Vyāsa then urges Dhṛtarāṣṭra to force Duryodhana to make peace with the Pāṇḍavas. We hardly need introduce Indra as a Vedic character. Surabhī however leads a Vedic life only as an adjective meaning "lovely". In the *Mahābhārata* and wider Purāṇic tradition, however, she is well known as a semi-divine cow. She is listed as one of the daughters of Dakṣa and a wife of Kaśyapa in several Purāṇas.[35] The *Mahābhārata* certainly knows Surabhī in this capacity and as the mother of all kine. She is described as such in the *Ādiparva* where she is also known as the grandmother of all horses and the mother of Vaisiṣtha's wonder-cow.[36] In the *Udyogaparva,* the fifth book of the *Mahābhārata,* she is described with her four daughters. She is also said to have been born from the *amṛta.*[37] She has a cameo in the *Śāntiparva* where she appears at the funeral of a particularly noble crane.[38] She also appears in the *Anuśāsanaparva* in a poetic reference to cows as "the family of Surabhī" (*Surabhīgotra*).[39] We can thus see that Surabhī is well known to the *Mahābhārata* and Purāṇas and not at all to the Vedas. This dialogue, nonetheless, associates Indra and his rain giving activities with a compassion for the plight of a suffering animal and with the dedication of a mother to her child. Notwithstanding Vyāsa's somewhat simple exegesis, the text resonates with the values of compassion and non-harm (*ahiṃsā*) that we mentioned first of all in our discussions of the contrary mongoose. At a more basic level, Vedic and post-Vedic characters are here presented as entering into dialogue in a non-specific past. Like the trial of Prahlāda, this dialogue is explicitly intended as a commentary on the main action of the plot but also suggests connections with later and more explicitly didactic portions of the *Mahābhārata*.

Another example of this sort of dialogue, drawn from the *Udyogaparva*, is that between Ātreya and the Sādhyas. In this short dialogue, the sage Ātreya, in the form of a swan, offers teachings to the Sādhyas, a class of divine being. We can see immediately that the *Udyogaparva*, which is, after all, the book of the endeavour (*udyoga*) for peace between the Pāṇḍavas and the Kauravas is having a shaping influence on the dialogues included within it:

> I have been taught, O deathless ones, that one is obliged to be resolute (*dhṛti*), tranquil (*śama*) and to pursue both truth (*satya*) and duty (*dharma*) and that, having undone all the knots (*granthi*) of the heart, one must develop a controlled nature in the face of both the agreeable (*priya*) and the disagreeable (*apriya*). When one is abused one should not abuse in return, when such affliction (*manyu*) is endured, the abuser will be consumed by it and you will enjoy a reward (*sukṛta*).
>
> *etat kāryam amarāḥ saṃśrutaṃ me; dhṛtiḥ śamaḥ satyadharmānuvṛttiḥ/*
> *granthiṃ vinīya hṛdayasya sarvaṃ; priyāpriye cātmavaśaṃ nayīta //*
> *ākruśyamāno nākrośen manyur eva titikṣitaḥ /*
> *ākroṣṭāraṃ nirdahati sukṛtaṃ cāsya vindati //*[40]

Here the emphasis is again on peace. However the focus is now on equanimity and on the moral reward of quietism. These are not what one would call classically Vedic values (though of course they are ideas that are present in the Upaniṣads) nor are they the hallmark of the *kṣatriya*. Yet this tale is more fully Vedic in its setting, as both dialogue partners are drawn from the Vedic corpus. Ātreya is known as a sage from the *Bṛhadāraṇyaka Upaniṣad* and the *Aitereya Brāhmaṇa*.[41] Ātreya, as a descendent of Atri, is also connected to the brāhmaṇical family of the Atris to whom the fifth book of the *Ṛgveda* is attributed in the *Kauṣītaki Brāhmaṇa* and the *Aitareya Āraṇyaka*.[42] Atri and the Atris are associated with a number of feats in the *Ṛg Veda*, including the rescue of the sun from the demon Svarbhānu.[43] The Sādhyas or "those who must be propitiated" are a class of divine being who are also mentioned in the *Ṛg Veda*.[44] According to the *Nirukta* (12.41) their world is said to be above that of the gods.[45] In the creation account of the *Manusmṛti* they are described as having refined natures and in the Purāṇas they become the sons of a supposed Vedic sage, Sādhya.[46]

This tale is also interesting because it occurs, like the tale of Prahlāda, more than once in the *Mahābhārata*: A variant form of the story of the Sādhyas and the Swan (this time not identified as the sage Ātreya) is told in the *Śāntiparva*.[47] In this, much fuller, version of the tale the teaching retains its focus on self-control and equanimity but offers a further great mystery:

Cursed, I never curse because I know that restraint (*dāma*) is the door to immortality (*amṛta*). I will reveal to you this divine mystery (*guhya*): *there is nothing better than humanity.*

> *nāhaṃ śaptaḥ pratiśapāmi kiṃ cid; damaṃ dvāraṃ hy amṛtasyeha vedmi/ guhyaṃ Brahmā tad idaṃ vo bravīmi; na mānuṣāc chreṣṭhataraṃ hi kiṃ cit //*[48]

In this new anthropocentric vision, the intention of a given act is of key importance:

That sacrifice in anger, that offering, the performance of those austerities, that oblation, Yama (Vaivasvata) keeps all of these. Fruitless (*mogha*) are the toils (*śrama*) of anger (*krodha*)!

> *yat krodhano yajate yad dadāti; yad vā tapas tapyati yaj juhoti / vaivasvatas tad dharate 'sya sarvaṃ; moghaḥ śramo bhavati krodhanasya//*[49]

Indeed, truth, which here approximates to a sense of correct intention, by which the text seems to suggest a certain quality of moral rectitude and self-control, is given high praise:

I have never discovered anything that is purer than the truth!
I declare, having made the acquaintance of both gods and men, that truth is a stairway to heaven as a boat is (a means of crossing) the ocean.

na pāvanatamaṃ kiṃ cit satyād adhyagamaṃ kva cit //
ācakṣe 'haṃ manuṣyebhyo devebhyaḥ pratisaṃcaran /
satyaṃ svargasya sopānaṃ pārāvārasya naur iva //[50]

Truth, in this sense, is productive of *mokṣa*:

Underlying (*Upaniṣad*) the Veda is truth, underlying truth is self-control, underlying self-control is *mokṣa*, this is the all-encompassing teaching (*sarva anuśāsana*).

vedasyopaniṣat satyaṃ satyasyopaniṣad damaḥ /
damasyopaniṣan mokṣa etat sarvānuśāsanam //[51]

There is, however, a resolute focus on the Vedas, they are, indeed, the locus of truth upon which self-control and, finally, *mokṣa*, or emancipation from rebirth, are founded. Here, in the *Mokṣadharmaparva* of the *Śāntiparva*, with its focus on that which is productive of release from the cycle of rebirth, the teaching of the swan becomes, rather than simply a pacifist homily, a rich emancipatory discourse. It is one that resonates with Buddhist teaching: Both in its focus on intention:

"Intention, I tell you, is kamma. Intending, one does kamma by way of body, speech, and intellect.[52]

and equanimity:

Likewise a monk without hate, without ill-will, pure, disciplined. Then a disciplined monk, at death, at the breaking up of the body, should attain to union with Brahmā – that is possible.[53]

And in its choice of metaphors:

Monks, I will teach you the Dhamma compared to a raft, for the purpose of crossing over, not for the purpose of holding onto. Listen & pay close attention. I will speak.[54]

This teaching is then an odd fit in a double sense. It is odd in Vedic terms in that it reflects, if at all, only the very latest, Upaniṣadic, stages of Vedic teaching. It is further replete with material that suggests Buddhist influence and perhaps even the universalising of the possibility of emancipation. Yet it retains a rhetorical emphasis on the Vedas. It is also an odd fit in terms of the main plot of the *Mahābhārata* in that it offers a doctrine of forgiveness that is cold comfort indeed to a king who has been constantly pressured into supporting acts of grotesque violence. Where the text 'fits' much more naturally is as a conservative brāhmaṇical synthesis offered to an immediately pre- and early common era audiences who are both aware of, and impressed with, a wide range of religious ideologies (many of which are non- or anti-brāhmaṇical). These audiences would also be more than aware of at least the human cost of the imperial impulse that swept the subcontinent from the Mauryan period onwards. If we presume a royal audience then the message becomes even simpler: The king should forgive; the king should be equanimitous; the king should support and recognize both the *Veda* and the brāhmaṇs. However we seek to imaginatively reconstruct the early South Asian audiences of these *saṃvāda*s (dialogues or colloquies), there can be no doubt that this text mobilizes the Vedic past in order to contextualize, and lend a certain authority to, a rather new set of religious ideas. At the same time, it achieves the conservative goal of protecting and underscoring the status of the Veda (and by extension the brāhmaṇs).

It is in the *Śānti-* and *Anuśāsanaparvas* of the *Mahābhārata* that these pseudo-Vedic dialogues are most common. In the *Anuśāsanaparva*, we find a rather lovely example of another quasi-Vedic dialogue that extols the virtue of the offering of incense and flowers to the gods.[55] It is in fact a dialogue within a dialogue. Bhīṣma initially introduces the conversation of Manu and the sage Suvarṇa in response to an enquiry from Yudhiṣṭhira as to the value of the gift of light (*āloka*, more than likely referring to, as we shall see, the light of the *dīpa*, the lamp lit as an offering to the gods).[56] Manu and Suvarṇa engage in reminiscences of the sages (*brahmārṣi*s), gods (*deva*s) and demons (*daitya*s) of ancient times (*purāṇa*).[57] Manu introduces a further dialogue, this time between Indra and Bali. Manu calls this narrative both an *itihāsa* and a *samvāda*.[58] Bali asks of the value of offerings of flowers (*sumanas*), of incense (*dhūpa*) and lamps (*dīpa*) to the gods. What follows is an extended description of the appropriate offerings to be made to a wide variety of classes of beings (*devas*, *asuras*, *rākṣasas*, *yakṣas*, *nāgas*, ancestors and human beings) by a householder. We need not discuss the Vedic pedigree of Indra. Vali, however, is not a Vedic character at all. Descriptions of his career as the sovereign of the Asuras are to be found in the *Mahābhārata* and throughout the Purāṇas, however.[59] He is the grandson of Prahlāda and the son of the very Virocana we encountered in our analyses of the dicing sequence of the *Sabhāparva* (and again in the *Udyogaparva*). He is associated in the Purāṇas with more developed forms of the *amṛtamanthana* mythology. He is also the antagonist in the story of Viṣṇu's incarnation as a dwarf (or *vāmana*—the fifth *avatāra* of Viṣṇu in the *daśāvatāra* or ten-incarnation scheme) in which he loses his dominance over the three worlds to the diminutive god incarnate. In this way, this rather homely dialogue concerning lamps and incense evokes a wide range of post-Vedic narratives. Focussing again on the content of the *saṃvāda*, Indra offers instruction on a range of small-scale domestic rites that speaks to audiences whose surroundings are considerably more humble than that of our grief-stricken, yet inquisitive, king Yudhiṣṭhira. This is particularly clear if we look at the offerings described in the text.

Offerings with flowers should be made to the gods consisting of soured milk and dilute curd that is pure, fragrant and pleasing to look at.

balayaḥ saha puṣpais tu devānām upahārayet /
dadhidrapsayutāḥ puṇyāḥ sugandhāḥ priyadarśanāḥ / /[60]

Compared to the lavishness of the gifts given in the grand sacrifices that stand at the heart of the *Mahābhārata*, however pleasing to the eye these gifts of milk, curds and whey are, they remain somewhat humble (and speak, once again, to an audience external to the text rather than to a great king!). In this *śloka*, there is also a Vedically related pun on the name of Bali, the demon king, in that the word for offering, attested in the *Ṛg Veda* (and elsewhere) in relation to both gods and kings is precisely *bali*.[61] In concluding its teachings, our text makes rather self-conscious use of this term on several occasions. The *bali* is here, however, being offered to a considerably expanded range of beings (in Vedic terms) from gods and anti-gods to the demons of the wilds (*rākṣasa*) and others. In this way, the dialogue valourises religious practices that are being undertaken to this day in Hindu temples across South Asia and in the diaspora. Even as it does this, it provides these activities with a Vedic, or at least Vedish, provenance.

We see then, in the dialogues that I have examined that Vedic and non-Vedic characters are brought together in order to locate, and guarantee, teachings and practices that are both distinctly non-Vedic, and which contain similarities to aspects of Buddhist thought as well as references to what were likely to be day-to-day religious practices. Compassionate, emancipatory or domestic, they speak to constituencies and contexts that seem to be as much beyond as within the text. As they innovate, however, they carefully situate themselves in a para-Vedic past. These dialogues are, then, revolutionary even in their apparent conservatism. They reflect without doubt both a plural religious context and a text uniquely well suited to integrating divergent religious ideologies. This is in marked contrast to the Hindi televisual *Mahābhārat*.

The Transmitted and Adapted *Mahābhārata*

The *Mahābhārata*, paraphrasing the great French antropologist Claude Lévi Strauss, has always been good to think with. There are a considerable number of excellent publications that take up the wide variety of ways in which the *Mahābhārata* has been interpreted in, and beyond, India both as a form of entertainment and as a means of expressing identity, preferred ideology and much else besides.[62] By no means all of these *Mahābhārata*s are dependent on the Sanskrit text. Within India, we find the *Mahābhārata* referred to in inscriptions at a very early stage and also reflected in art and architecture and *belles lettres*.[63] Beyond India, [64] we find the *Mahābhārata* referred to in Cambodian inscriptions as early as the sixth century, as well as depicted in narrative friezes (some up to forty-nine meters long) in the great Khmer city of Angkor Wat (c. twelfth century). In Thailand, portions of the *Mahābhārata* have been adapted, such as in the *Krishna Son Nong,* which is drawn from the *Āraṇyakaparvan*, the third book of our great tale. While in Indonesia, one can hardly overestimate the significance of the *Mahābhārata*: Eight *parvans* of the text are extant in Old Javanese and the story lives on through shadow puppetry (*wayang*) performances, which are based on short adaptations of *Mahābhārata* material known as *lakons,* to this day. Even as far afield as Mongolia and Japan, there are *Mahābhārata* adaptations to be found: A Mongolian commentary (which revises a Tibetan original), the *Subhashidi-yin tayilburi cindamani-yin tulkigur kemegdeku,* provides a summary of the *Mahābhārata;* while in Japan, the well-known Kabuki drama *'Narukami'* takes up the tale of the innocent sage Ṛṣyaśṛṅga, whose story is told in the *Mahābhārata*. If we move from the global to the relatively local, we find, in South Asia, countless forms of adaptation of the *Mahābhārata* story: These range from those in Sanskrit, to vernacular versions, to an extraordinary range of regional performance traditions, to modern cinematic, televisual and comic book versions.

I will take up only two examples in this paper. The first is Sanskrit, while the second is in a North Indian vernacular, Marāthī. The first is more than a thousand years old, while the second brings us to the modern period and the beginning of the twentieth century and the momentous changes that took place in India at that time. The first explores the moral and emotional *aporia* of the *Mahābhārata*, while the second exploits its potential for political allegory.

Bhāsa's *Breaking of the Thighs*

It is in the work of the playwright Bhāsa that we find some of the richest engagements with the *Mahābhārata*. There is considerable controversy over his date. A.K. Warder placed him in the second century CE.[65] This was on the basis of features of the style of his work on the fact that Kālidāsa cites a Bhāsa.[66] However, in the works of the brothers Pisharoti and subsequently in those of Herman Tieken, it has been argued that Bhāsa is not an individual at all, and that his putative works are in fact anonymous compositions belonging to the Keralan dramatic repertory of about the seventh century CE.[67] Whatever their precise date, the works that are attributed to Bhāsa are rather different to those of dramatists such as Kālidāsa.[68] The plays are shorter, more action-packed and lack the long lyric episodes designed to evoke one of several highly formalised aesthetic responses from the audience (known in Sanskrit dramaturgy as *rasa*, juice, flavour or essence and, by extension, sometimes translated as 'mood').[69] This is not to say Bhāsa wrote in ignorance of at least early forms of Sanskrit dramatic theory. His plays reflect genres established, for example, in the *Nāṭyaśāstra*.[70] Nonetheless, there is a marked brevity to his work. His engagement with the *Mahābhārata* is sustained (with six plays written about it) and he tends to emphasize ambivalent events in the tale. It is in the *Urubhaṅga* that this tendency is most fully expressed and it is this text that we will now turn.

The *Urubhaṅga*, or "*The Breaking of the Thighs*", is a one-act play that takes up the mace duel between Bhīma and Duryodhana at the close of the *Śalyaparva* of the *Mahābhārata*. This marks the end of the formal Bhārata war and precedes the events of the brutal night attack of Aśvatthāman in the *Sauptikaparva* (the Book of the Night Attack), in which the remainder of the Pāṇḍava forces are butchered in their camp. Bhāsa's text, even in the prologue, exhibits a clear consciousness of the horrors of the *Mahābhārata* war:

> *Your honour, Why do these*
> *Men roam about testing each other's valour*
> *Their bodies marked by the tusks of wild elephants?*
> *And limbs scarred by sword and axe? Is it for heaven*
> *That they pour out their bodies' libation on the altar of war.*[71]

The prologue is oddly truncated for a Sanskrit drama. Neither the play nor the author is named. The main action commences with three unnamed soldiers wandering across Kurukṣetra. The emphasis on the horror of war is unremitting and reminiscent of the *Strīparva* of the *Mahābhārata*. Birds pepper the field of battle with their "beaks wet with flesh" (vs. 7) and "headless corpses twitch from the habit of life" (vs.10).[72] There is a certain aestheticization of death as well.

> *Their fearless upturned faces, like a silent lotus lake*
> *Made to bloom by the sun of valour shining in the sky of war!*
> *For stalks, I see swords bearing buds of diadems; for filaments,*
> *Frowns; for petals, lips; for bees, those sightless eyes!*[73] *(vs.13)*

Bhāsa here takes up, amongst other things, the favoured dramatic figures of the brow and the bee. In other contexts, these form the stock-in-trade of rather more delicate descriptions of heroes and heroines:

> Śakuntalā: [in confusion] Aiee! Disturbed by my watering, a bee has flown out of the Jasmin into my face [She shows every sign of being attacked by a bee]
>
> King: [longingly] Wonderful! Even this threat enhances her charm:
>
> Where the bee flies
> There fly her eyes,
> Beneath her lovely knitted brows,
> She darts an ardent glance,
> Inspired by fear.
> Mere practice, for on other days,
> Such looks shall match a lover's gaze
> In pure desire.[74]

The *Urubhaṅga* transforms such delightful scenes into meditations on the death of the warrior. In so doing, Bhāsa emphasizes the ambivalence inherent in his glorification of the battlefield. This is reinforced when Bhāsa employs the simile of the degenerating text:

> The battlefield is heaped with dead horses, elephants, kings and men
> Like a wormy manuscript whose characters are corrupt.[75]

This is a comparison that he returns to later in the play:

> Aśvatthāman: Listen-
> With a wave of my sword I will rid you of Kṛṣṇa,
> Anall the sons of Pāṇḍu; I will throw them away like a manuscript of blotted characters![76]

The simile of the degenerating text lends a certain self-referentiality to Bhāsa's work. Even as corpses rot, and as heroes die, so too does the written word degenerate and disappear. This reading is reinforced by Bhāsa's reference to the *amṛtamanthana* myth. Duryodhana, after he has been unfairly struck and defeated by Bhīma, is described as follows:

> He lies like Vāsuki in the primal sea, exhausted,
> shedding his skin
> After churning the ambrosia: of no use to god or demon![77]

Here, Bhāsa refocuses attention upon Vāsuki, the snake that plays an integral role in the story of the churning of the elixir of immortality, the *amṛtamanthana,* which is told in the *Mahābhārata*. In this famous creation narrative, Vāsuki is wrapped around Mt. Mandāra in order to churn the ocean of milk so as to obtain the *amṛta,* the elixir of immortality, and the fundaments of divine and human existence. However, for Bhāsa, the snake is an exploited and disregarded figure. He introduces a moral ambivalence into the churning narrative that is entirely absent from the version of it told in the first book of the *Mahābhārata*. This can be read on a number of levels: it helps to rehabilitate Duryodhana, and cast him in a new and more noble light; it might be a reference to the "exploitation" of human agents fated to die as a consequence of the unburdening of the earth (the cosmic justification of the Mahābhārata war); or it might be a rather more straightforward plea for the socially exploited. In any case, Bhāsa is far from unequivocal in his view of the Pāṇḍavas. The sheer fact that the Pāṇḍavas say so little in this drama, allows the spotlight to shine on Duryodhana.[78] The pathetic scence of Duryodhana's encounter with his young son as he lies, dying, on the battle field is especially moving.

> Duryodhana: Affection for him consumes my heart, even in my misery!
>
> Durjaya: Papa! I want to sit in your lap! [He climbs.]
>
> Duryodhana: [Restraining him.] Durjaya! Durjaya, my boy! Be careful!
>
> This young moon of my heart's joy
> Who has so often delighted my sight
> Assumes, in my misfortune, the strange
> Shape of a scorching fire!

Durjaya: Why won't you let me sit in your lap?
Duryodhana: Sit somewhere else!
This too familiar place
Henceforth is not for you![79]

We are in a position to see now the extent to which Bhāsa plumbs the pathos of the death of Duryodhana and the wider loss of life at Kurukṣetra.[80] The play ends as abruptly as it starts and promises only the night attack (told in the *Sauptikaparva* of the *Mahābhārata*). Balarāma, the most vocal critic of the Pāṇḍavas at this point, speaks the benediction: "May the king protect the earth, his enemies appeased".[81] This suggests perhaps a rather bleak closing irony: On one level, the protection of the earth is precisely what the *Mahābhārata* war achieves, yet Bhāsa seems to focus far more on the human cost of war. Bhāsa dwells on the ambivalences and *aporia* in the *Mahābhārata* in order to stimulate emotional response and to point to the complexity of human action and the conundrums of divine or cosmic constraint.

Where Bhāsa focuses on moral ambivalence in the *Mahābhārata* tale, the author of the next adaptation of the *Mahābhārata* story that we shall consider focuses on moral certitude. He requires the *Mahābhārata* only in order to furnish exemplars of inequality and exploitation as a means of criticising the forces of colonial rule in India, namely the British.[82]

Khaldilkar's *Mahābhārata*

Krishnaji Prabhakar Khadilkar takes the story of the death of Kīcaka, told in the fourth book of the *Mahābhārata*, and transforms it into what Rakesh Solomon calls "a militant anticolonial melodrama on the Pune stage".[83] The story of Kīcaka takes place when the Pāṇḍava brothers and their common wife Draupadī are living, in exile and incognito, in the court of one king Virāṭa of Matsya. Kīcaka is the chief general of king Virāṭa. On seeing the beautiful Draupadī (who is in disguise as a chambermaid and is known as Sairandhri), he attempts to woo her. Kīcaka is singularly unsuccessful. Eventually, finding that conventional means fail him, he seeks to molest Draupadī. Humiliated and enraged, Draupadī pleads with her husbands. The irascible Bhīma agrees to help Draupadī. Disguising himself as a woman and hiding in his wife's bedclothes, he tricks Kīcaka into bed with him and promptly pounds him to death. Such is the beating that Kīcaka is given, indeed, that he is reduced to a single ball of flesh.

Solomon gives the following pithy summary of the allegorical force of Khadilkar's 1907 production:

> Kichaka, representing the hated Viceroy Curzon, lives up to his sinful portrait...Kichaka's attack on another man's wife alludes to Curzon's attempted rape of another man's land, while Kichaka's public betrayal of his virtuous wife (which Khadilkar focuses upon) alludes to Curzon's betrayal of his own nation's ideal of liberal democracy. Kichaka even defies Shiva's awesome manifestation, Bhairava, the deity of the temple where Sairandhri is banished (in the play): "This Bhairava actually cleans my bed and cleans my spittoon... Sairandhri, I am the god of gods—the king of kings. So accept my garland." Kichaka's mockery of Hindu values further justifies violent action against him, and by extension against British rule.[84]

Khadilkar's adaptation, whilst repudiating British rule, incorporates several features of Western theatrical tradition. Not least of all the staging of the drama under the proscenium arch and the very theatrical form of the melodrama. As Solomon states:

> These Marathi playwrights forged a potent anticolonial performance that successfully blended Indian history, ancient narratives, religious sentiment, popular taste, Sanskrit theatre conventions and contemporary nationalists with Western Political thought and contemporary Western dramatic and theatrical conventions.[85]

It is worth noting that such a description sounds, in some of its aspects, more than a little like the beginnings of the genre of Indian film that is now known as "Bollywood". Indeed, the story of Kīcaka was to prove irresistible to early Indian film makers, with versions of the story produced in 1920 (directed by Buburao Painter), 1933 (directed by V. Shantaram), and 1939 (directed by Kanjibhai Rathod). It might also be noteworthy that we see such a rash of adaptations of this particular story *before* Indian independence. It would be too much to claim for the *Mahābhārata* the modern edifice of "Bollywood", but the emergence of the *Mahābhārata* as a critical resource for the expression of political sentiments that would have been quite unfamiliar to its original authors is a tribute to the pathos and "plastcicity" of its content. Something that we have seen was both inherent to the design and thematics of the original Sanskrit text and apparent, perhaps to a morbid degree, to another of its gifted interpreters, Bhāsa. This brings me to the close of my brief and summary discussion of the very plural applications of the *Mahābhārata* story.

In direct contrast to the *Mahābhārata's* own boast, which I paraphrase here, that "what is not within it is nowhere else", I would like to make quite the opposite claim for this section of my paper. My consideration of even those scant materials that I have mentioned has been largely dependent on the excellent scholarship of others and is far from complete. However, each example that I have taken up, of the transmitted and adapted Mahābhārata, supports this paper's central hypothesis: that the *Mahābhārata* is a plural phenomenon and has been used to mean many things to many people (indeed, in English we need only two examples for a plural and in Sanskrit three). It is therefore disturbing to find a version of the *Mahābhārata* that seeks to repress this intrinsic and extrinsic dialogue and which, instead, seeks to forge a *Mahābhārata* that acts as a charter for a rather more restricted religious and political identity (in a way that differs from the foregoing examples of religious and political adaptation). This is the Hindi televisual version of the *Mahābhārata*. Ironically, despite its best efforts, it nevertheless stands only as a further demonstration of the adaptability of the *Mahābhārata* story.

The Doordarshan *Mahābhārat*

I should say at the outset that it is not my intention to judge the Doordarshan *Mahābhārat* against the Sanskrit *Mahābhārata*, nor do I see the latter text as an "adaptation" of the Sanskrit text in a workaday sense of that term. I wish only to contrast the alternate strategies in the two texts, which after all take up the same events and characters, with regard to religious and political ideology. That being said, I will commence my analysis with a stark contrast. Far from preserving, or reflecting, the complex interlocutory structure of the Sanskrit *Mahābhārata*, the Doordarshan *Mahābhārat* has a univocal narrator: Time itself. The narration of the history of the Bhāratas is entirely encompassed by this single narrative agency. As a narrator, Time is depicted at the beginning of each episode as the vague outline of a person projected against a cosmic background of stars and planets. His resonant voice intones, in refined Hindi, not, then, from a specific location in time and space, but rather from all-space and with the voice of all-time, and the audience is completely elided. Instead of a selective exploration of the significant past of both brāhmaṇical and kṣatriya interest groups, as we had in the Sanskrit text, we are presented with universal history, that is to say in Hindi, with *itihās* in a new, and as we shall see politically charged, sense. Time denies the possibility of their being any other witness, "no one else can narrate the story since I alone saw it happen", in this way, the unfolding narration is given a narrator with a universal reach and near total authority. Time then goes on to describe itself in the three roles of "mother, teacher and sage" in the opening episode of the series. It thus underscores its authority with an appeal not to Vedic status (as one might find in a Sanskrit text) but to traditional familial, religious and pedagogic institutions.

Early on in the series, Time declares that he is free of all relationships, a disinterested observer. Thus we are presented with an authoritative, all-seeing and wholly neutral narrator in stark contrast to the dialogue-based Sanskrit text. Indeed, the viewer is only explicitly alluded to by Time in the context of the narration of the childhood exploits of Kṛṣṇa (which are actually a fusion of materials from the Harivaṃśa, Parāṇas, and later Braj biography inserted into the main body of the *Mahābhārat*) where he or she is described as a *disciple*. This is, of course, a very different power dynamic to that between a king (Janamejaya) and a brāhmaṇ narrator (Vaiśampāyana) and a professional storyteller (Ugraśravas) and a brāhmaṇ patron (Śaunaka)! It also, potentially at least, excludes non-Hindu, or indeed non-Vaiṣṇava, viewers.

Time also emphasizes the linearity of his narrative and its connection to the history of the Indian nation state: This is achieved by commencing the *Mahābhārat* with the reign of Bhārat (which receives sparse treatment in the Sanskrit text). Time states, again and again, "*our* country is named after him" (the use of pronouns here is equally revealing about the presupposed audience of the text – that is to say of a presumed national constituency). Time's presentation of the narrative configures viewer expectations of a linear account of the past. His agency is part of a broader movement in the televisual version that transforms the ongoing situational analyses of the Sanskrit text into a linear history of a nation state. Though we have also seen that the Sanskrit *Mahābhārata* has its own political visions and that these are also exclusive (we need only think of the perfected realm of Prājāpati in the *Bhūmiparva* in this regard)

The Doordarshan *Mahābhārat* drastically delimits narrative embedding: there are never more than two concurrent narrations at any one time in the programme (and this includes the narration of the main plot by Time itself). Thus in contrast to the Sanskrit text, which habitually has three narrative layers, and which can juggle up to six concurrent tales, we are left with a very simple use of embedded narrative as a flashback technique for clarification rather than as a model of the creative exploration of the past. Indeed, the telling of a story within a story occurs rarely within the television version (the only examples in the Hindi version that I could find are the narration of the curse of Gaṅga and the Vasus and the reason for the enmity of Dhrupad and Droṇa). The Sanskrit text's retrospective and episodic 'back-formation' of the histories of its characters such as that of Bhīṣma and, in our example, Karṇa, is replaced with a serial unfolding of life histories as part of the encompassing history of the descendants of Bhārat and thus of the Indian nation state. This is certainly not wholly alien to the Sanskrit *Mahābhārata*, at least in terms of its presentation of a rhetorically Vedic and brāhmaṇ-centred vision of the past and the place of *Bhāratavarṣa,* but it is not the whole story, as we have seen.

An overview of some of the key terms that circulate in the televisual *Mahābhārat* is also instructive: In the abridged DVD version of the Doordarshan *Mahābhārat* Democracy (*lokatantra/ prajātantra*) is mentioned explicitly four times, the nation (*rāshtra/desh*) is mentioned eight times. The term 'Tradition' (*paramparā*) is mentioned at least ten times most of which are compounded with the designation for the modern Indian nation state (*Bhārat*) (which is used some thirty times). Motherland (*matribhūmi*) is also used four times. *itihās* is the recurring term for both history (which is invoked on a regular basis – some twenty two times at a rough count) and for the *Mahābhārat* itself, which competes as a self-designation with *kathā* (literally 'story' which also peppers the television version). Indeed, *itihās* and *kathā* seem to circulate in the text in such a way that their interaction serves to semantically approximate the European conception of epic,[86] that is to say, as the expression of a national past and national tradition:

> The world of the epic is the national heroic past: it is a world of 'beginnings' and 'peak' times in the national history, a world of fathers and of founders of families, a world of 'firsts' and 'bests.'[87]

The *Mahābhārat* is, in this way, by both the narrative agency of time and the strategic deployment of a range of lexical items, transformed into the "the great epic of the India nation". This epical quality is further developed by the construction of key characters and events as reflective of a falling away from a national tradition of democracy. Very early on in the televisual *Mahābhārat*, the founder of the Bhārata dynasty is described as 'the flower of democracy'. The reason for this is his nomination of one Bhūmanyu as *yuvarāja*, or crown prince, ahead of his own sons (who he considers less worthy). This act is interpreted in the Hindi *Mahābhārat* as a proto-democratic experiment on the part of Bharata which emphasises "worth over birth".

Later on, the birth of Bhīṣma is an occasion for the

extension of this proto-democratic rhetoric: Gaṅgā, Bhīṣma's mother, states that the "Indian Tradition" is one of "action not birth, doers not inheritors!." She states that her son is not necessarily "worthy", although in matter of fact he is worthy and is declared *yuvarāja* in due course. Bhīṣma's achievement of this status is based on a moving speech he makes in favour of the forgiveness of an enemy king: He states that "India is an ideal nation" and that it must have a "secure and progressive future" and that this can only be achieved by forgiveness. Political rhetoric becomes, here, the basis for "election" to office.

The epical concerns of the text are even clearer in the treatment of Bhīṣma's voluntary giving up of the status of crown prince in order to allow his father to marry again. Bhīṣma's terrible vow, renouncing both the crown and his reproductive rights, is interpreted as the beginning of the difficulties of the descendants of king Bharat in the televisual text, as it contradicts the meritocratic and proto-democratic ideals of its founder-king; it is thus the critical catalyst for the sequence of events that end in the horrific battle of Kurukṣetra. In this way, the text becomes an epic account of the falling away from a series of social and political ideals.

The allegorical potential of such an account of a falling away from the high ideals of a founding figure hardly needs labouring in post-Independence South Asia. The allegorical dimensions of the text, are made absolutely clear to the viewer, however, considerably later in the series, in the context of the *partition* of the ancestral lands of the Bhāratas between the Kauravas and Pāṇḍavas. In a moving speech, Bhīṣma states that when politics (*nīti*) stumbles, the nation (*desh*) suffers. King Vasudev also states, "Partition is not the solution, it reduces both kingdoms." Thus, recent historical experience configures the construction of the significant past as it is played out in the *Mahābhārata*. In addition, ideas of democracy and nationhood are naturalized, and made authoritative, by being projected into that past. The Hindi *Mahābhārat* sketches out, then, both a national constituency and a political tradition.

Of critical importance in this regard is the way in which

the Dordarshan *Mahābhārat* sets itself up as a linear history of the Indian nation state and then incorporates within itself a wide range of Vaiṣṇavite literature that is external to the *Mahābhārata* tradition itself. The childhood exploits of Kṛṣṇa are given centre stage, and the entire text is presented as the story of Lord Kṛṣṇa when Time states: "Kṛṣṇa is the great hero of the tale!" And "The Story of Braj is essential to Mahābhārat as Kṛṣṇa is the great hero of the Mahābhārat...the essence of India!" In this way, devotion to Kṛṣṇa, and indeed devotion to a particularly Purāṇic and medieval Kṛṣṇa, is inserted into the linear progression of the narrative in a way quite unlike that of the Sanskrit text (in which the life of Kṛṣṇa is included as an appendix—the *Harivaṃśa*). This again may reflect popular understandings of the *Mahābhārata*, which have replaced the theological emphasis on Kṛṣṇa in the *Mahābhārata* with a biographical one.

Kṛṣṇa is emphasized in both dialogue and in song in the Doordarshan *Mahābhārat* as an *avatāra;* an incarnation of lord Viṣṇu sent to restore *dharma* in the world. The Sanskrit *Mahābhārata's* descriptions of almost all its major characters as incarnations of various divine and demonic beings in order to unburden the earth of a fractious warrior caste is replaced with a unified, Kṛṣṇa-focussed, *avatāra* doctrine (which is again, of course, not wholly alien to the Sanskrit *Mahābhārata* but certainly not its only theology). The dominance of *bhakti,* or devotional, values reaches a fever pitch of intensity in the context of the disrobing of Draupadī, where Kṛṣṇa intervenes to protect her virtue: As we have seen, in the Sanskrit text, the agent of Draupadī's protection is given various identities in different manuscript traditions, but in the televisual version it is Kṛṣṇa, and only Kṛṣṇa, who intervenes in a scene which is dramatic precisely for its lack of drama: instead what we find is a hugely extended scene of some three minutes in which Kṛṣṇa is depicted, in the top right hand corner of the screen, in a beatific pose, replenishing Draupadī's sari as quickly as Duśāsan can tear at it. This scene functions not dramatically but devotionally: Its extended duration ruptures the linear progression of the narrative and offers the opportunity for the establishment of a charged relationship between deity and devotee, a form of televisual *darśan*.[88] This is implicitly exclusive, and rather different from the *dharma* focussed ambivalence of the Sanskrit text. The text may not demonize "the other", but it most certainly *divinizes*, and its exclusion of the other is perhaps more politically chilling than the *demonization* processes that Sheldon Pollock sees as so central to the Rāmāyaṇa tradition.[89] By this I mean that there is, at times, no room for the other *at all* in the Hindi televisual text (just as there was no room for Buddhist ideology in the *Mahābhārata*). Indeed, the Doordarśan *Mahābhārat* implicitly and explicitly excludes all those who do not subscribe to its historical vision. The text finishes with the following, somewhat chilling, statement by Time:

> 'Vyās' poem ends today, this tale will solve your problems, it is your armour and your weapon, use this tale to recognize the evil ones in this society. Evil flourishes today as it did in Hastinapur, today's Droṇas sit in the camps and make unreasonable demands, silence implies they are partners in *adharm*. O man, strike out on a new path or you also will be dragged into darkness like Karna, be the heir to *dharm*.

Taken together this material (and I have only scratched the surface), suggests that the televisual Mahābhārat is a text that presents the past in such a way that it is closed off from debate and subordinated to the delineation of a national ideal (and the exploration of the consequences of the falling away from that ideal) and which articulates as normal, natural and obvious a vision of India that is "aboriginally" democratic, Hindu and indeed Vaiṣṇavite, culturally gangetic, Hindi Speaking, and which posits South Asia in its entirety (that is to say an un-partitioned South Asia) as a nation state.[90] I am not suggesting that this agenda was an overt one. It appears to me that the assumptions at work in the Hindi *Mahābharat* are just that: assumptions. That is to say, presuppositions with regard to the necessarily 'bounded' nature and form of religion, culture and nation were so widely internalized by the late 1980s in India (as they are the world over, I should add) that this seemed the normal and natural way to interpret the *Mahābhārata*. This takes us a long way from the Sanskrit text in which we saw such a concern with divergent religious ideologies, moral *aporia* and the integration of new ideas (albeit disguised as old ones). We have moved from a text of *pṛthaktva* (differentness) to one of *Bhāratatva* (Indian-ness) and from plurality to its opposite.

Concluding Remarks

In the Sanskrit *Mahābhārata,* we saw a restless capacity for innovation and embedded commentary; this was also the case in Bhāsa's engagement with the *Mahābhārata* story. Khadilkar, meanwhile, in his politicized adaptations of portions of the Sanskrit text, exploited the potential for new layers of allegory to be added to the *Mahābhārata* story. In contrast, in the Doordarśan adaptation, we found a text that presented a profoundly linear, "epic" (in a European sense) and "universalized" account of the Indian national past. One might broadly characterize these engagements with the *Mahābhārata* story in relation to two abstract concepts; of differentness (or plurality), *Pṛthaktva,* and Indian-ness, *Bhāratatva*:

1. *Pṛthaktva*: Is marked by a restless textual ambivalence and a complex orientation to its participants both within and outside of the text.
2. *Bhāratatva:* Is marked by the "nationalization of the past" and the projection of contemporary norms, practices, and theological perspectives into a linear and authoritative historical account.

The Sanskrit *Mahābhārata* both reflects and projects *pṛthaktva* and plurality. The Doordarśan *Mahābhārata* does not (though implicitly, of course, it reflects a complex blend of performance traditions, genres and media technologies). It is of critical importance to contemporary political discourse in South Asia (and beyond) that lessons are learned from pre-modern literature such as the *Mahābhārata*. Chief amongst these is that narrative is a tool for debate and not solely for coercion. The period before and after the beginning of the common era in South Asia was replete with challenges (dynastic instability, environmental and agrarian uncertainties, as well as invasion from the North West of the subcontinent) and ideological innovation (institutionally consolidated forms of Buddhism and Jainism, for example) and yet much of the brāhmaṇsical literature of the period (notwithstanding its probable 'elite' authorship) is marked by a determined responsiveness to change and to ideological plurality (even if the *Mahābhārata* has a few tricks up its sleeve with regard to Vedicizing new and alien ideas, as we have seen). One can only hope that we, in the present moment, respond with a similar degree of rigour and flexibility.

ENDNOTES

1. This was the view of a variety of European scholars of the 19th century. For example, Winternitz called the text a *literarisches Unding*, a "literary unthing". His view, and those of other scholars who saw the *Mahābhārata* as an essentially composite entity, has been critiqued by Alf Hiltebeitel in his *Rethinking the Mahābhārata: A Reader's Guide to the Education of the Dharma King*, University of Chicago Press, Chicago, 2001. For an excellent overview of *Mahābhārata* studies, from the nineteenth century to the present, see Adam Bowles' introduction to his *Dharma, Disorder and the Political in Ancient India: The Āpadharmaparvan of the Mahābhārata*, E.J. Brill, Leiden, 2007.
2. It is also the case that the critical edition of the *Mahābhārata*, in so far as we may trust its reconstructions, offers us a text that very much includes embedded, digressive materials. While the reconstituted text is not perfect, of course, we have no external evidence for the vagaries, or indeed fidelity, of the Mahābhārata tradition in the first millennium that is not 'circumstantial' (literary and epigraphic – with the sole exception of the incomplete *parva* list preserved in the Spitzer manuscript. For a recent discussion of these materials, see John Brockington's "The Spitzer Manuscript and the Mahābhārata" in E. Franco and M. Zin, eds., *From Turfan to Ajanta*, Lumbini International Research Institute, Lumbini, 2010). The text we have is an approximation, to be sure, and some materials appear to be highly likely to be later than others in the reconstituted Pune text, but this does make the text composed of *interpolations all the way down*. This would be a highly artificial, and counter-intuitive, way of looking at a literary text (unless one had fairly concrete evidence that this was its mode of composition).
3. The range and depth of work in this area is beyond summary in a note. However, mention must be made of the contributions of

the work of James Fitzgerald and Alf Hiltebeitel in elucidating the range of ideological concerns at work in the Sanskrit text. See Fitzgerald, J.L., "The Great Epic of India as Religious Rhetoric: A Fresh Look at the Mahābhārata", *Journal of the American Academy of Religion*, vol. 51, 1, 1983, p. 611–30 and his "Making Yudhiṣṭhira the King: the dialectics and the Politics of Violence in the Mahābhārata." *Rocznik Orientalistyczny*, 54, 1, 2001, pp. 63–92. See also, in addition to A. Hiltebeitel, *Rethinking the Mahābhārata*, "Conventions of the Naimiṣa Forest", *Journal of Indian Philosophy*, 26, 1998, pp. 161–71, and "Weighting Orality and Writing in the Sanskrit Epics" in P. Koskallio, ed., *Epics, Khilas and Purāṇas: Continuities and Ruptures*, Proceedings of the Third Dubrovnik International Conference on the Sanskrit Epics and Purāṇas, Academia Scientiarum et Artium Croatica, Zagreb, 2005. pp. 81–113, as well as many others (a full list of which cannot be given here). New and exciting work includes two recent monographs by Adam Bowles (mentioned above) and Simon Brodbeck (*The Mahābhārata Patriline: Gender, Culture and the Royal Hereditary*, Ashgate, Farnham, 2009). I may mention my own monograph entitled *Religon, Narrative and Public Imagination in South Asia: Past and Place in the Sanskrit Mahābhārata*, Routledge, London and New York, 2012.

4. *Mbh*, 14.92.1.
5. *Mbh*, 14.92.4.
6. *Mbh*, 14.92.5.
7. *Mbh*, 14.92.5.
8. This regionalization of Vedic schools has been explored by Michael Witzel in his "On the Localisation of Vedic Texts and Schools (Materials on Vedic śākhās, 7)" in G. Pollet, ed., *India and the Ancient World: History, Trade and Culture Before A.D. 650.* Orientalia Lovaniensia Analecta 25, Departement Oriëntalistiek, Leuven, 1987, p. 173–213, and in his "The Development of the Vedic Canon and its Schools: The Social and Political Milieu (Matrials on Vedic Śākhās, 8)" in Michael Witzel, ed., *Inside the Texts, Beyond the Texts*, Harvard Oriental Series, Opera Minora 2, Cambridge, 1997, pp. 257–345. The use of narrative to express differences between brāhmaṇical interest groups is explored in the early Upaniṣads by Brian Black in his *The Character of the Self in Ancient India: Priests, Kings and Women in the Early Upaniṣads*, SUNY Press, Albany, 2007.
9. I translate *tapas* here, more generally translated as penance or austerity, as gleaning as this makes more sense in this particular narrative context. Manu also suggests, at 11.237, that the *tapas* of the *ṛṣi* or sage is to feed on fruits (*phala*) and roots (*mūla*). See

Patrick Olivelle, *Manu's Code of Law: A Critical Edition and Translation of the Mānava-Dharmaśāstra* (*M.Dh.*), Oxford University Press, New York, 2005, p. 228 (English) and p. 881 (Sanskrit). In the above, one might risk a bolder translation of *tapas* as simply poverty - if one wished to suggest that the message of the text was more revolutionary and socially-focussed. I thank Simon Brodbeck for this interesting suggestion (in a personal communication).

10. *Mbh*, 14.93.91-93.
11. We will have more to say on this in the sequel.
12. This somewhat free rendering of the term *ārjava* as either 'moral rectitude' or 'sense of fair play' reflects the occurrence of *satya*, here meaning sincerity or truthfulness, in the line that follows.
13. Perhaps because their generosity is celebrated as unsurpassed in the *Ṛg Veda* (1.37.7 and 2.5.2).
14. *Mbh*, 14.94.22.
15. It is worth noting that *kṣetra* can simply mean cultivated lands in opposition to *jaṅgala*, or wilds and that the opening challenge of our pugnacious mongoose referred to the *kurukṣetra-nivāsinaḥ*, the residents of the land of Kuru and not exlusively to brāhmaṇs
16. *Mbh*, 14.94.34. It is worth noting that my point would not be undermined by a more standard translation of *tapas* as austerity or asceticism here.
17. All of this is refracted through an emphasis on an ethical preference for poverty that might have been quasi-monastic, renunciative or simply socially conservative depending on how you read the accumulating narratives.
18. The *Mahābhārata*'s engagement with the Bhārgavas is sustained and elaborate and has been the subject of a number of studies. See, for example, the classic study of V.S. Sukthankar, "Epic Studies: VI. The Bhṛgus and the Bhārata: A Text Historical Study", *Annals of the Bhandarkar Oriental Research Institute*, 18, 1936.
19. *Mbh*, 14.96.12.
20. *Mbh*, 14.96.14.
21. For an exhaustive study of the *Mahābhārata* patriline, see Brodbec's *The Mahābhārata Patriline: Gender, Culture and the Royal Hereditary.*
22. The references to the main war of the *Mahābhārata* are too numerous to list. A fairly typical example may be found in the *Udyogaparva* when Duryodhana states: '*Karṇa* and I have laid out the battle-ritual (*raṇayajña*), having made Yudhiṣṭhira the sacrificial offering (*paśum*). We two are consecrated (*dīkṣitau*), O bull of the Bhāratas' - *ahaṃ ca tāta karṇaś ca raṇayajñaṃ vitatya vai/ Yudhiṣṭhiraṃ paśuṃ kṛtvā dīkṣitau bharatarṣabha* / /*Mbh*, 5.57.13.

Further examples may be found at: *Mbh*, 5.64.13; 5.139.53; 7.77.18;.9.59.22–25; 10.5-9;10.7.12–14

23. *Mbh*, 1.2.209
24. *Bhāratamañjarī*. 14.190-214.
25. See the introduction to Shekhar Sen's *The Jaimini Āśvamedhika Parva in the Mahābhārata (JAp)*, ed. Pradip Bhattacharya, Writer's Workshop, Calcutta, 2008.
26. *JAp*. 67.12.
27. *JAp*. 67.17–17. Shekhar Sen, *Jaimini*, p. 468.
28. *Mbh*, 2.61.60–80.
29. One way in which we can actually track deliberative response to the events of the *Dyūtaparvan* is in the shifting identification of the being responsible for the replenishing of Draupdī's skirts. Unnamed in the critical text we find versions that tell of Kṛṣṇa's intervention in a star passage (2*543.0–11) or, alternatively, Dharma's intervention (2*0544.1–4). Star passages are examples of textual variants in the manuscript tradition of the *Mahābhārata*. They are included in the critical edition of the Sanskrit *Mahābhārata*.
30. The title itself refers to the 'lake of the acts of Rām', with each of its books being a 'step', or *sopān*, leading to it.
31. Philip Lutgendorf, *The Life of a Text: Performing the Rāmcaritmānas of Tulsīdās*, University of California Press, Berkeley, 1991, pp. 25-6.
32. *Mbh*, 5.35.
33. *Mbh*, 14.26.6-11. Cf. *Bṛhadāraṇyaka Upaniṣad (BU)*, 5.2.
34. *Mbh*, 3.10.10.
35. See V.R. Dikshitar, *The Purāṇa Index*, vol. 3, Motilal Barnarsidass, New Delhi, 1995, (1955), p. 658.
36. *Mbh*, 1.60.65;1.93.8.
37. *Mbh*, 5.100.1.
38. *Mbh*, 12.167.3.
39. *Mbh*, *13.14.82
40. *Mbh*, 4.36.4–5.
41. *BU*, 2.6.3 and 4.6.3 and *Aitareya Brāhmaṇa (AB)*, 8.22.
42. *Kauṣītaki Brāhmaṇa*, 24.3 and *AB*.2.2.1.
43. *Ṛgveda (RV)* 5.40.
44. Ibid., 10.90.16.
45. *Nirukta*, 12.41.
46. *Mbh*, 1.22. For Purāṇic references, see Dikshitar, *The Purāṇa Index*, vol. 3, p. 581.
47. *Mbh*, 12.288ff
48. *Mbh*, 12.288.20
49. *Mbh*, 12.288.27 One should remember our mongoose, who was

krodha, who was Dharma!

50. *Mbh*, 12.288.30&31.
51. *Mbh*, 12.288.240
52. *Aṅguttara Nikāya*, 6.63.5
53. *Dīgha Nikāya*, 13.81
54. *Majjhima Nikāya*, 22.13 – this, and the other Buddhist materials cited here, are in the translation of Thanissaro Bhikku and are available at http://www.accesstoinsight.org/tipitaka.
55. *Mbh*, 1.101.
56. *Mbh*, 13.101.1.
57. *Mbh*, 13.101.7.
58. *Mbh*, 13.101.10.
59. Dikshitar, *The Purāṇa Index*, vol. 3, p. 471.
60. *Mbh*, 13.101.59.
61. *RV*.1.70.9, 5.1.10, 8.100.9, and to kings *RV*.7.6.5 and 10.173.6.
62. A good start in this regard is Kalyan Kumar Chakravarty, ed., *Text and Variations of the Mahābhārata: Contextual, Regional and Performative Traditions*, Munshiram Manoharlal, New Delhi, 2009.
63. For visual culture and the *Mahābhārata*, see Brockington's "Visual Epics", *Rocznik Orientalistyczny*, 54, 1(2001), pp. 111–31. More generally, see his *The Sanskrit Epics*, E.J. Brill, Leiden, 1998. See also chapter five of my *Religion, Narrative and Public Imagination.*
64. See Chandra, L., "The *Mahābhārata* in Asian Literature and Arts" in Kalyan Kumar Chakravarty, op. cit., pp. 25–37.
65. A.K. Warder, *Indian Kāvya Literature*, vol. 2: *The Origins and Formation of Classical Kāvya*, Motilal Barnarsidass, Delhi, 1990 (1974), p. 262.
66. E. Gerow, "Ūrubhaṅga: The Breaking of the Thighs" in Arvind Sharma, ed., *Essays on the Mahābhārata*, Motilal Banarsidass, Delhi, 2007 (1991), p. 57. Warder, *Indian Kāvya Literature*, vol. 2, p. 263.
67. A.K. and K.R. Pisharoti, "Bhāsa's Works – Are they Genuine?", *Bulletin of the School of Oriental and African Studies*, vol. 3, 1923, pp. 107–17, and Tieken, H., "The So-called Trivandrum Plays Attributed to Bhāsa", *Wiener Zeitschrift für die Kunde Südasiens*, 45 (2001), pp. 91–124.
68. For convenience, I will continue to refer to him as the author.
69. The poetic *rasa* are as follows: *śṛṅgāra*, love, *vīra*, heroism, *bībhatsa*, disgust, *raudra*, fury, *hāsya*, mirth, *bhayānaka*, terror, *karuṇa*, compassion, *adbhuta*, wonder, *śānta*, equanimity.
70. See Warder, *Indian Kāvya Literature*, vol. 2, p. 265.
71. This is Gerow's translation. See, "Urubhaṅga....", p. 68.
72. Gerow, "Urubhaṅga....", p. 69
73. Gerow, "Urubhaṅga....", p. 70.
74. W. Johnsons's translation from Act 1 (verse 20a) of the

Abhijñānaśākuntalam. See his *The Recognition of Śakuntalā*, Oxford University Press, Oxford, 2001, p. 13.

75. Gerow, "Urubhaṅga....", p. 68.
76. Gerow, "Urubhaṅga....", p. 81.
77. Gerow, "Urubhaṅga....", p. 74.
78. David Gitomer has provided an excellent analysis of ways of reading Duryodhana both wthin and beyond the epic text in his "King Duryodhana: The *Mahābhārata* discourse of sinning and Virtue in Epic and Drama", *Journal of the American Oriental Society*, 112 (1992), pp. 222–32.
79. Gerow, "Urubhaṅga....", p. 77.
80. The play also demonstrates a rich consciousness of the wider action of the *Mahābhārata*. This includes, the dicing, the exile of the Pāṇḍavas (vs.63), the slaying of Hiḍimbā (vs.34) and the night attack (vs.66).
81. Gerow, "Urubhaṅga....", p. 82.
82. See Rakesh Solomon, "Culture, Imperialism, and National Resistance: Performance in Colonial India", *Theatre Journal*, 46 (1994), pp. 323–43.
83. Nor was he the only playwright engaging in this sort of activity. See Solomon's full article for details.
84. Solomon, "Culture, Imperialism and Nationalist Resistance", p. 25.
85. Ibid., p. 331.
86. For a concise statement of this view see Schiller and Goethe's 'Über epische and dramatische Dichtung' in Goethe, J.W., *Sämtliche Werke*, Jubiläums-Ausgabe, Stuttgart and Berlin, 1902-1907, vol. 36. pp. 149–52. This is without commenting at length on the way in which the figure of Time itself in the Hindi version seems to reflect an unobtainable ideal of the perfect historian: Disinterested and Omniscient.
87. Bakhtin, M., *The Dialogic Imagination: Four Essays* by M.M. Bakhtin, trans. C. Emerson and M. Holquist, University of Texas Press, Austin, 1998, p. 13.
88. The ritual act of seeing, and being seen by, an empowered being.
89. See above, note 28.
90. For an analysis of how these feature of the text are reflected in details of dress, soundtrack and other aspects of the production of the Doordarshan Mahābhārat see Anand Mitra, *Television and Popular Culture in India: A Study of the Mahabharat*, Sage, Delhi, 1993. This work has a useful and sophisticated sociological orientation but is marred by a somewhat superficial analysis of the narrative of the actual televisual text.

Section IV

NUDITY AND SEXUALITY: DIVINE AND HUMAN

9

The Nude Goddess or "Shameless Woman" in Western Asia, India, and South-Eastern Asia*

*H.D. Sankalia***

Nude, or semi-nude female figures are not new to India. The question here is the introduction of certain specific types into Indian art and iconography, and the spread of identical and similar types in South-East Asia,[1] as far as the Celebes. This is discussed against a background of Roman and prehistoric Egyptian evidence, and the data gathered from stratified excavations during the last ten years in India.[2]

M.A. Murray,[3] while writing on "Female Fertility Figures" classified them into three groups as follows:

(1) The Universal Mother or Isis type
(2) The Divine Woman or Ishtar type
(3) The Personified Yoni or Baubo type.

Briefly the characteristic of each are as follows:-

The Universal Mother

This is the true "mother" goddess represented in three ways:-

---

* Reprinted from *Artibus Asiae*, vol. 23, no. 2, 1960.

** The type here discussed is different from the types included by Dr. Ananda Coomaraswamy in his article "Archaic Indian Terracottas", *Mārg*, VI, 2, pp. 22–35.

(a) With full breasts, often exaggerated in size or number.
(b) With a child in her arms, either being suckled or held up to her face.
(c) As a pregnant woman.

In these figures the child is an essential part, actual or implied.

Of these types, two are here illustrated. The first (Fig. 2) is a surface find from a Chalcolithic and Early Historic mound at Bilwali, near Dhar, Madhya Pradesh; the second (Fig. 1) is from the Chalcolithic layers of the latest excavations at Nevasa, District Ahmadnagar. Both the figures in essence belong to the same type in which the buttocks are exaggerated, and little or no attention is paid to the delineation of other features: head, nose, arms and even breasts. The antiquity of the Bilwali type can be traced back to Neolithic Anatolia and Crete, [4] that of the Nevasa one to Upper Palaeolithic Europe.[5] This would be "the archaic style" figurine of Gordon,[6] though those illustrated by him are a little elaborate. So also are the "Mother Goddess" type from Ahichchhatra,[7] Kausambi,[8] Sonepur[9] and Somnath.[9]

The Divine Woman

In the second type, "the figure is always that of a young woman, hardly more than a girl, and the rounded limbs are made as beautiful as the skill of the sculptor permits." She is sometimes nude, sometimes lightly clad and sometimes completely clothed. "Such figures", as Murray has rightly remarked, "should not be called a 'mother goddess', for she has not yet borne a child." It represents "the divine woman whom man desires—beautiful, exquisite, alluring, potential mother but still a virgin."

Personified Yoni or Baubo

In the third type, as Murray showed by discussing examples from Neolithic Egypt as well as much later figures from the same country, and also from England and Ireland, the whole emphasis is laid on the pudenda. And "in the ancient world, the most realistic of such figures belong to Egypt, where they represent the goddess Baubo. Though these figures are of the Roman period, they are not necessarily of Roman origin, they are merely an ancient goddess in a new form." "The figure is commonly represented as seated on the ground, the legs spread out so as to display the pudenda, which are strongly marked and often exaggerated in size." In some cases the figure is squatting with the knees raised and turned outward. This Murray calls the Baubo-Phryne or "frog" attitude. "In every case the outward spread of the thighs is essential. The pose of the arms is varied; sometimes they are raised in the so-called 'attitude of prayer', sometimes they are held forward as in invitation, sometimes the hands are laid on the thighs to stretch the legs apart and so emphasize the pudenda. This last was not uncommon in late Roman times."

Codrington followed up this publication with an article "Iconography: Classical and Indian",[10] in which he cited a small female terracotta figure in the form of a toad, now in the Indian Museum, London. Though its exact provenance and date were not known, from other associated red stone figures and stylistic evidence, he assigned it to Mathura in the Kushan period (early second century AD). He also thought that similar naked goddesses or Yakṣinīs from Bharhut, Mathura, Sanchi etc. belonged to the Baubo and the Sheila-na-gig class, and the small toad figure, specially inspired by the Baubo figures. This inspiration, he attributed to the increased overland contacts with Western Asia during this period.

Codrington probably suspected Roman influence in the handing down of this inspiration, when he used the words "the provincial Roman art of Sirkap, the Taxila of the first century BC must be taken into consideration as the witness of special contacts."

Excavation during the last ten years has conclusively shown that the first two centuries of the Christian era and probably the first century BC witnessed a prosperous maritime as well as overland trade with the Roman world. This was not confined to Taxila or Mathura, as the principal seats of Kuṣāṇa power, but was felt all over India, and more by the sea-ports on the western and eastern coast of India This is exemplified, besides Roman coins, by amphora sherds from Arikamedu, Chandravalli, Kolhapur, Nevasa, Junnar and Ujjain. Associated with this is a fine Red Polished ware, some of it, as at Nasik and probably at Nevasa, and other Andhra sites, being of Roman origin or done in imitation of the Roman ware.

It was with such sherds that the principal figure (Fig. 3) discussed here was brought from Ter, Osmanabad District, Bombay (now Maharashtra) State. Ter is the ancient Tagara. It lay on the trade route from Masulipatam in the east coast to Junnar or Broach in the west *via* Paithan. Until recently it was known chiefly for its early structural Caitya-like temple.[11]

Extensive mounds at the sites were noted by Cousens in his short visit,[12] but their age was never suspected. Recently, a number of finds from Ter were brought to my notice. Among these, I found the famous Black-and-Red pottery, the Red Polished ware, beautiful kaoline boyheads, the terracotta goddesses and a feeding cup, also in fine Red Polished Ware. Though not stratified, there is no doubt, from the evidence afforded by Nevasa, Kolhapur and Maheshwar and the unstratified evidence from Kondapur, that we can confidently assign all the objects to the first second centuries AD. In fact small excavations[13] there during 1958 have confirmed this inference, and a figure (Fig. 4) like the one discussed here was found in the excavation, in association with Red Polished Ware etc. and assigned to the 1st-3rd centuries AD.

Of these, I would like to discuss in some detail the terracotta female figure (Fig. 3). It measures about 1 inch to 2 inch, about inch thick, and is cast in a single mould, the back side being flat. The surface is fine, red polished all over. The female is shown seated as described by Murray, with the thighs spread out. The arms are supposed to be on the sides. *But there is no head*. This is intentional. Round the neck is a beaded necklace, a thick girdle encircles the waist, and there are heavy anklets. In the stratified figure (Fig. 4) there seem to be a large number of girdles, the torso is very much shortened, and there are four rosettes—two on the top, and two below.

An almost identical figure (Fig. 5) on a circular terracotta plaque was found by Marshall in his excavations at Bhita.[14] It is now exhibited in the Indian Museum at Calcutta. Though headless like the Ter figure, it differs in having a lotus flower with petals falling over the shoulders, while the hands are upraised like those of a toad; the waist is very narrow and decorated by a girdle, and on the legs are worn a heavy anklet and a series of rings, and bangles on the arms. This figure, though heavily ornamented, is nearer the Baubo type than are those from Ter.

Marshall, probably because of the association, assigned it to the Kuṣāṇa period, but thought that it might be Gupta. He further drew attention to a similar figure from Kosam exhibited in the Indian Museum.

The former really is of the Kuṣāṇa period, as it was found just after (if the numbers in dark black were given on the field or indicate the order in which the objects were discovered) what Marshall called a "water bottle".[15] Since the Kolhapur finds[16] this has been recognized as a characteristic vessel in Red Polished Ware and dated to the second century AD.

Similar figures are also found sculptured in caves and temples. The first (Fig. 6) is from a cave at Siddan Kotte, north of Kelur in Northern Karnatak. This was copied by the late Mr. Chapgar and is reproduced from his diary.

The figure of a goddess (Fig. 7) with a female attendant on either side in Cave No. 21 (Rameshwar) at Ellora seems similar, but may be in fact different. The goddess is seated in *utkatikāsana* with thighs spread apart, prominently showing the pudenda region. But the latter appears to be repaired, as are some other portions of the sculpure, and it is not certain whether the figure was originally nude. If it indeed was, then one might say that this type of mother goddess was accepted into the Rāṣṭrakūṭa pantheon. She was in fact turned into a regular goddess, as shown by the attendant figures.

Were some doubt left about such a development, it is removed by a tiny but highly significant stone sculpture (Fig. 8) from Vadgaon, near Satara. It was brought to me by Shri Inamdar of the Aundh State Museum. The goddess, again headless, is shown exactly as in the two terracottas discussed above, but in addition with a bull—Nandi—to her right. She is regarded as a form of Durgā or Pārvatī. That this was again a widespread feature is being proved by the occurrence of an almost identical figure from the excavations at Nevasa, in 1959–60. The stone figure (Fig. 9) was found from the foundation debris of Period VI and is thus assignable to Period V (c. 100–300 AD).

This goddess was even accepted in the early Buddhist pantheon, as is shown by a terracotta from Nagarjunikonda. In this, the upper part of the goddess is in the form of a stūpa (Fig. 10). Baubo's Indianization is thus complete.

Stella Kramrisch has identified a similar figure—a stone sculpture—in the museum at Alampur, now in the Andhra Pradesh, with Aditi-Uttānapad[17] (Fig. 10A). But before accepting this interpretation, it should be pointed out that we have no early identical figures from the Ṛgvedic period (whatever be the date of that period) or from a period before the first-second century AD. The Alampur and other figures are at least five or six centuries later than the first introduction of this figure in India. So the identification of the figure with Aditi-Uttānapad may be justified as a later apotheosis of an idea or symbolism which was probably foreign, as pointed out here. How this gradually took place has been shown. And it must be emphasized once again that it was not only in the brāhmaṇic religion, but also in the Buddhist that this symbol was deified.

An explanation of the survival (if not the first introduction) of such a goddess in India was provided by the late Shri Chapgar. He has noted that the figure is called "Lajjā Gaurī" that is "a shy woman". But this is euphemistic. Really it means "a shameless woman". Hence her head is never shown. Now-a-days, women who do not get children worship "Lajjā Gaurī". Butter and red lead are applied on the vagina and breasts and they pray for children.

This explains one of the reasons why such figures occur not only in Indian art and iconography, but in European, West Asiatic, Egyptian and even South-East Asian monuments. There might be psychological reasons too, as pointed out by Murray, and that is how such figures could find a place even on Christian churches and in Indian temples.

It is interesting to find that such figures (Figs. 11–16) *but with heads* continue to be made even now, or were made until recently in such far of places as Kampong and Sanga, Middle and West Celebes, and Palau and Java from where figures were carried to Japan, as drawings, photographs and information kindly supplied to me by Dr. Carl Schuster[18] and his friends prove.

In India, the inspiration was most probably received from Egypt through the Romans in about the first-second centuries AD. It is to this that may be attributed the occurrence, in late Andhra or Sātavāhana layers, of another goddess, seated in European style. Cast in double mould, and perhaps nude or in diaphanous dress, she has pleasing, benign features. She might well be the "Divine Woman" or "the Ishtar type",[19] wherein the figure is always that of a young woman, hardly more than a girl, and the rounded limbs are beautifully shown.

So far, such "Divine Woman" figures have come from Kolhapur (Fig. 17), Nasik, Nevasa, Ter (Fig. 18), Tripuri,[20] and Nagarjunikonda,[20] all belonging to the first-second centuries AD.

Mother goddess figures probably of similar inspiration can be had from Mathurā and elsewhere. Hārītī and Ambikā are well-known. But towards the later Andhra or early Gupta period, i.e. about 300-500 AD and later, deterioration in type had developed as shown by the stratigraphical evidence from Kolhapur,[21] Nevasa,[22] Maheshwar[23] and Ahichchhatra[24] and Kausambi.[24] All these sites have produced a figure, cast in single mould, as if in half relief. The woman is shown standing, with her right arm at her side, and with the left supporting a child. Agrawala called such figures *aṅkadhātrī*. On the contrary, Northern Gujarat, including the former Idar State,[25] has given us some of the finest mother-and-child stone sculptures in Indian art.

From this rapid review of certain types of female figures can we say definitely that these were introduced from Western Asia in the early Roman period. Except for the Piprawa (Lauriya Nadangadh) gold leaf image,[26] and now the Rupar stone relief[17] (600–200 BC), we have few well-documented figures of this nature from the Early Historical Period. It is a far cry to Mohenjodaro and the so-called Mother Goddess figures of that civilization are differently made, though the motive or purposes might be the same. As against this, there is good stratigraphical, evidence from a number of sites in India to suggest the importation of the type during the first centuries BC or AD with the Roman and West Asiatic trade. However, as with Graeco-Iranian and other motifs, the figures were soon Indianized, so much so that in figures from Gujarat, it would be difficult to see even a trace of foreign influence.[28]

When and how the Baubo type figures reached Indonesia (Java and the Celebes islands) is also worth investigation. The figures resemble the Mathurā toad figurine so much in certain particulars that Indian influence[29] may not be ruled out. However, allowance must be made for other sources of such influences. This might be directly Roman or early European in the 15th-16th centuries.

Within India, two other sources are likely, though it is possible that both are quite independent of each other, and also of the Baubo type figure under discussion. The earlier chronologically[30] (Fig. 19) suggesting the human sex act is a drawing on a pot found from the Chalcolithic site of Daimabad on the Pravara river, District Ahmadnagar, in 1959. Almost identical male and female symbols are carved on a pillar of a dormitory at Raisu by the Bhuiya and Muria Gonds[31] (Fig. 20). So it may be argued either that the Murias carry on the prehistoric tradition, or that they have borrowed the symbolism from the figurines of the Early Historical period;[32] or that the figurines themselves are based on this old tradition and have nothing to do with the Egyptian, Roman and the Western Asiatic influences.

Perhaps the earliest representation of this goddess in Iran is to be found on a votive bronze "pin" from Luristan. On one piece illustrated by Ghirshman, *Iran*, p. 102, Pl. 8a, this goddess is shown squatting in child-birth. She holds her breasts—a gesture which is shown on other objects. It is said that thousands of figurines of similar nature are found in Near Eastern sites (Western Asia), particularly at Susa, where under the Elamite name of Kiririsha this fertility goddess was worshipped through the centuries. Under the name of Nanaia her cult continued down to the Parthian period and many terracotta figurines are found in the Parthian cemetery at this important site.

It is in this way that we are able to get a link between Egypt and India in about the 7th-8th century BC. As mentioned in the article, the goddess was taken to India under the Roman impact.

ENDNOTES

1. I cannot adequately express my indebtedness to Dr. Carl Schuster. After I showed him the figures from Ter in Poona, on his return to the United States, he ransacked all the literature bearing on this subject in South-East Asia and beyond, photographed the relevant material from books and also requested his friends—who are also my friends now—to send me the original photographs. After waiting for nearly three years to do justice to all this material I thought it advisable to publish merely the bare facts without trying to go into greater details about the origin and spread of the motif discussed here.

   If the matter is inadequately treated, the fault is mine; but I remain profoundly thankful to Dr Schuster, Prof. C. Tj. Bertling of Koninlijk Institut Voor de Tropen, Amsterdam, Dr. J.H. Jager Gerlings, Curator, for a photo of the house model in Rotterdam Museum, Van Heekeren of Java (now in Holland), Prof. Heine-Geldern (Vienna), Prof. Galestin, Amsterdam, and Prof. Franz Termer, Director of the Museum in Hamburg for kindly allowing me to publish the two photos of *Dilsuki* from his forthcoming (now probably published) monograph, Dr. Roland W. Force, Curator of Oceanic Archaeology and Ethnography, Chicago Natural History Museum, for photocopy of the "shameless woman" on the gables of the houses in Palau.
2. For reproducing photographs from these, I am obliged to Shri A. Ghosh, Director General of Archaeology in India, Dr. P.M. Joshi, Director of Archives and Archaeology in the State of Maharashtra, and the Superintendent of Indian Museum, Calcutta.
3. *Journal of the Royal Anthropological Institute of Great Britain and Ireland*, vol. LXIV, 1934, pp. 93–100.
4. See Evans, *The Palace of Minos at Knossos*, I, figs. 12–13.
5. For instance in MacCurdy, George Grant, *Human Origins*, I, figs. 125, 159, 160, 162–64, or the more recent appraisal by Absolon,

Karel, "The Diluvial Anthropomorphic Statuettes and Drawings, especially the so-called Venus Statuette, discovered in Moravia", *Artibus Asiae*, vol. XII, p. 201 (ff. Cf. also op. cit. p. 104, Salmony, Alfred, "Some Palaeolithic Ivory-Carvings from Mezine (in Ukraine)."

6. Gordon, D.H., "Early Indian Terracottas", *Jour. Ind. Soc. of Oriental Art*, vol. IX (1943), p. 143 and pp. IX, 1–5. See also Das Gupta, C.C., "Unpublished Ancient Indian Terracottas" in the Musée Guimet, Paris, *Artibus Asiae*, vol. XIV, pp. 283–305, Figs. 1–24, and from the British Museum; and Coomaraswamy, op. cit., pp. 22–3.
7. Agrawala, V.S., "Terracotta Figurines of Ahichchhatra", *Ancient India*, no. 4, p. 106, ff. and pl. XXXIA.
8. Kala, Satish Chandra, *Terracotta Figurines from Kausambi*, Allahabad, 1957, p. 14, pl. I and III, and Sharma, G.R., *The Excavations at Kausambi (1957–59)*, Allahabad, 1960, p. 75 and pl. 44, 3. (This is however more primitive looking than the "archaic" ones.)
9. *Indian Archaeology—A Review* (*IAR*), 1956–57, pl. XXVA and pl. XVIIIV, 5 respectively.
10. *Man*, XXXV, I935, no. 70, p. 65.
11. Cousens, *Archaeological Survey of India, Annual Report* (ASIAR), 1902–03, p. 196.
12. Op. cit.
13. See *IAR*, 1957-58, p. 23. Preliminary Report on the work by Dr. B.N. Chapekar of the Deccan College has been submitted to the Director of Archives, Bombay, for publication.
14. *ASIAR*, 1911-2, p. 75, pl. XXIII, no. 40. A figure similar to this is described and illustrated by Kala as from Kausambi, though the latter is not clear. See Kala, op. cit., p. 30, figs. pl. XVII, A and C.
15. Marshall, op. cit., P1. XXX, fig. 52.
16. Sankalia, H.D., and Dikshit, M.G., *Excavations at Kolhapur (Brahmapuri)*, Poona, 1952, pl. XIX, A and pl. XXXIII, D.
17. Stella Kramrisch, "An Image of Aditi-Uttānapad", *Artibus Asiae*, vol. XIX, p. 259. Cf., however, Coomaraswamy, op. cit., p. 32 who says, "we cannot with any security attach a name to the Indian nude goddess", and suggests several alternations.
18. See note 1 on page 1 and figs. 11–16 from Java (11–13), Palau (14A-B), Toradja, Central Celebes (15-16).
19. Op. cit., p. 94.
20. Dikshit, Moreshwar, G., *Tripuri—1952*, pl. XXXIII and p. 95, and *IAR*., 1956-57, pl. LXIA.
21. Sankalia, H.D., and Dikshit, M.G., *Excavations at Kolhapur (Brahmagiri)*, pl. XXII A.

22. Sankalia, H.D. and Deo, S.B., *From History to Prehistory at Nevasa*, (Poona 1960), fig. 179, 16.
23. Sankalia, H.D., and Subbarao, B., and Deo, S.B., *Excavations at Maheshwar and Navdatoli* (Poona and Baroda 1958), fig. 105, 1, 2.
24. *Ancient India*, no. 4, pp. 146–8, pl. LI-II, and *Bulletin, Museum and Picture Gallery, Baroda*, XII (1955–56), p. 3.
25. Shah, U.P., *Sculptures from Śāmalāji and Roda*, Museum and Picture Gallery, Baroda, 1960, figs. 29, 31, 37, 39, 40.
26. Bloch, T., "Excavations at Lauriya", *ASIAR*, 1906-07, and Coomaraswamy, op. cit., p. 31, no. 36.
27. Sharma, Y.B., "...Excavations at Rupar" in *Lalit Kala*, no. 1-2, p. 125, fig. 13; see also fig. 14.
28. For Roman influence on Indian art and architecture, see Goetz, Hermann, "Imperial Rome and the Genesis of Classic Indian Art" in *East and West*, vol. 10. (1959), pp. 153–81; 261–8.
29. One of the ways to ascertain this is to study minutely the Angkor Vat and other monuments from Java, Sumatra and Cambodia. If they depict any such figures, then presumably the source will be Indian.
30. Seen at the exhibition in Bhuvaneshwar in October 1959 and reproduced here with the courtesy of the Director General of Archaeology and Shri M.N. Deshpande. See also *IAR*, 1958–59, p. 16, fig. 7 (phase III, left bottom corner).
31. Elwin, Verrier, *The Muria and their Ghotul* (1947), Fig. 46, brought to my notice by Dr Schuster. Here fig. 18. Cf. also fig. 59 on p. 337.
32. A terracotta, probably Early Gupta, now in the Bikaner Museum, seems to depict the *yoni* over an *ekamukha liṅga*, thus giving the symbolism a definitely religious turn. Cf. Agrawala, "Two Interesting Śaiva Terracottas in the Bikaner Museum", *Artibus Asiae*, vol. XIX, p. 161, fig. 2.

Fig. 1: Mother Goddess of Upper Palaeolithic type from the Chalcolithic deposits at Nevasa

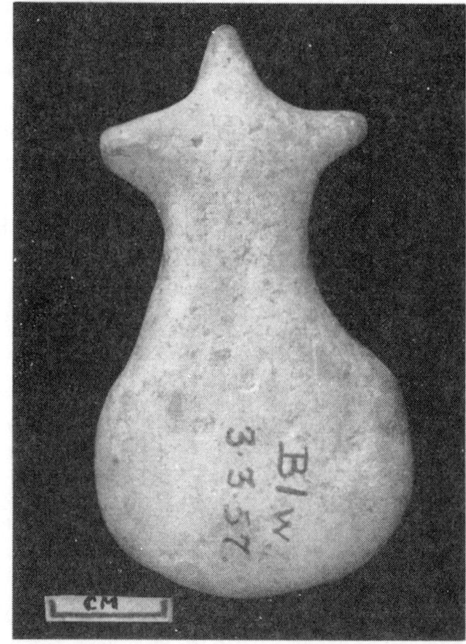

Fig. 2: "Fiddle" or West Asiatic Neolithic type Mother Goddess from the Chalcolithic and Early Historic Mound at Bilwali, Dhar, Madhya Pradesh

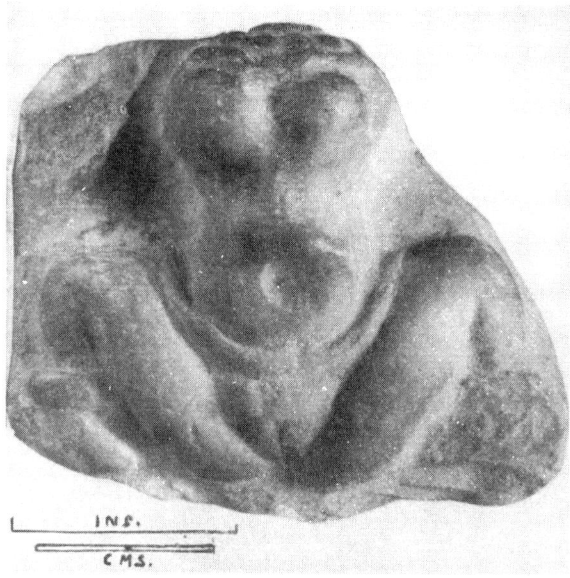

Fig. 3: Nude Goddess or "Shameless Woman" from Ter, Osmanabad District, Maharashtra

Fig. 4: Nude Goddess from Ter excavation

Fig. 5: Nude Goddess or "Shameless Woman" from Bhita, Uttar Pradesh

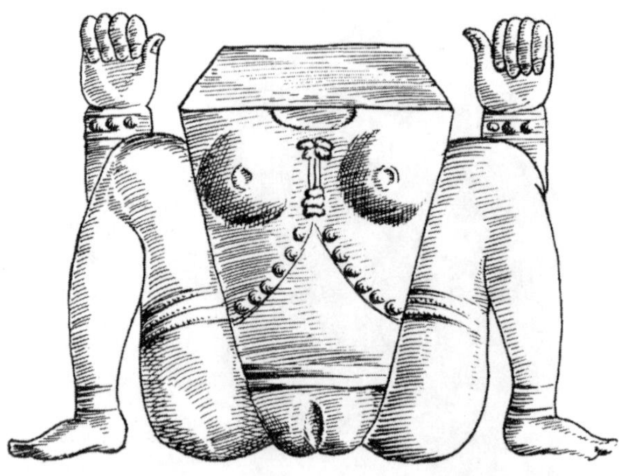

Fig. 6: Drawing from a painting of a nude goddess in Siddan Kotte Cave, Kelur, North Karnatak, Mysore

Fig. 7: Nude (?) Goddess with attendants from Cave 21, Rameshwar Cave, Ellora, Maharashtra

Fig. 8: Nude headless goddess with a Nandi from Vadgaon, Satara, Maharashtra

Fig. 9: Nude headless Goddess from Nevasa excavation, District Ahmadnagar

Fig. 10: Nude Goddess with stupa head from Nagarjunikonda, District Guntur, Andhra Pradesh. Photograph by courtesy of the Department of Archaeology, Government of India

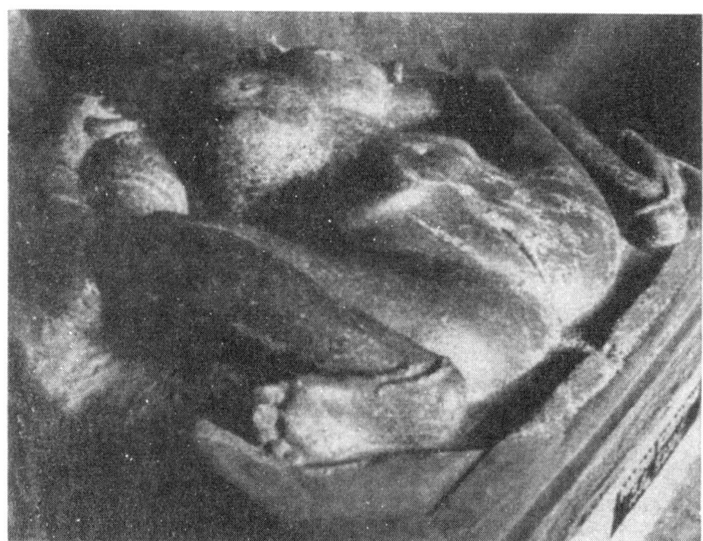

Fig. 10A: Aditi-Uttānapad from Alampur, now Andhra Pradesh

Fig. 11: Nude Goddess on a Hindu Javanese gold pendant, Java. (Courtesy: Dr. Konigswald)

Fig. 12: Nude Goddess on a Stone Sarcophagus, West Sumba, District Laoli, Kampong, Java. (Courtesy: Museum für Volkerkunde, Basel)

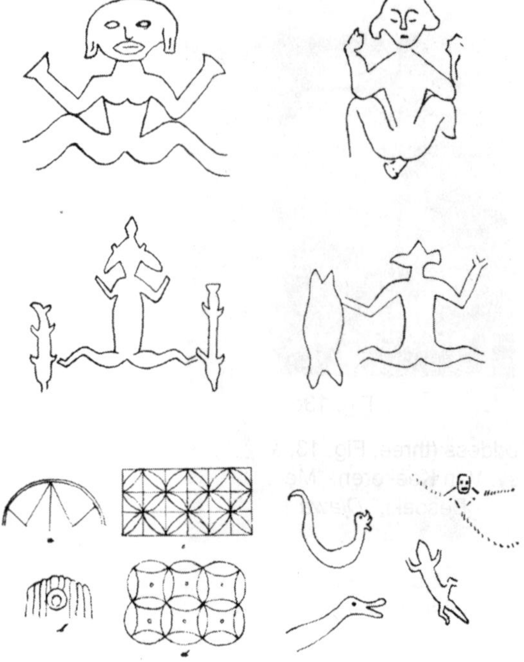

Fig. 13a

Fig. 13b

Fig. 13c

Fig. 13: Nude Goddess (three, Fig. 13, a-c) on Dolmen-like graves in Java. (Courtesy: Van Keekeren, "Megalithische Overblijfselen in Besoeki," *Djawa* 11, 1931)

10

Erotic Nudity, Barren Sexuality and Ferocious Goddesses

Jae-Eun Shin

One of the persistent themes in the art history of India is the sensuous female image. There is "scarcely a single female figure represented in early Indian art without erotic suggestion of some kind, implied, or explicitly expressed and emphasized."[1] The innumerable images of goddesses or feminine semi-divine beings that have ample, curvaceous, beautiful and naked body are often interpreted as the symbol of abundance, prosperity and fertility. They are a sign of the auspiciousness.

On the other hand, there is the other group of images in which feminine divinities are depicted having voluptuous and naked (or semi-nude) body with wholly exposed breast and even genital organ. Even though their sexuality is highly emphasized, it does not have any positive connotation. They are neither a sign of fertility nor auspiciousness. For instance, Ḍākinīs, known as protean and flying witchlike beings, are sexually voracious, but their sexual vigour does not have any relation with reproduction and prosperity. Rather, they are malevolent, and cause sickness, infertility and death to humans and animals. Yoginīs, who are usually naked and pleased with offerings of bodily and sexual excretion, appear as highly ambivalent beings with the power to bestow life and to snatch it away. Moreover, several ferocious goddesses clustered in the group of ten Mahāvidyās are radical and sexual; Kālī, Tārā and Chinnamastā are often described as naked young women who have sexual intercourse with Śiva in reverse pose at the cremation ground in their *dhyāna* mantras. They are often called "mā", but remain "childless" women.

The images of these unusual Tantric feminine divinities have provoked various theoretical discussions, especially among western scholarship. Though the eccentric qualities of Tantric goddesses were recast, reinterpreted, and reshaped in diverse ways, there are three pervasive paradigms in academic discourse. First, ever since the publication of Heinrich Zimmer's pioneering work in 1926, Indologists have interpreted Tantric art including sexual and terrifying images of goddesses just as "a ritual expedient and ritual meditation itself as a means leading to identification with the deity, and finally salvation."[2] Another interpretation of Tantric images is based on the concept of "anima" in Jungian psychology, an archetype of the feminine, embedded in the psyche of male. Jung identified anima with personal subjectivity. It is the inner life which is the reverse of public persona, in which one's private dreams, impulses and imagination hold sway and, in which sexual and dangerous feminine spiritual beings, represent all that man is lacking and for which he yearns.[3] Moreover, they are deemed to be a "shadow" or a "necessary counter image to represent all those dark elements suppressed in each woman as well as in society as a whole".[4] Thirdly, a more recent model in academic discourse is inspired by feminist ideas. While the androcentric hypotheses and ethnocentric interpretive frameworks on women within Tantric traditions were strongly criticized in the light of feminist agenda,[5] the role of sexual and ferocious goddesses was positively evaluated. It is claimed that goddess such as Vajrayoginī served women as "divine prototypes and archetypal images of their own potential."[6] The most violent goddess, Kālī, is considered as "the embodiment of terrifying and radical womanhood which challenges the notion of dharma."[7]

Though the above mentioned three paradigms have

facilitated our understanding of different aspects of the sexual and ferocious goddesses, there is a common tendency which makes us shift our focus from a tactile presence of bodies to a mystique of higher meanings; from a social reality to an abstract symbol; and from a contextual understanding to an essentialist generalization. Therefore, those goddesses are viewed as the most precious symbol of inner spiritual journey, the reflection of male fantasy, or the icon of feminist agenda. I do not deny various possible meanings and implications of these extraordinary images of Tantric goddesses. But I am not inclined to subscribe to these assumptions and prefer to view these images in their proper context. In the present paper, I focus on some of the fierce goddesses of the group of ten, known as Mahāvidyās,[8] and argue that their concept and iconographical features associated with nudity and sexuality were constructed through the continuous interaction between sedentary and non-sedentary societies and that they had nothing to do with creativity and fertility.

The Sanskrit word "*mahāvidyā*" is a combination of the adjective "*mahā*", meaning great or supreme, and the noun "*vidyā*" which is from the verbal root "*vid*" meaning, to know, to learn, to ascertain, to experience. *Vidyā* denotes knowledge in general as well as a branch of knowledge such as science, philosophy, logic, and metaphysics in particular.[9] However, the term *vidyā* does not have a strictly limited meaning. The age-old fascinating stories of *vidyādhara*s (literally meaning bearers of knowledge) demonstrate various kinds of supernatural ability called *vidyā*, which may be identified as mental and spiritual knowledge, as knowledge in spell or as knowledge in medical herb.[10] It liberates its possessor from his human limitations and provides him with superhuman faculties. Therefore, it is suggested that the word *vidyā* is virtually synonymous with 'magic'.[11] In Theravāda Buddhism, a *vijjādhara* may be one, who acquires a dreadful kind of magic (*ghora*) and becomes invisible by use of herbs, or may recite a *mantra*, fly in the sky and show a fourfold military array, or one who, carrying a weapon and flying in the Himalayas, presents the Buddha Sumedha with a flower.[12] The two great epics, the *Rāmāyaṇa* and the *Mahābhārata*, also mention the supernatural and mythical beings called *vidyādharas*. The *Bṛhatkathāślokasaṃgraha* of Budhasvāmin gives us several detailed descriptions of *vidyādharas* with their special magical powers: a *vidyādhara* is able to fly; he moves through the air in *vimānas* (heavenly chariots); he can make himself invisible; he traces someone whose whereabouts are not known; he uses his magical knowledge to obtain his object and so on.[13] *Vidyā* thus denotes the knowledge of appropriate formulas and spells that give one entire control over one's destiny.[14] For that reason, *vidyā* came to be used as an alternative term for *mantra* (magical formula), and *mantra, dhāraṇī, hṛdaya* and *vidyā* mean very much the same.[15]

It is significant that the presiding deity of *vidyā* is female[16] as attested by numerous textual references in which goddess(es) is associated with it. In the *Mahābhārata, Vidyā* appeared as a feminine divinity in the royal procession of Pārvatī along with Gaurī, Gāndhārī, Keśinī, Sumitrā and Sāvitrī.[17] *Vidyā* is often personified as and identified with the goddess Durgā in the *Kathāsaritsāgara*. She is even said to have composed prayers and magical formulas.[18] In the *Devīmahātmya*, she is referred to as Vidyā as well as Mahāvidyā.[19] In fact, the idea that goddess(es) is an embodiment of knowledge, learning and wisdom had evolved from the early phase of history and continued in brāhmaṇical as well as Śramanic traditions in various ways. For example, Sarasvatī, the most well known goddess of knowledge in brāhmaṇical pantheon, rules over speech as the means of conveying traditional knowledge consisting of the Vedas and the Śāstras, which she often inspires by entering the mouth or body of a famous sage (*ṛṣi*).[20] Since knowledge plays a fundamentally important role in Jainism, Sarasvatī has remained as one of the popular Jain goddesses. Her iconography demonstrates her close association with learning, art, and spiritual attainment.[21] In Buddhist traditions, the goddess Prajñāpāramitā (Perfection of Wisdom) is believed to be a personification of transcendental knowledge, embodied in the *Prajñāpāramitā-sūtra*. She hypostatizes the wisdom that is most often designated in this literature by the feminine noun '*prajñā*' (literally meaning wisdom, knowledge, and intelligence). She is celebrated as the ultimate teacher. One of the main titles of Prajñāpāramitā is the "Mother of All Buddhas" (*sarva-buddha-mātā, or sarva-jina-mātā*.[22]

Nevertheless, these goddesses are scarcely associated with the magical knowledge or spell called *vidy*ā. The domain of knowledge presided over by Sarasvatī and Prajñāpāramitā is rather closely related to the intellectual, literary and artistic activity of brāhmaṇs and the metaphysical contemplation and spiritual attainment of Buddhist monks and devotees. That the magical power (*vidyā*) is different from the knowledge embodied in the form of benevolent and intelligent goddesses can be gleaned from the story of Vegavatī (a daughter of *vidyādhara*) narrated as follows by Buddhasvāmin in his *Bṛhatkathāślokasaṃgraha* (14.1-77):

> There is a mountain called Āṣāḍha, ... the abode of a clan of *vidyādhara* (*vidyādhara-kula*). There the king of the *vidyādhara* is Vegavān and his chief queen is Pṛthivī. In their quest for a son they started to worship the clan wisdom goddess, Manaḥputrikā (*manaḥputrikā nāma kula vidyāṃ*). Some time passed and the queen gave birth to a son called Mānasaveg and a daughter called Vegavatī. One day the king noticed that his hair was turning grey. So, as required by family tradition, he abdicated the throne and went to forest to become an ascetic. After sometime had passed, Vāyu-muktā (a daughter of the king Mātaṅga), who had *vidyā* to fly, came to Āṣāḍha with a group of friends. While Vāyu-muktā flew into the sky with her friends like young female swans, Vegavatī was unable to fly because she had not yet mastered the family's *vidyā* (*kula-vidyā*). The queen asked two ministers to take Vegavatī to the forest where her father was practicing his austerities. There she spent her days doing various jobs and austerities. One day her father gave her *vidyā* because the hermits were content with her ascetic practice (*tapas*). Her father declared that the power obtained by her asceticism would be four times greater than her brother's.

In this account *vidyā* can be viewed as a kind of special magical power, which is 1) owned by particular family or clan (*kula*) in a mountain; 2) personified in the form of goddess; 3) associated with tribal groups such as Mātaṅgas; 4) obtained by ascetic practice or by residence in the forest; 5) regarded to be far more strong than the power of a sovereign ruler.

A close association between *vidyā* and the people living on the periphery is corroborated by a tale of Mahāvidyādharī (a great sorceress) in the *Divyāvadāna*.[23] In this story, the mother of a Mātaṅgī is called "Mahāvidyādharī". Here the term *vidyā* denotes the magical power which works by means of *mantras*, and *vidyādharī* means a woman possessing the magical power by which she can attract and control others. Though Mahāvidyādharī is not depicted as a goddess, some of her characteristics bear similarities to those of Yoginīs as well as to those of goddesses categorized as Mahāvidyās.

It is noteworthy that Mahāvidyādharī is a wife of Mātaṅga, a hunter king of forest, and her magical power is comparable to that of Vāyu-muktā, a daughter of king Mātaṅga, who figures in a story of the *Bṛhatkathāślokasaṃgraha* related above. Both of them are Mātaṅgīs, the women living in the forest who were closely identified with Śavareśvarīs, mistresses of the Śavaras.[24] The Śavaras are a tribal people living in forest and often described in unfavorable terms in Sanskrit literature.[25] The portrayal of forest dwelling women like Mātaṅgīs as possessing magical power can be explained by the antonymous connotation of *vana* (forest) and *kṣetra* (sedentary society).

According to Sontheimer, *vana* stands for a wild space, forest or jungle which harbours the hermitage, tribals, *sannyāsī* and the *āśrama*, whereas *kṣetra* denotes an inhabited space with regular plough agriculture and village settlements. The *vana* has "its ambivalence and ambiguous values as seen from the *kṣetra*. It may be considered deadly, chaotic, primordial, full of *bhūta*s, *daitya*s and *rākṣasa*s, but it also had very much its positive values. It was the source of creation and renewal of life."[26] Therefore, the forest and other wild places have been closely associated with various kinds of ambiguous feminine divinities and their mysterious power from the early phase of history.[27]

The dichotomy between the *vana* and *ksetra*, however, is not absolute. They are not mutually exclusive, but complementary or a continuum.[28] The first was gradually transformed into the second through a historical process of the expansion of agrarian settlements into non-agricultural regions and the assimilation of tribal groups into a sedentary society facilitated by the brāhmaṇical order over the centuries.[29] The spread and proliferation of agrarian settlements in the erstwhile peripheral areas caused multi-dimensional cultural transactions and cult assimilations. In this process, various elements and practices of *vana* were absorbed into those of the *kṣetra*,[30] and the ambiguous power of non-sedentary area and its people was abstractly conceptualized and defined as *vidyā*.[31] Thus the Sanskrit term, *vidyā*, originally meaning knowledge in general, came to denote various kinds of popular religious practices which largely originated in or were associated with the forest,[32] and the supernatural power owned by those living beyond the confines of settled agrarian society.

Another important aspect of the *vidyā* was the destructive and dangerous power of the marginalized people related to black magic.[33] In this context, *vidyā* denotes the supernatural knowledge of terrifying and destructive power by which one can subdue or defeat one's enemy. In fact, the ten Mahāvidyās are believed to bestow various vicious powers such as *māraṇa* (destruction or killing), *uccāṭana* (ruining an adversary) *kṣobha* (shaking), *mohana* (depriving of consciousness or perplexing) and *drāvaṇa* (putting to flight). It is said, therefore, that they must be kept concealed.[34] Most of these powers are categorized as the Tantric six acts (*ṣaṭkarmas*)[35]—all of them except one (that is, *Śānti*) being grouped collectively as '*abhicāra*' which may be translated as black magic.

Questions such as who could access and appropriate the magical and destructive power (*vidyā*) and how it was granted or transmitted to its recipient are important for appreciating the significance of the sexual symbolism of several ferocious Mahāvidyās such as Kālī, Tārā and Chinnamastā. An interesting story from the *Rājataraṅgiṇī* tells us how the mysterious power of Yoginīs was conveyed to a man. It is said that a Kashimiri royal minister, Sandhimat, was wrongly accused of treason and put to death on a stake. Wild wolves fed on his body, reducing it to a skeleton, until one night a group of divine Yoginīs arrived, put his body back together and recalled his spirit. Each Yoginī then had sex with him; in yogic parlance they consumed his sexual fluids. Subsequently, he was made king, which meant the Yoginīs repaid his sexual offering with kingship.[36] This story clearly indicates that the sexual intercourse is a kind of conduit through which the devotee can access and obtain the magical power of goddesses,[37] that in the Tantric tradition it generally takes place in the cremation ground which is the most polluted and dangerous place[38] and that the person who is supposed to get the magical power through the sexual intercourse or ritual is as a rule a male practitioner. A conjunction of the sexual intercourse and cremation ground is the most important feature of the iconography of several ferocious Mahāvidyās as is shown below.

Kālī, known as Ādyavidyā (the first *vidyā*), displays an explicit sexual symbolism. Her most popular form in eastern India, known as Dakṣiṇakālikā, is often described as a naked, ferocious and young woman copulating with Śiva in reverse pose in the cremation ground.[39] Sometimes Kālī, portrayed as standing naked on Śiva indicating her dominance during intercourse,[40] is worshipped in some parts of West Bengal (for example, Navadvipa) during the festival known as *Śaktirāsa*, when she is called Śavāśivā.[41] Though Dakṣiṇakālī shares some of her features with Kāli-Cāmuṇḍā, the well-known warrior goddess in the *Devīmāhātmya* (7.4-7), there are noticeable differences between them: the former is naked, haunts the cremation ground, and copulates with Śiva, whereas the latter is not naked and has nothing to do with the cremation ground and sex. In fact, the form of Mahāvidyā Kālī, seated naked on the inert body of Śiva, and immersed in the pleasure of reverse sexual intercourse, is rarely used outside esoteric worship.[42]

The iconography of the second Mahāvidyā, Tārā, originally important in the Buddhist tradition, also demonstrates the conjunction of two imageries, namely, the sexual intercourse and the cremation ground. She is more like Kālī in appearance than any of the other Mahāvidyās, and the name Tārā is often employed to denote Kāli in many Śākta texts. In several *dhyānas*, she is said to be dwelling in the cremation ground and standing on the corpse.[43] Though she is not as erotic as Kālī, she is also depicted as a sexually powerful woman in several images.[44]

The iconography of the most awful goddess Chinnamastā (or Chinnamuṇḍā), the fifth Mahāvidya, is characterized by several striking elements such as self-decapitation, nudity, vivid sexual symbolism and so on. Like Tārā, Chinnamastā was a Buddhist goddess who came to be incorporated in Śākta Tantric tradition during the early medieval period.[45] She was known as Vajrayoginī, the 'leader of Yoginī hordes' in the Vajrayāna pantheon,[46] visualized as naked in the cremation ground and sexually impassioned and 'steaming' with blood.[47] The earliest Hindu image of Chinnamastā has been identified by Donaldson in a sixteenth century Caṇḍī temple in Orissa.[48] The goddess here is shown as assuming a walking posture, while standing on a lotus. She is naked, wears a garland of skull, and holds her severed head in her left hand and a sword in her right hand. Three streams of blood spring from her throat and fall into the mouth of her severed head and the mouths of two attendants. These female attendants hold a sword and a skull bowl in their hands.

The most arresting iconographic feature of Chinnamastā is probably her sex organ which is distinctively depicted in many images. For instance, a miniature painting of Chinnamasta by Molaram (late eighteenth century) depicts her squatting naked above Śiva and having sexual intercourse in reverse position.[49] Her depiction as headless with prominently exposed genitalia has led some scholars to suggest a linkage between Chinnamastā and the headless and nude goddess, the so-called 'Lajjāgaurī'.[50] However, the symbolic meaning of the headless and nude Chinnamastā is quite different from that of Lajjāgaurī. The former suggests her aggressive sexuality and destructive power, whereas the latter is rather related with women's fertility and life-giving power.[51] The *Śaktisaṅgama*

Tantra relates an interesting story about Chinnamastā's domineering sexuality according to which the goddess was in reverse sexual intercourse with Śiva, and she dismounted Śiva before he ejaculated.[52] This implies that their sexual intercourse is not aimed at reproduction or sexual satisfaction of a man.

The Tantrik imagery of sexual intercourse may be interpreted as the supreme union of two aspects of reality, represented by Śiva, the male/inert principle, and Śakti, the dynamic aspect of creation. The choice of the cremation ground for the intercourse of the ferocious Mahāvidyās is due to its being a place where the barrier between the visible and invisible worlds is most permeable; it is a place of traffic of spirits, of coming and going from one world to another, a liminal place, betwixt and between worlds, where radical transformation takes place.[53] Moreover, the cremation ground is unique for its location, situated neither within nor outside the society. Comparable to *vana* on one hand[54] and marginal to *kṣetra* on the other, it was perceived as dangerous and polluted and, at the same time, as an important source of uncontrollable and unpredictable power. This apparently paradoxical perception of the cremation ground grew out of the interaction between sedentary and non-sedentary societies over the centuries during which *vana* elements were assimilated by the dominant brāhmaṇical ideology of *kṣetra* and were given a new meaning. For instance, Mātangī, the goddess of the forest and jungle, came to be worshiped in the cremation ground.[55] Although she is called "Uccisṭa-Caṇḍālinī (Caṇḍāla women who take left-over)" in one Tantric text,[56] she often appeared as a *vidyādharī*, the possessor of ambiguous magical power of *vana* in the earlier tradition, and became the goddess of pollution and low-caste people.[57] This change demonstrates how the obscure and unbound supernatural power was viewed, categorized, and conceptualized differently in the course of time.

The Tantric ritual manuals and texts often claim that women from low caste or tribal groups are suitable sexual partners of male practitioners. According to the *Kulārṇava Tantra* (7. 42-43), Caṇḍālī (untouchable), Carmakārī (leather worker), Mātangī (Mātanga tribe woman), Pukkasī (huntress), Śvapacī (woman who cooks a dog), Khaṭṭakī (meat seller), Kaivartī (fisher woman) and Viśva-Yośitā (wife of all, that is prostitutes) are considered as the representative "eight Kula-Śaktis". Further, it enumerates the "eight non Kula-Śaktis" as follows: Kandukī (cook), Sauṇḍikī (wine seller), Śastrajīvī (fighter), Rajjakī (dyer), Gāyakī (singer), Rajakī (sweeper), Śilpī (artisan) and Kaulikī (weaver). The *Hevajra Tantra* (3.10) also tells us the name of eight Yoginīs who were originally the women of the lowest class: they are Garuī, Caurī, Vetālī, Ghasmarī, Śavarī, Caṇḍalī, Ḍombinī and Pukkasī. Living as they did on the fringe of the agrarian society, they were personifications of the goddess(es) of marginality, and according to the Tantric beliefs and practices, sexual intercourse with them was the way to obtain the power of "others" who were segregated and excluded from the social mainstream. By choosing a sexual partner from among such a group of people, male Tantric practitioners could fulfill their religious aim while retaining conventional gender relation and causing only minimal disruption of social order.[58]

It appears from the above discussion that the concept of Mahāvidyās is incompatible with the long cherished view of the female power (*Śakti*) as the material cause of creation, that is, the cosmic 'Mother'.[59] The "Mother Goddess" has been the generic term for a number of goddesses and the concept of "fertility" dominates the interpretation of their sensuous images. But our survey of the images of ferocious and sexually voracious goddesses makes us reconsider this essentialist approach which presupposes the "Śaktihood of all women".[60] They are naked, sexual, and vigorous, but have nothing to do with reproduction. Their power does not derive from any inherent creativity, but from their polluting potential and destructiveness as perceived from the brāhmaṇical and male-centered perspective of the sedentary society over centuries.

ENDNOTES

1. A.K. Coomaraswamy, *History of Indian and Indonesian Art*, Dover Publications, New York, (rep.) 1965, p. 64.

2. K.R. van Kooij, "Iconography of the Battlefield: The Case of Chinnamastā" in J.E.M. Houben and K.R. van Kooij, eds., *Violence Denied: Violence and Rationalization of Violence in South Asian Cultural History*, E.J. Brill, Leiden, 1999, p. 257.
3. For a critical survey of Jung's impact on the studies of Ḍākinīs and other ferocious Tantric goddesses see J. Simmer-Brown, *Ḍākinī's Warm Breath: The Feminine Principle in Tibetan Buddhism*, Shambhala Publication, Boston and London, 2001, pp. 5–17.
4. In Jungian psychology a "shadow" means the sum of all qualities repressed from the self-image of a single person or society because they oppose or even threaten the moral attitude dominating the respective person or group. Based on the concept of shadow, Herrmann-Pfandt discusses the anti-ideal character of Ḍakinīs or Śākinis in Indian society: ("The Good Woman's Shadow: Some Aspects of the Dark Nature of Ḍakinīs and Śākinīs in Hinduism", in A. Michaels, C. Vogelsanger, and A. Wilke, eds., *Wild Goddess in India and Nepal*, Peter Lang, Bern, 1996, pp. 39–70.
5. M. Shaw, *Passionate Enlightenment: Women in Tantric Buddhism*, Munshiram Manoharlal, Delhi, 1998, pp. 4–19. Idem, 'Is Vajrayogini a Feminist?' in A. Hiltebeitel and K.M. Erndl, eds., *Is the Goddess a Feminist?: The Politics of South Asian Goddesses*, Oxford University Press, Delhi, 2000, pp. 173–5.
6. M. Shaw, "Is Vajrayogini a Feminist?", p. 172.
7. S.K. Patro, *A Feminist Reading of Womanhood in 'Dark' Kālī Tradition*, Indian Society for Promoting Christian Knowledge, Delhi, 2005, pp. 258–64.
8. The cluster of ten goddesses known as the Mahāvidyās (Kālī, Tārā, Tripurāsundarī, Bhuvaneśvarī, Bhairavī, Chinnamastā, Dhūmavatī, Bagalāmukhī, Mātaṅgī and Kamalā), is the most comprehensive Śākta Tantric feminine pantheon, which was formed in the conjunction of various religious streams in eastern India. Although some of the above mentioned goddesses (Kālī, Tārā and Kamalā) are traced back to the very early phase of history, the Mahāvidyās are known as a distinctive group from the 12th century as is attested by the *Mahābhāgavata Purāṇa* and the *Devībhāgavata Purāṇa*. For the process of formation of the pantheon, see J.E. Shin, "Daśa Mahāvidyās in Lower Ganga and Brahmaputra Valleys (7th-15th Centuries)", unpublished Ph.D. Dissertation, University of Delhi, 2007, pp. 86–121.
9. In the *Atharvaveda* (vi. 116, 1; xi. 7, 10; 8, 3), the *Taittirīya Saṃhitā*, (II. I, 2, 8; v. I, 7, 2) and the *Aitareya Brāhmaṇa* (VIII. 23, 8, 9), *vidyā* denotes knowledge, especially that of three Vedas, which are called *trayī vidyā* (the three fold knowledge). In a more special

sense *vidyā* occurs in the lists of objects of study in the *Śatapatha Brāhmaṇa* (XI. 5, 6, 8), see A.A. Macdonell and A.D. Keith, *Vedic Index of Names and Subjects*, vol. 2, Motilal Banarsidass, Delhi, (rep.) 1995, p. 299.

10. J. Grafe, "Outlines of a Classification of *Vidyādharas*", in *Archiv Orientalni*, vol. 67, 1999, p. 233.
11. J.A.B. van Buitenen, "The Indian Hero as Vidyādhara", in Ludo Rocher, ed., *Studies in Indian Literature and Philosophy: Collected Articles of J.A.B. van Buitenen*, American Institute of Indian Studies, Motilal Banarsidass, Delhi, 1988, p. 140.
12. As to the textual information on *vijjādhara* in the Theravāda Buddhist canons, see J. Grafe, op, cit, p. 232.
13. *Bṛhatkathāślokasaṃgraha* by Budhasvāmin, (*The Emperor of the Sorcerers*), trans. by Sir James Mallinson, New York University Press and J.C.C. Foundation, New York, 2005, 14.3 ff.; 20.327; 20. 324; 20.116.
14. For instance, the *Raghuvaṃśa* (ed., G.R. Nandargikar, Motilal Banarsidass, Delhi, 1982, XI, 9) explains a special *vidyā* as follows: one day, a brāhmaṇ Kauśika asked Rāma to guard his sacrifice from assaults of the demons. The king ordered Rāma to go with the Muni together with Lakṣmaṇa. By the power of the two magical spells called *bala* and *atibala* (*balātibalayo vidyāyoḥ*) which they were taught by the Muni, the two princes felt no more fatigue on the way.
15. D.L. Snellgrove, *Indo-Tibetan Buddhism: Indian Buddhists and Their Tibetan Successors*, Serindia Publications, London, 1987, p. 141
16. The *Yoginī Tantra*, ed., B. Shastri, Bharatiya Vidya Bhavan, Delhi, 1982, II.7.28, mentions that *mantras* are proclaimed to be male deities, *vidyās* are known to be female deities.
17. *Mahābhārata* ed., V.S. Sukthankar et al., Bhandarkar Oriental Research Institute, Poona, 1942, 3. 221, 20.
18. *Kathāsaritsāgara* by Somadeva (tr. James Mallinson, New York University Press, 2007), 10.95; 18.218, 227, 240; 33.170, 178; 37.186; 38.54; 42.32, 34, 38; 45.280, 290; 52.161.
19. *Devīmāhātmya*, (*Durgāsaptaśatī Saptaṭīkā-saṃvalitā*), ed., H. Sharma, Venkatesvara Press, Bombay, 1988, 1.44; 4.8 and 1.58; 11.21.
20. For a recent comprehensive study of the goddess Sarasvatī, see C. Ludvik, *Sarasvatī: Riverine Goddess of Knowledge: From the Manuscript-Carrying vina Player to the Weapon-Wielding Defender of Dharma*, E.J. Brill, Leiden, 2007.
21. As to detailed information on the iconographic features of the earliest image of Sarasvatī in Jain tradition see P. Pal, *The Peaceful*

Liberators: Jain Art from India, Thames & Hudson, Los Angeles, 1994, pp. 26, 171.

22. M. Shaw, *Buddhist Goddesses of India*, Princeton University Press, Princeton, 2006, pp. 166–9.
23. Once upon a time, a Mātaṅgī girl called Prakṛti or Caṇḍāla loved Ānanda, disciple of Buddha. To attract Ānanda, she asked help of her mother, Mahavidyādharī. By her magic (*vidyā*), Ānanda left the monastery to seek Prakṛti out. Arriving there, he stood near the mother's altar and began to weep. He prayed to the Buddha to rescue him, and the Buddha, aware of his predicament, nullified the power of the Caṇḍāla woman's *mantras*. Ānanda returned to the monastery: *Divyavadana*, story 33: *śardūlakarṇa*, 314–25.
24. In her thousand name hymn from the *Nandyāvarta Tantra*, Mātaṅgī bears several epithets that associate her with Savareśvarī. For instance, she is described as one "who lives in the forest", "who knows the forest", and is also called "Śavarī". In her *dhyāna mantra* in the *Śāradātilaka Tantra* (12.128), Raja-Mātaṅgī is said to listen to the chattering of green parrots, to play a *vīnā*, to have paintings of leaves on her forehead, and to wear flower garlands in her hair and conch sells as earrings. She is also said to control all wild animals (12.98) (D. Kinsley, *Tantric Visions of the Divine Feminine: The Ten Mahāvidyās*, Motilal Banarsidass, Delhi, 1998, p. 219).
25. *The Kādambarī* (C.M. Ridding tr., Mushiram Manoharlal, Delhi, 1974, pp. 28–31) describes the life of Śavaras as follows; "... their one religion is offering flesh to Durgā... their Śāstra is the cry of the jackal... their kingdom is in deserted woods... their friends are the bows that work their cruel deeds." It also tells us that the leader of the Śavaras is named Mātaṅga who was Ekalavya in another birth.
26. G.D. Sontheimer, "The *Vana* and the *Kṣetra*: The Tribal Background of Some Famous Cults", in G.C. Tripathi and H. Kulke, eds., *Religion and Society in Eastern India*, The Eschmann Memorial Fund, Bhubaneshwar, 1994, pp. 129–30. Some scholars have, however, made a distinction between *grāma* (village) and *araṇya* (forest). According to Malamoud, for example, *grāma* is maintained and sustained by *dharma*, i.e. social rules, whereas *araṇya* is the other world, the world of the gods. See C. Malamoud, *Cooking the World: Ritual and Thought in Ancient India* (translated from the French by David White), Oxford University Press, Delhi, 1998, pp. 74–81.
27. For example, '*matṛgaṇa*' (a group of mothers) is said to live in trees, caves, mountains, crossroads, and cremation grounds. See

Mahābhārata, Śalyaparvan, 45.39. Similarly, Mahādevī Durgā is said to dwell on summits of mountains, terrible places, rivers, caves, forests and groves. *Harivaṃśa*, ed., P.L. Vaidya, Bhandarkar Oriental Research Institute, Poona, 1971, vol. II. no. 8, 7–8.

28. G.D. Sontheimer, op. cit, p. 128.
29. R.S. Sharma, "Social Changes in Early Medieval India" in his *Rethinking India's Past*, New Delhi: Oxford University Press, 2009, pp. 257–63; V. Nath, *The Purāṇic World: Environment, Gender, Ritual and Myth*, Manohar, New Delhi, 2009, pp. 220–45 and B.D. Chattopadhyaya, *The Making of Early Medieval India*, Oxford University Press, Delhi, 1994, p. 16ff.
30. Elsewhere, I have dealt with this process focusing on the transformation of the cult of a local goddess, Kāmākhyā, and her association with different groups of multiple feminine divinities (J.E. Shin, "Yoni, Yoginīs and Mahāvidyās: Feminine Divinities from Early Medieval Kāmarūpa to Medieval Koch Behar", *Studies in History*, vol. 26, no. 1, 2010, pp. 1–29). For the brāhmaṇical transfiguration of autochthonous goddesses like the group of Mātṛkas, see J.E. Shin, "From *Mātṛgaṇa to Sapta Mātṛkās*: Brāhmaṇical Taransformation of Autochthonous Goddesses", *Toyobunkakenkyujo Kiyou (the Memoirs of Institute for Advanced Studies on Asia)*, no. 116, 2011, pp. 566–92.
31. It has been argued that in the formation of Hinduism "the process of metamorphosis is dominated by the mediation of the *brāhmaṇa* and his text... dominant *kṣetra* element puts a new meaning into what could originate in the *vana*" (B.D. Chattopadhyaya, "Reappearence of the Goddess" in his *Studying Early India: Archeology, Texts and Historical Issues*, Permanent Black, Delhi, 2003, p. 186).
32. The compounds such as *sarpavidyā* (knowledge of or connected with serpents), *devajanavidyā* (knowledge of demon), *devavidyā* (mythology), *bhūtavidyā* (demonology), and *nakṣatravidyā* (astrology and astronomy) indicate that the term *vidyā* is used to indicate the secret knowledge or the special skill related with popular religious practices (J. Gonda, *History of Indian Literature: Vedic Literature*, vol. I, fasc. 1, Otto Harrasowitz, Wiesbaden, 1975, p. 408 n).
33. The *Sūtrakṛtānga Sūtra* mentions the art of Caṇḍāla among evil occult sciences which include, among others, the art of making one miserable, lose wits, fall asleep, fall down, immobile or sick, and impregnating a woman, and states that its practitioners were to be reborn among the Asuras and evildoers. Their aboriginal background is suggested also by a reference to Śavaras, Draviḍas,

Kalingas, Gauḍas and Gāndhāras (*Jaina Sutras*, Book II, Lecture II, Part II., p. 366–7).

34. *Mahābhāgavata Purāṇa*, (P.K. Sharma, ed., Eastern Book Linkers, Delhi, 1942) 8.72-75. The *Bṛhaddharma Purāṇa* (H. Shastri, ed., Krishnadas Academy, Varanasi, 1974), however, gives a slightly different list including *māraṇa, uccāṭana, kṣobhaṇ, mohana, drāvaṇa, jṛmbhaṇa* (causing to yawn), *stambha* (make immobile or paralyze), *saṃhāra* (destruction) *vāñchit-ārtha* (fulfillment of wished benefit) and so on (Madhyakhaṇḍa, 6.131-133).
35. The *Yoginī Tantra* (I.4.3) enumerates the six acts as *Śānti* (peace), *vaśya* (subjugation), *stambhana* (making immobile), *vidveṣaṇa* (generating enmity), *uccāṭana* (eradication) and *māraṇa* (killing), though the list found in different Tantric texts may not be the same. For the importance and implication of the Tantric six-acts, see G. Bühnemann "Six Rites of Magic" in D. G. White, ed., *Tantra in Practice*, Motilal Banarsidass, Delhi, 2001, pp. 447–62.
36. *Rājataraṅgiṇī* (M.A. Stein, tr., Motilal Banarsidass, Delhi, 1961), vol. 2. 65b-117b.
37. D. G. White, *Kiss of Yoginī: 'Tantric Sex' in its South Asian Contexts*, The University of Chicago Press, Chicago, 2003, p. 195
38. For the practice of sexual yoga in the cremation ground see S. Tsuda, "The Cult of Śmaśāna, the Realities of Tantrism", in T. Goudriaan, ed., *Sanskrit Tradition and Tantrism* (Panels of the 7th World Sanskrit Conference, General Editor: J. Bronkhorst, vol. II, E.J. Brill, Leiden, 1990, p. 104. In Tantric ritual, especially the Yoginī cult of the non-dual Śaiva Trika, the sexual fluids, along with other polluting bodily substances, were offered to the Yoginīs in the cremation ground. According to Sanderson, "the goal of initiate was to force or entice these Yoginīs to gather before him and receive him into their band (*Yoginīgaṇaḥ*) sharing with him their miraculous powers and esoteric knowledge"("Śaivism and Tantric Tradition", in S. Sutherland et al., ed., *The World's Religion: Religions of Asia*, Routledge, London, 1988, p. 671).
39. For a discussion of the *dhyānas* of Dakṣiṇakālikā as given in the *Tantrasāra* see D.C. Sircar, "Tantrasāradhṛta Dhyānamālā', (reprinted from *the Journal of Ancient Indian History*, vol. 6, 1972–1973), Calcutta: University of Calcutta, 1973, p. 83.
40. D. Kinsley "Corpse, Severed Heads, and Sex" in C.A. Humes and R.F. McDermott, eds., *Breaking Boundaries with the Goddess: New Directions in the Study of Śāktism*, Manohar, New Delhi, 2009, p. 143. The *Bṛhaddharma Purāṇa* (23.11–17) describes Kālī as standing naked on Śiva lying on his back like a dead body. She has a smiling face, and is engaged in drinking wine and blood. She is adorned with ornaments and is surrounded by Yoginīs

who dance and drink blood and wine. During the worship, the worshippers are singing '*Mālasī* song' and utter words expressive of male and female generative organs. Besides, animals are to be sacrificed, and cloths, ornaments, *pāyasa* etc. are to be offered. Though the bit about reverse copulation is omitted in this description, the sexual connotation of Kālī worship is explicit.

41. P. Pal, *Hindu Religion and Iconography according to the Tantrasāra*, Vichitra Press, Los Angeles, 1981, pp. 64–5.
42. S. Gupta, "The worship of Kālī According to the *Toḍalatantra*" in D.G. White, ed., *Tantra in Practice*, p. 466.
43. *Kālikā Purāṇa* (B. Bisvanarayan, ed., Nag Publishers, Delhi, 1992), 61:63b–68 and D.C. Sircar, op. cit, p. 25ff.
44. For example, Tārā is shown copulating with Śiva in the painting by Molaram (late 18th century, Garhwal, Himachal Pradesh). It is presently kept in Bharat Kala Bhavan, Varanasi. For this image of Tara, see D. Kinsley, *Tantric Visions of the Divine Feminine:The Ten Mahāvidyās*, Motilal Banarsidass, Delhi, p. 101.
45. Regarding the Buddhist origin of Chinnamastā, see E.A. Benard, *Chinnamastā: The Aweful Buddhist and Hindu Tantric Goddess*, Motilal Banarsidass, Delhi, 2000, p. 58.
46. For different images of Vajrayoginī see E. English, *Vajrayoginī, Her Visualizations, Rituals and Forms: A Study of the Cult of the Vajrayoginī*, Wisdom Publications, Boston, 2002, pp. 50–107. According to English, among various forms of Vajrayoginī, Trikāyavajrayoginī is known as Chinnamastā, ibid., p. 44.
47. *Sādhanamālā*, ed., B. Bhattacharyya, Oriental Institute, Baroda, pp. 452–3.
48. T.E. Donaldson *Hindu Temple Art of Orissa*, E.J. Brill, Leiden, 1985–87, p. 742, fig. 1827.
49. For this image, see D. Kinsley, *Tantric Visions of the Divine Feminine*, p. 158.
50. P.K. Agrawala, "The Headless Nude Goddess and Her Identification", in T.S. Maxwell, ed., *Eastern Approaches: Essays on Asian Art and Archeology*, Oxford University Press, Delhi, 1992, pp. 63–73 and D. Kinsley, *Tantric Visions of the Divine Feminine*, p. 146. Though the name Lajjāgaurī is quite arbitrary, it has been used to describe a nude feminine deity who appears in various forms and found in several places in India. For the diverse forms of Lajjāgaurī see C.R. Bolon, *Forms of the Goddess Lajjā Gaurī in India Art*, Motilal Banarsidass, Delhi, 1997.
51. It has been suggested that Lajjāgaurī's sitting posture is similar to a woman who is about to deliver a child. Moreover, a lotus which replaces the head of her image is the symbol of procreation

and recreation: J.B. Bapat, "The Lajjāgaurī: Mother, Wife or Yoginī", in J.B. Bapat and I. Mabbett, eds., *The Iconic Female: Goddesses of India, Nepal and Tibet*, Somaiya Publications, Mumbai, 2009, pp. 84–9.

52. *Śaktisaṃgama Tantra*, vol. 4: *Chinnamastā Khaṇḍa* 5.152-73 cited in D. Kinsely, *Tantric Visions of the Divine Feminine*, p. 148.
53. D. Kinsely, "Corpse, Severed Heads, and Sex", p. 147.
54. G.D. Sontheimer argues that in Tamil "*kāṭu*" means forest as well as *śmaśāna* (op. cit., p. 130)
55. P. Pal, *Hindu Religion and Iconography*, p. 89.
56. According to the story of Mātangī's origin found in the *Prāṇatoṣinī Tantra* (Basumati Sahitya Mandir, Calcutta, 1928, pp. 379-81) Pārvatī disguises herself as a Caṇḍāla woman and attracts Śiva. While they make love, Śiva himself changes into Caṇḍāla. After that Pārvatī asks Śiva for a boon. Her request is: "as you made love to me in the form of a Caṇḍālini, this form will last forever and will be known as Uccista-Caṇḍālinī. Only after performing suitable worship to this form will you be worshipped and your worship be made fruitful", cited in D. Kinsley, *Tantric Visions of the Divine Feminine*: p. 213.
57. Regarding the close linkage between the goddess Mātangī and low caste people, see D. Kinsley, *Tantric Visions of the Divine Feminine*, pp. 217–8.
58. The presence of low-caste women in the Tantric ritual is a very complicated issue and it is certainly far more complex than a matter of sexual availability or sexual exploitation of women. I have discussed this point elsewhere. See J.E. Shin, "Tantric Gender Ideology: The Images of Female in Shakta Tantricism in Early Medieval India", *Social Science Probings*, vol. 16, no. 1, 2004, 85–109.
59. For the concept of Śakti, see S. Gupta, "Women in the Śaiva/Śākta Ethos", in J. Leslie, ed., *Roles and Rituals for Hindu Women*, Motilal Banarsidass, Delhi, 1991, p. 206 and F.A. Marglin, *Wives of God-King: The Rituals of the Devadāsīs of Puri*, Oxford University Press, Delhi, 1985, pp. 98, 231–2, 290–1, 302–03.
60. This assumption became another theoretical stereotype in many cultural and feminist studies. For instance, based on Marglin's concept of transformative principle, Shaw has claimed that this power [*Śakti*] supersedes and transcends hierarchy because its efficacy does not depend upon the social status of the beneficiary. By virtue of their occupations, low caste women possess and embody transformative power, or female energy. See M. Shaw, *Passionate Enlightenment*. p. 61.

11

Homosexuality in Ancient Indian Literature

Shalini Shah

For a long time, the perception in the academic world was that 'sex' which refers to the erogenous capacities and genital functions of the human body, could only be a matter of study by sexologists like Havelock Ellis, Alfred Kinsey, Masters and Johnson, or by social anthropologists like Malinowski.[1] But while there could be no history of sex, there could be histories of sexuality, which was a cultural interpretation of the human body's sexual capacity. After all, sexuality is intelligible only in relation to the warp and woof of the entire social fabric, which itself is made of marriage, family, behavioural conventions, aesthetic values, moral codes, gender roles, and even the paradigms of sexual excitement. If it was difficult to write the history of sexuality, it was even more difficult to write about seemingly deviant/unconventional sexual behaviour like homosexuality, because here one had to deal with erasures and silences of the sources.

Homosexuality has often been regarded as an alien[2] sexual practice which, it has been argued, was thrust into the Indian public cultural discourse only due to the influence of malevolent western media. A small, but fairly vehement, section of Indian society also argues that homosexual emotions and the act of buggering came into the Indian sub-continent under the influence of Islam; and *Bāburnāma*, which honestly records the young Bābur's homoerotic feelings, is much bandied about as its evidence.

In contemporary India two major public debates on this issue occurred when Deepa Mehta's film *Fire* was released. The plot of the film revolved around the lesbian sexual coupling of the two sisters-in-law. Various civil groups have also come together to successfully challenge the colonial-era Indian Penal Code laws which treated sodomy as a criminal offence. But even as civil society grappled with the reform of criminal law, the issue of homosexuality was once again thrust into the public eye by the media persecution and institutional victimization of a homosexual professor in a premier Indian university. More recently speculations on the homoerotic relationship between Mahatma Gandhi and his German friend and sponsor in South Africa Hermann Kallenbach have received much media attention. The present paper, beginning with a brief discussion of some important studies of homosexuality in ancient Greco-Roman society, attempts a historiographical survey of the same sex love in ancient India and argues that it was part of Western as well as Indian cultural traditions though its visibility and reception in them may have differed.

I

Contrary to the popular Indian middle-class perception that the idea of homosexuality has always been centre-stage in the western cultural discourse, it came to the 'public' attention in the West only in the nineteenth century with the rise of gay movement in Germany,[3] though the educated men of Europe with their training in the Classics were aware of it even earlier. Even so, Friedrich Karl Forberg, who extensively illustrated Greek and Latin sexual practices in his *Apophoreta*,[4] published in 1824, did not refer to paederasty.[5]

Another German scholar, writing a century later, Paul Brandt, however, devoted 88 pages to the practice of paederasty in his *Sexual Life in Ancient Greece*, published in 1928 and more than four decades later, in 1976, Vern L. Bullough, sought to study such variant practices as homosexuality, bestiality, masturbation, incest, rape etc. in his *Sexual Variance in Society and History* (1976).[6] His work was followed by the publication of K.J. Dover's *Greek Homosexuality in 1978.*[7] It was a pioneering work on the varying aspects of homoerotic behaviour and attitudes in ancient Greece, and also provided an invaluable analysis of the iconographical representation of such activities culled from the extensive repertory of attic vase paintings. But the most celebrated work on the western classical world's sexual philosophy and practice has been *A History of Sexuality*[8] by Michel Foucault, first published in French between 1976 and 1984. He commented extensively on male homosexual practices as mentioned in classical sources, but completely ignored lesbian desires articulated by Sappho in her poetic corpus.

Since the publication of Foucault's work, however, feminist scholars in the West have tried to highlight the homoerotic as also the homo-social world (a range of relations between females, and not just genital sexual contact) of Greco-Roman women in antiquity. An important work that inaugurated the academic discussion on lesbianism was the influential paper "Compulsory Heterosexuality and Lesbian Existence" by Adrienne Rich(1980).[9] She was the first to argue that heterosexuality was the central organizing principle of patriarchy, which had prevented female bonding. She coined the term "lesbian continuum" to refer to a women-connected existence, which may or may not be a genital sexual experience. Bernadette Brooten's *Love between Women: Early Christian Response to Female Homoeroticism* (1996)[10] was a study of women who preferred women in Roman and Christian societies in late-antiquity. An important aspect of Brooten's study was to show how the female homo-erotic relation was situated differently from male homosexuality in early Christianity. The *Lesbian Desire in the Lyrics of Sappho* (1997) by Jane Snyder,[11] and *Among Women: From the Homo-social to the Homoerotic in the Western Ancient World* (2002)[12] edited by Rabinowitz and Auanger are other important works in this genre. The ideological and theoretical vigour of much of all the above-mentioned works on the issue of male and female homosexuality derived from the political context of the early-1980s with its lesbian and gay liberation movements in the West, as also the academic engagement with writing the history of sexuality.[13]

While there is little doubt that homosexuality was a part of the civilizational ethos of the Greco-Roman world, it was also present in other cultures. Van Gulik[14] points out that in ancient Chinese medical and alchemical lore connected with sexuality, homosexuality was not considered an illness or disorder. However, in case of the Indian civilization, the overall impression of many scholars has been that the erotic was firmly entrenched in heterosexual practices. A.L. Basham in his celebrated work *The Wonder that was India* (1954)[15] took the view that "the erotic life of ancient India was generally heterosexual. Homosexualism of both sexes was not wholly unknown; it is condemned briefly in the law books, and the *Kāmasūtra* treats it cursorily and with little enthusiasm. Literature almost ignores it. In this respect ancient India was *far healthier* than most other ancient cultures" (emphasis ours). D.D. Kosambi[16] in his brilliant introduction to the edited volume of Vidyakara's *Subhaṣitaratnakoṣa* (1957), does not fail to appreciate, like Basham, the lack of same-sex erotica in this work. In fact he talks of "certain healthiness in the sexual depiction, where we hear little of prostitution and nothing of *homosexuality or other abnormalities*" (emphasis ours).

Of late, the heterosexual normativity of ancient Indian civilization has been problematized by scholars, both Indian and foreign. They have analysed a vast corpus of ancient Indian literary texts of all genres and all sectarian hues—in Sanskrit, Pāli, Prākrit and Tamil—to illuminate how sexual desire was conceived for members of the same sex. One of the earliest writings on this subject was Arvind Sharma's paper "Homosexuality and Hinduism",[17] published in 1993, which seeks to provide a survey of evidence for homosexual practices in ancient Indian texts classified by him under the headings of *dharma, artha, kāma,* and *mokṣa.* Its inadequacy is evident, among other things, from the fact that most of the time Sharma cites evidence from secondary sources and does not subject the various genres of the text to any systematic analysis. For example he does not analyse even the evidence from the *Kāmasūtra*, which is the text par excellence on eroticism in ancient India and also refers to homosexual practices. Its author, Vātsyāyana, states that two men friends (*nāgaraka*), who have complete trust in each other may unite (*paraspara parigraham*) and does not make any value judgement or elaborate his statement.[18] But his commentator, Yaśodhara,[19] attributes the homosexual practices to the marginals of society–young servants (*paricārakāḥ*), old men (*gatavayaśa*), impotent (*mandarāga*), and those for whom women are not available (*strīsvabdhavṛtāya*). Similarly, Vātsyāyana[20] refers to anal sex being practiced by the people of the South (*dakṣiṇātya*) in a non-pejorative tone, a fact also corroborated by the Tamil epic *Śilappadikāram* in which there is a reference to a thousand, brilliantly attired *kanjuka* boy-prostitutes who are sent as a gift for Cera king Śenguṭṭuvan.[21] But Yaśodhara refers to this act as 'the wrong way' (*vimarga*), since it is not the place for the secretion of the semen and, in fact, considers it appropriate for the members of the third sex (*tṛtīyaprakṛti*). Further, Vātsyāyana[22] also refers to lesbian practices in the polygynous royal household and attributes their prevalence to the the non-availability of men. He says that they either dress up some women as men and satisfy themselves, or they use dildos (*apadravya*) of various kinds, which are seen as the substitute for penile penetration. While Sharma ignores all the above evidence, Kumkum Roy[23] does not see any evidence of lesbian sex in these verses and maintains that such sex is defined in terms of categories of heterosexual intercourse where some women act or are dressed like men and that it was either marginalized or given recognition only by assimilating it into various heterosexual roles which had legitimacy within the dominant tradition. Also, the obsessive focus on male penetration as the cause for women's erotic satisfaction explains why lesbian relations were all but invisible outside the realm of sexuality, and within it they were couched in terms of lack of masculine presence as is implicit in Yaśodhara's statement that women of secluded quarters (*antaḥpuragatāḥ*) indulge in mouth congress (*auparisṭakam*) with each other.[24]

Arvind Sharma not only ignores the *Kāmasūtra* evidence but is also dismissive of the information available from other sources. "...In the vast corpus of tantric literature", he tells us, "there is a not a single case of homosexuality proper",[25] though he himself refers to a profusion of variant sexual practices mentioned in it.[26] His reference to what he calls "symbolic homosexualism"[27] in some forms of devotional Hinduism remains unexplained[28] just as his statement that homosexual practices are not evident in early Indian erotic art[29] is without any basis and is too sweeping to inspire confidence. Similarly his view that medieval and modern Hinduism tends to associate the homosexual practice "with an outcrop with whom its encounter has not been pleasant or peaceful" echoes the narrow Right-wing perception according to which it was transported to India by Islam and Christianity, and amounts to a denial of its prevalence in early India.

Many scholars have, however, examined early Indian texts to show the prevalence of homosexual practices in pre-Islamic India. For example, in his paper published in 1992, Leonard Zwilling analysed the issue of homosexuality with reference to its ethical and psychological implications on the basis of the Pāli texts. He also examined the status of homosexual clergy and laity in Buddhism, and drew attention to the references to effeminate men or *paṇḍakas* and to their homoerotic tendencies in the early Vinaya literature[30] which describes *Asittapaṇḍaka* as a person who satisfies his sexual desires by fellating another to ejaculation.[31] Both Buddhist and Jain texts see this class of people as habitually soliciting homosexual sex.[32] Such people were denied ordination in both Buddhist and Jain monastic orders[33]and one of the grounds on which a Jain monk could be expelled from the community was homosexual behaviour which is defined as sexual intercourse between two males (*puruṣayuga*) involving the mouth and anus. The Vinaya texts also show an awareness of the homoerotic tendencies rampant in closed, same-sex communities, which the monastic orders would be. They refer to mutual masturbation among nuns, though the practice seems to have been less common among them than among the monks; for explicit references to it are fewer in the *Bhikkunīvinaya* than in the *Bhikkuvinaya*.[34] In order to minimize the occasion for homosexual activity among the inmates of the *samgha* it was laid down that two nuns could not share the same bedcover, and two novices could not serve one monk. It is, however, interesting to note that in both Buddhism and Jainism, a sexual relation with a woman was treated as a greater offence than any homoerotic relationship; the former, in fact, necessitated the monk's immediate expulsion from the monastic Order. This does not mean that the Buddhist religion was more tolerant of homosexuality than Jainism. Buddhaghoṣa,[35] in his commentary on a passage of *Dīghanikāya* describing the progressive degeneration in the lifespan of human beings, explains the expression "wrong conduct" (*micchādhamma*) as "sexual desire of men for men and women for women". Thus, for him, homosexuality was a causal factor for the general decline and decadence. This sentiment is not unique to the Buddhist texts but finds expression in the brāhmaṇical sources as well. The *Mahābhārata*,[36] quite unambiguously, links it to societal decay presaging its destruction. The sage Mārkaṇḍeya, in his account of the degenerate Kali age, refers to women using their mouths as a vagina (*mukhebhagaḥ striyo rājan bhaviṣyanti yugakṣaye*) and being promiscuous. The lawgiver Manu[37] views the practice of the homosexual act as a cause of loss of caste status (*jātibhramsa*). Kalhaṇa[38] states that indulging in paederasty was a reason for the notoriety of the rule of King Kṣemagupta who was said to have male favourites (*lalitaka*), and whose court was said to be filled with, among others, corrupters of boys (*bālakadrogdhrnirbhara*).

Michael J. Sweet and Leonard Zwilling in their essay published in 1993, examined the ancient Indian Āyurvedic texts[39] according to which homosexuals, both male and female, were genetic abnormalities (*vikṛti*) and homosexual practices themselves were a deviance (*viprakṛti*). One of the terminological classifications for homosexuals elaborated by Caraka and Suśruta, say Sweet and Zwilling, is *nārīsaṇḍa*, i.e. a lesbian female. Caraka describes such a woman as man-hating (*nṛdvesinī*) and breast-less (*astanī*). Both Caraka and

Suśruta are convinced that they suffer from a diseased uterus (*yoniroga*). The male homosexuals,[40] according to them, include fellators (*asekyapuruṣa*), and the effeminate males (*strīceṣṭikakara/ narasaṇḍa*). The common causal explanation for the origin of these homosexuals is that the parents did not perform the 'correct role' (virile model of sex with man on top) during coitus. Suśruta treats the behaviour of the anal-receptive male (*kumbhika*) as acquired from "the unchaste and others (*abrahmacaryādi*) who treat their own anus as a man does women".[41] Ḍalhaṇa, in his commentary on Suśruta, explains away such people as lascivious, but also having a weak libido.

In one of their seminal papers,[42] Leonard Zwilling and Michael Sweet have discussed the linkage of homoeroticism with the third sex identity and have argued that the former was usually not central in its construction in India and that impotency was often a reason for classifying people as *tṛtīya prakṛti*. They have pointed out that it is only the *Kāmasūtra* which views same sex orientation as a crucial determinant of the third sex in both the male and female variants and refers to the third gender as bereft of both masculinity and femininity,[43] and as divided into those who resemble men and those who resemble women in terms of appearance, dress and behaviour.[44] Vātsyāyana, as also his commentator Yaśodhara, points out that both the male and female variants of the third sex engage in homosexual acts, taking the receptive role in fellatio. The female variety of *tṛtīya prakṛti* earn their livelihood openly as professional fellatrices, whereas the males take up "the profession of masseurs" using massage as a pretext to excite their clients and perform oral sex on them.[45] The *kāmasāstrīya* texts also refer to certain coital postures which may be interpreted as referring to homosexual acts. One such is the *vāḍava* coital posture. *Vāḍava* is referred to in the *Taittirīya Saṃhitā* and the *Gopatha Brāhmaṇa* as an androgynous male horse mounted by other males as if he were a mare.[46] That the members of the third sex resorted to homoerotic practices is also gleaned from narrative texts. In Vararuci's *Bhāṇa Ubhayābhisārikā*,[47] the *Viṭa* tells the eunuch Sukumārikā that she has a major advantage as compared to the other *nāyikā* for the man/*nāyaka*. When she (that is, Sukumārikā) embraces (the *nāyaka*) the breasts do not intervene. She is not afflicted with monthly periods (*ṛtu*) which is the cause of loss of attachment (*rāgadhvamsa*). She also does not get pregnant (*garbhinī*) which is the cause of the destruction of beauty (*rūpa*) and grace (*śrī*) and youth (*yauvana*) in the *nāyikā* (woman). With so many advantages (*saguna*), if the man shows no affection for her then he is certainly not fit to celebrate the love festival (*ratyutsavaṁ*).

A landmark historical study of sexuality in India is Giti Thadani's *Sakhiyani*,[48] (published in 1996), which specifically looks at lesbian desire in ancient and modern India. Though short on documentation, Thadani's monograph is rich in new insights and perspectives. Particularly useful is her chapter which documents the lesbian representation in art, sculpture as well as miniature paintings and goes against Arvind Sharma's assertion that there is no homosexual representation in the Indian erotic art. Lesbian desire, as Thadani theorizes it, is essentially a physical, erotic act amongst women. Her definition of lesbian relations is not based on a 'lesbian continuum' or women-connected existence as Adrienne Rich suggests.[49] In her discussion on ancient India Thadani focuses in particular on the Vedic texts, and reading against the grain, traces feminine cosmogonies to the lesbian couplings, that is *Jamī*.[50] However, it is difficult to accept Thadani's reading of *Jamī* exclusively as dual deities of the same sex (mainly the feminine sex). Although some *Jamīs* were pairs like mothers or sisters, others were twin brothers like Aśvins,[51] as also twin brother and sister pairs like Yama and Yamī. Furthermore, Uṣas and Varuṇa are also described in the *Ṛgveda* as *Jamī*.[52] *Jamitva* or the relationship between the *Jamīs* is based on sameness and equality. In the exorable march of Vedic society towards greater stratification along both class and gender lines, the *jamitva* fell into disuse. Kumkum Roy points out that in the *Aitareya Brāhmaṇa* a sacrificial ritual justified exclusion of the *Jamī*, who was replaced by the *patnī*.[53]

The most in-depth and systematic analysis of homosexuality has been presented by Ruth Vanita and Salim Kidwai in their *Same Sex Love in India* (2000). They not only deal with an enormous number of literary texts ranging from the Vedic to the modern Indian literature, but also provide a more expansive definition of same-sex love which is not limited to gay/lesbian 'sexual acts', but include other types of romantic same-sex attachments as well. Vanita,[54] who analyses the material for the ancient Indian section, takes pains to define the methodology of reading the texts for this form of love. She sees change of sex, rebirth,[55] cross-dressing, intense life-defining friendships, and resistance to marriage[56] as tropes for homoerotic desires. The celebrated tale of Śikhaṇḍin's change of sex in the *Mahābhārata* is interpreted from a homoerotic angle. The deep friendship between Kṛṣṇa and Arjuna is also opened to analysis for its strong homoerotic overtones; for in the *Padmapurāṇa*, the motifs of sex change and deep friendship coalesce when we find Arjuna changing into the woman Arjunī in order to sport with Kṛṣṇa.[57] The interpretation of the Kṛṣṇa-Arjuna relationship as homoerotic may be more than mere speculation as I have argued elsewhere on the basis of the evidence of the *Mahābhārata*.[58] It refers to them as *priyasakhā*,[59] which may have sexual overtones, and describes Kṛṣṇa as asking Indra for a boon of eternal friendship with him (*prītim pārthena śāśvatim*).[60] In the *Vana Parva*,[61] Kṛṣṇa declares to Arjuna "you are mine and I am yours". At another place he states that Arjuna is more important to him than his wife's children or even his kinsmen.[62] His love for Arjuna surpasses all other loves.[63] He calls Arjuna half his body[64] (*śarīrārdha*). Interestingly, the term *śarīrārdha* is exactly the same as the term *ardhāṅga*, and this term in its feminine gender stands for the word "wife". We can only speculate whether the use of the term *śarīrārdha* was original or whether it was substituted for the term *ardhāṅga* by the redactors because they were uncomfortable with its implications. Kṛṣṇa proclaims that Arjuna was dearer to him than even his own life, and that he has no desire to enjoy anything without him.[65] Throughout the *Mahābhārata* we get many references to Kṛṣṇa and Arjuna enjoying pleasure trips in each other's company[66] and the term used to describe their romp is *ramate* as in *ramatepārthamādhavo*,[67] a word for pleasurable enjoyment.[68]

Vanita also locates homoeroticism in the medieval *Bhakti* ideology, especially in the *sākhya* form of worship which was of major significance in Vaiṣṇava theology. Within this mode of worship the devotee's relation to the deity is one of tender and intimate love, often expressed in the image of two mirrors facing one-another.[69] As the image implies, perfect devotional love involves the loss of the separate identity—it is impossible to tell which mirror reflects which being. Vanita states that here the emphasis on sameness, rather on difference, is crucial to the relationship. This seems to be a throwback to the Vedic notion of *jamitva*, which was non-differentiated, non-hierarchical, and also many-a-time homoerotic. In fact, as Dimock[70] points out, in the *sākhya* form of worship, the stimuli are such sensations as may be caused by the sound of a flute, and the sight of a handsome youth.

The significance of the Sapphic love in the patriarchal world, which has not been discussed by Vanita, finds place in my work[71] (1995) based on the *Mahābhārata*, according to which Pañcacūḍā tells Nārada that when women find no males at hand, they satisfy each other's desire.[72] This reference to lesbian sexual bonding as if by default, could be interpreted as denial of the reality that some women could be actively blocking sexual access to men and the patriarchal ethos, unable to accept this behaviour, sought to explain it away as an aberration on the part of women who were, by circumstances, denied sexual/ emotional bonding with men. In the *Mahābhārata*[73] we find reference to Aṣṭāvakra's visit in the *uttara diśā* where he meets a woman who is said to be living in a women-only community. Such references attest to the prevalence of women-connected existence which did not get subsumed under patriarchy's diktat of a compulsory heterosexual existence[74] and remind us of Vātsyāyana's *Kāmasūtra*[75] which refers to *strīrājya*,[76] where lesbian sex was practiced. The location of *strīrājya* is never specific; the *Mahābhārata*[77] describes women's kingdom as far off and distant, grouping it with barbarians, the *yavanas* and the Chinese. Apparently in these liminal elsewhere spaces, new kinds of intimacies could be explored. Not surprisingly the *Mahābhārata*[78] refers to sexually liberated women or *svairiṇī*, meaning self-willed, independent, and unrestrained,[79] but translated by Neumeier-Dargyay as "one who makes love with her own kind."[80]

In my recent work[81] (2009), where the concept of homoeroticism, especially female eroticism, has been discussed in greater detail, the attitude to homosexuality as reflected in the texts of various genres has also been studied. It would appear that while the brāhmaṇical law books and Āyurvedic treatises are condemnatory of homoerotic tendencies, the *kāmaśāstrīya* discourse is ambivalent. In the *dharmaśāstras*, the notion of sex was rooted in the idea of the reproduction of the species, and hence, in their view, heterosexual coitus was the ideal form of sexuality. Any deviance in the form of homosexuality (tellingly referred to as *klībya*, that is, impotence) and lesbianism earned the ire of the law givers. According to Manu,[82] one who unites in sexual union with a man loses his caste and his commentator Medhātithi[83] agrees with him that such a man should perform atonement for this sin. As for lesbian lovers Manu[84] says that if the offender is a maiden herself she can get away with a lighter punishment (of lashes) without her crime being publicized, but if it is a mature woman, her guilt has to be publicly proclaimed and she has to be paraded on a donkey. Perhaps this was because a more mature and active partner was seen as directly threatening the patriarchal family and conjugal rights of men. Medhātithi,[85] however, states that there being no authority for such a view (punishment) it should be ignored. In the Āyurvedic texts also the woman's body is valued for the reproductive role and any alternative model of sexual gratification like lesbian love was denounced. Thus, both Suśruta and Ḍalhaṇa tell us that a boneless monstrosity (*alpakomalāsthi*) is the outcome of a sexual act in which both partners are female, and their *śukra* (here in the sense of sexual secretions) unites somehow or the other in the womb of one of them.[86]

It is only in the narrative texts that we find a positive space for homoerotic feelings. Thus, *Kathāsaritsāgara* tells us about princess Padmāvatī whose confidante and personal maid Manohārikā tells her that "even women who see you are so much in love with your beauty that they desire to become men".[87] In the same text we get a reference to the man-hating (*puruṣadveṣinī*) princess Malayavatī who amused herself by marrying her female attendants to one-another (*kanyākanyonya vivāhādi vinodanaiḥ*).[88] An interesting verse in Jalhaṇa's *Sūktimuktāvalī*[89] also makes an oblique reference to lesbian love. It states that when female friends (*sakhī*) of the lotus-eyed one saw her heavy lower part (*jaghana*) while she was asleep, they all turned men in their heart.

In the early-medieval classical Sanskrit literature we also find some free-standing verses by poetesses that are preserved in the Sanskrit anthologies. There is little escaping the fact that these verses of poetesses are essentially about heterosexual desire and display an ardent aspiration for male companionship; for we do not find any clitoral imagery herein. Yet there is one cryptic verse by the poetess Jaghanacapalā which refers to the love of a (married) woman for another (man?). She says that "on a bad, rainy night when dark clouds cover the sky and it is difficult to walk through the deserted city streets, and when the husband is away in a foreign country, Jaghanacapalā feels immensely happy". If in this verse "husband" is interpreted as the husband of an un-named (suggested) "other" (rather than as the husband of Jaghanacapalā) who is away on a journey, a fact which makes Jaghanacapalā happy, then this interpretation could lend itself to the possibility that the narrator Jaghanacapalā was engaged in a lesbian love relationship with that unnamed "other".[90]

In conclusion, one may state that homosocial and homoerotic tendencies have not been peculiar to any one specific cultural complex. They may be more unambiguously displayed in some cultures (as for instance, ancient Greece) or be muted in others, but human nature and emotions find their own outlet. As Jain philosopher Śākaṭāyana states in a matter of fact manner, "... a person may be capable of being sexually aroused by the same-sex, the opposite-sex, or even by an animal".[91] Vātsyāyana, in his *Kāmasūtra*,[92] gently reminds the readers/listeners of his *kāmaśāstriya* discourse that: "It is by taking into account the country (*deśa*), the period (*kāla*), custom (*prayogam*), the injunction of *śāstra*, as well as one's own liking (*ātmānam cāpi samprekṣya*), that one decides whether or not to practice these kinds of sexual relations". Referring to mouth-congress (*auparisṭakam*), Vātsyāyana states: "practiced according to one's fantasy and in secret, it is difficult to know who, how and why one does it (*kaḥ kadā kim kutaḥ kuryāditi ko jñatumahṛti*)".

This historiographical survey of homosexuality in ancient Indian literature confirms not only its presence but also attests to a polyphony of reception which this sexual practice received within Indian cultural tradition.

ENDNOTES

1. B.M. Malinowski, *The Sexual Life of Savages in North-Western Melanesia*, Routledge and Kegan Paul, London, 1957.
2. Jawaharlal Nehru comments that homosexual relations of the ancient Greek variety and the conception of the beloved as a male in Persian literature is absent in Sanskrit literature. He goes on to say that "Homosexuality was evidently neither approved nor at all common in India" (*The Discovery of India*, The John Day Company, New York, 1946, p. 146).
3. M.B. Duberman, M. Vicinus, and G. Chauncey, eds., *Hidden From History: Reclaiming the Gay and Lesbian Past*, New American Library, New York, 1989. David M. Halperin, *One Hundred Years of Homosexuality and Other Essays on Greek Love*, Routledge, New York, 1989. For gay movements in Germany see Robert Beachy, "The German Invention of Homosexuality", *Journal of Modern History*, vol. 82 (Decembr 2010), pp. 801–31.
4. F.K. Forberg, *Apophoreta*, English translation by J. Smithson as *Manual of Classical Erotology*, 2 vols., Manchester, 1884, Reprint, Newyork, 1966
5. David M. Halperin, J. Winkler, and F. Zeitlin, eds., *Before Sexuality: The Construction of Erotic Experience in the Ancient Greek World*, Princeton, 1990, pp. 10–11.
6. Vern L. Bullough, *Sexual Variance in Society and History*, John Wiley, New York, 1976. This book also commented on the variant sexual practices in the non-Western world such as Islamic culture, China and India.
7. K.J. Dover, *Greek Homosexuality*, Vintage Books, New York, 1978.
8. Michel Foucault, *A History of Sexuality*, vol. 2, Penguin, 1987; vol. 3, 1990, London.

9. Adrienn Rich, "Compulsory Heterosexuality and Lesbian Existence", *SIGNS: Journal of Women and Culture in Society*, vol. 5, no. 4 (Summer 1980), pp. 631–60.
10. Bernadette Brooten, *Love between Women: Early Christian Response to Female Homoeroticism*, University of Chicago Press, Chicago, 1996.
11. Jane Snyder, *Lesbian Desire in the Lyrics of Sappho*, Columbia University Press, New York, 1997.
12. Nancy Rabinowitz, and Lisa Auanger, eds., *Among Women: From the Homosocial to the Homoerotic in the Western Ancient World*, University of Texas Press, Austin, 2002.
13. Sue Morgan, ed., *The Feminist History Reader*, Routledge, London, 2006, p. 98
14. A.B. Van Gulik, *Sexual Life in Ancient China*, E.J. Brill, Leiden, 1961, pp. 91–169.
15. A.L. Basham, *The Wonder That Was India*, Rupa, Delhi, 1988, p. 173.
16. D.D. Kosambi, "Íntroduction" to the *Subhāsitaratnakoṣa of Vidyākara*, Harvard University Press, Cambridge 1957, p. xli.
17. Arvind Sharma, "Homosexuality and Hinduism" in Arlene Swidler, ed., *Homosexuality and World Religions*, Valley Forge, Pennsylvania, 1993, pp. 47–80
18. *Kāmasūtra* (2.9.36) with commentary of Yaśodhara, ed. and tr., Madhavacharya, vols. I and II, Khemraj Srikrishna Prakashan, Bombay, 1995
19. Ibid., 2.9.35
20. Ibid., 2.6.49
21. Ruth Vanita and Salim Kidwai, eds., *Same-Sex Love in India: Readings from Literature and History*, St. Martin's Press, New York, 2000, p. 27
22. *Kāmasūtra*, 5.6.1-2
23. Kumkum Roy, "Unravelling the Kāmasūtra", *Indian Journal of Gender Studies*, vol. 3, no. 2 (1996), p. 159.
24. *Kāmasūtra*, 2.9.36
25. In the *Śāktatantra* the serpent power (*kuṇḍalinī*) is found in its latent form around the sex organ (*mūladharacakra*). This *cakra* is located in the anus (*gudā*) and is an important centre of psychic energy in the human body. Its significance is repeatedly emphasized in tantric literature with what might be called homosexual overtones: Arvind Sharma, op. cit., p. 65.
26. Ibid., pp. 48–9.
27. Within the *Śāktatantra*, for example, all believers aim to become

identical with the Tripurāsundarī, and as part of this *sadhanā* all followers, even male, habituate themselves to think that they are women.

28. Arvind Sharma, op. cit, p. 68.
29. Ibid.
30. Leonard Zwilling, "Homosexuality as Seen in Indian Buddhist Texts", in Jose Ignacio Cabezon, ed., *Buddhism, Sexuality and Gender*, Indian edition, Satguru Publications, 1992, pp. 203–14 (p. 205).
31. Ibid., p. 204.
32. Michael J. Sweet and Leonard Zwilling, "The Evolution of Third Sex Constructs in Ancient India: A Study in Ambiguity", in Julia Leslie and Mary McGee, eds., *Invented Identities: The Interplay of Gender, Religion and Politics in India*, Oxford University Press, Delhi, 2000, pp. 99–132 (p. 117, fn. 62).
33. Zwilling and Sweet, "Like A City Ablaze: The Third Sex and the Creation of Sexuality in Jain Religious Literature", *Journal of the History of Sexuality*, vol. 6, no. 3 (1996), pp. 359–84 (373–4).
34. Zwilling, op. cit., 1992, p. 207.
35. Ibid., p. 209.
36. *Mahābhārata* (3.186.35) (ed., V.S. Sukthankar, et al., 19 vols., Poona, 1933-72).
37. *Manusmṛti* (11.68). (tr., Wendy Doniger and Brian Smith, Penguin, New York, 1992).
38. *Rājataraṅgiṇī* (6.152, 159) (ed. and tr., Ramjet Shastri, Pandit Pustakalaya, Kashi, 1960).
39. Sweet and Zwilling, "The First Medicalization: The Taxonomy and Etiology of Queerness in Classical Indian Medicine", *Journal of the History of Sexuality*, vol. 3, no. 4 (1993), pp. 590–607 (pp. 593, 597).
40. Ibid., p. 593.
41. Ibid., p. 596.
42. Sweet and Zwilling, "The Evolution of Third Sex Constructs...", pp. 99–132.
43. *Kāmasūtra*, 1.5.27
44. Ibid., 2.9.1-2.
45. Ibid., 2.9.6-9.
46. Sweet and Zwilling, "The Evolution of Third Sex Constructs...", p. 104.
47. *Sṛṅgārahāṭa: Caturbhāṇī*, ed. and tr., Motichandra and V.S. Agrawala, Hindi Granth Ratnakar, Bombay, 1960, p. 137.
48. Geeti Thadani, *Sakhiyani: Lesbian Desire in Ancient and Modern*

India, New York, Cassel, 1996, pp. 21, 48.

49. Adrienne Rich, op. cit., pp. 631–60.
50. Geeti Thadani, op. cit., pp. 21, 48.
51. Vanita and Kidwai (eds),, op. cit, p. 17, fn. 44.
52. Kumkum Roy, *The Emergence of Monarchy in the North India: 8th–4th Centuries BC*, Oxford University Press, Delhi, 1994, p. 166.
53. Ibid., p. 277.
54. Vanita and Kidwai, op. cit, p. 2.
55. Vanita (ibid., p. 28) sees the rebirth motif as the single most significant factor in the Indian understanding of same-sex love. This motif occurs both in the ancient texts as also in folk-tales.
56. Vanita (ibid., pp. 19–21) refers to the Tamil epic *Maṇimekalai,* whose eponymous heroine spurns all attempts at matrimony.
57. Ibid., pp. 90–3.
58. Shalini Shah, "The Principle of Kāma Puruṣārtha in the Mahābhārata", in Kalyan Kumar Chakravarty, (ed.), *Text and Variations of the Mahabharata: Contextual, Regional and Performative Traditions* Munshiram Manoharlal, Delhi, 2009, pp. 321–9. In an expansive essay Robert P. Goldman discusses the tales of trans-sexuality or sex change found in ancient Indian texts and reads in them a deeply longed-for metamorphosis that makes possible an erotic liaison with a powerful and desired male. Trans-sexualism, in his view, is nothing but a metaphor for homosexual longings: ("Transsexualism, Gender and Anxiety in Traditional India", *Journal of American Oriental Society*, vol. 113, no. 3, (July-September, 1993), pp. 374–401.
59. *Mahābhārata*, 1.210.5
60. Ibid., 1.225.13
61. Ibid., 3.13.36
62. Ibid., 10.12.27
63. Ibid., 7.56.23
64. Ibid., 7.56.30
65. Ibid., 7.157.40-41.
66. Ibid., 14.15.3-6; 14.51.33; 2.14.33.
67. Ibid., 1.214.29.
68. It has been pointed out that the term *ramate*, which is used to describe pleasurable enjoyment, is the same for both homosexual and heterosexual companionship (Vanita and Kidwai, eds, op. cit, p. 4).
69. Ibid., p. 66.
70. Dimock, Edward, *The Place of the Hidden Moon: Erotic Mysticism*

in the Vaiṣṇava Sahajiya Cult of Bengal, Motilal Banarsidass, Delhi, 1991, p. 23.

71. Shalini Shah, *The Making of Womanhood: Gender Relations in the Mahābhārata*, Manohar, Delhi, 1995, pp. 56–7.
72. *Mahābhārata*, 13.42.17–19.
73. Ibid., 13.20.64-69.
74. Shalini Shah, *The Making of Womanhood*, pp. 56–7.
75. *Kāmasūtra*, 2.5.27.
76. Ibid., 2.5.27.
77. *Mahābhārata*, 3.48.21.
78. Ibid., 1.114.65.
79. Monnier Williams, *Sanskrit-English Dictionary*, Munshiram Manoharlal, Delhi, 1994, p. 1279.
80. Serenity Young, ed., *Encyclopedia of Women and World Religion*, Macmillan, New York, 1999, vol. II, p. 585.
81. Shalini Shah, *Love, Eroticism and Female Sexuality in Classical Sanskrit Literature 7th-13th Centuries*, Manohar, Delhi, 2009, p. 187.
82. *Manu*, 11.68
83. Medhātithi on Manu, 11.174 (Manusmṛti with the bhāṣya of Medhātithi, tr. Ganganath Jha, 5 vols., Calcutta University, 1920-26)
84. *Manu*, 8.369-370
85. Medhātithi on Manu, 8.370
86. *Suśrutasaṃhitā*, (Śarīrasthāna, 2.47). (ed., Trikamji and Narayan Ram Acharya, Chowkhamba, Varanasi, 2003).
87. Shalini Shah, *Love, Eroticism and Female Sexuality in Classical Sanskrit Literature*, p. 187.
88. Ibid.
89. *Sūktimuktāvalī*, (188.77). (ed., E. Krishnamacharya, Oriental Institute, Baroda, 1938).
90. Shalini Shah, "Poetesses in Classical Sanskrit Literature: 7th-13th Centuries CE", *Indian Journal of Gender Studies*, 15(1) (January-April, 2008), pp. 10–11.
91. Padmanabh S. Jaini, *Gender and Salvation*, Munshiram Manoharlal, Delhi, 1992, pp. 89–90.
92. *Kāmasūtra*, 2.9.44–45.

About the Contributors

James M. Hegarty, Ph.D., is senior lecturer in Indian Religions at Cardiff University. He was educated at the University of Manchester, where he specialized in Sanskrit religious literature and, in particular, the *Mahābhārata*. He has an abiding interest in the role of narrative in the transmission and adaptation of religious knowledge in pre-modern South Asia. He is the author of numerous scholarly articles on Sanskrit, Pali and vernacular Indian sources. He is also the author of *Religion, Narrative and Public Imagination: Past and Place in the Sanskrit Mahābhārata* (Routledge, 2012).

D.N. Jha was a professor of history at the University of Delhi until his retirement in 2005. He is the author of *Revenue System in Post-Maurya and Gupta Times* (1967), *Ancient India* (1977, 1998), *Studies in Early Indian Economic History* (1979), *Ramjanmabhumi-Baburi Masjid: A Historians' Report to the Nation* (1991, jointly with R.S. Sharma et al), *Economy and Society in Early India* (1993), *Early India* (2004), *Holy Cow: Beef in Indian Dietary Traditions* (2001), reprinted as *The Myth of the Holy Cow* (2002, 2004, 2009), and *Rethinking Hindu Identity* (2009): all these works have been translated into Hindi and other Indian languages. His edited volumes include the *Society and Ideology in India* (1993), *The Feudal Order* (2001), *Mind and Matter: Essays on Mentalities in Medieval India* (2009, jointly with Eugenia Vanina), and

The Many Careers of D.D. Kosambi (2011). His current interests focus on heretic traditions, colonial and post colonial construction of Hinduism, and the land, power and caste in early India.

Suvira Jaiswal is a former professor of history at the Jawaharlal Nehru University, New Delhi. She obtained her Master's Degree in History from Allahabad University in 1953 and Doctorate from Patna University in 1963. She was the President of the Ancient India Section of the Indian History Congress in 1977 and its General President in 2007. She was also elected the General President of the Andhra Pradesh History Congress in 2002. Her main area of research is religion and society of early India. Her publications include *The Origin and Development of Vaisnavism* (Munshiram Manoharlal, Delhi, 1967 and 1981) and *Caste: Origin, Function and Dimensions of Change* (Manohar, Delhi, 1998) and have received wide acclaim.

H.D. Sankalia (d. 1989) was a professor of prehistory and protohistory at the Deccan College of Postgraduate Research and Institute, Pune, until his retirement in 1973. During his tenure at the Institute he oraganized an active team of archaeologists with whose assistance he was able to explore and excavate a large number of sites, especially in Maharshtra and Gujarat. He introduced new techniques in archaeological explorations and excavations and provided insightful perspectives in Indian field archaeology and rescued it from the effete and obsolete antiquarian approach. Sankalia's remarkable achievement lay not only in excavating a large number of sites but also in publishing the results of his findings. Apart from coauthoring with his colleagues the numerous excavation reports, he himself authored several seminal works like those on Nalanda and the Ramayana. His *Prehistory and Protohistory of India and Pakistan* (1974) remains a landmark publication in the field of Indian archaeology.

Nabanita Dev Sen is a former professor of comparative literature at the Jadavpur University, Kolkata. Recepient of numerous honours including the Sahitya Akademi Award, and a writer in residence at several international artists' colonies, she has authored about eighty books which include fiction, short stories, satires, one-act plays, poems and travelogues and children's literature. Although most of her writings are in Bengali, she knows a number of languages and writes also in English. Her current interest is focused on India's epic traditions on which she has written extensively and lectured at many centres of education and culture. Her essay in the present anthology is an abridged version of her S. Radhakrishnan Memorial Lecture delivered at Oxford.

Shalini Shah is a senior associate professor in the Department of History, University of Delhi. She has authored *The Making of Womanhood: Gender Relations in the Mahābhārata*, Delhi 1995, Revised Edition 2012 and *Love, Eroticism and Female Sexuality in Classical Sanskrit Literature Seventh to Thirteenth Centuries*, Delhi 2009. She has published widely on gender issues in prestigious Journals.

Jae-Eun Shin took Ph.D. from Department of History, University of Delhi in 2008 and worked on religious history of East India with special focus on Śākta traditions. She is currently Junior Research Fellow at Research Institute for Languages and Cultures of Asia and Africa, Tokyo University of Foreign Studies. Her published articles include 'Yoni, Yoginīs and Mahavidyas: Feminine Divinities from Early Medieval Kāmarūpa to Medieval Koch Behar', 'Transformation of the Goddess Tārā with Special Reference to Iconographical Features', 'From Mātṛgaṇa to Sapta Mātṛkās: Brāhmaṇical Transfiguration of Autochthonous Goddesses'.

Mahima Singh is a postgraduate in early Indian history from St. Stephen's College, University of Delhi, and has studied Cognitive Semiotics of Visual Art (University of Aarhus, Denmark). She has worked as a Faculty Assistant with the Vidya Bhavan Education Resource Centre, Udaipur, Rajasthan and has collaborated with many educationists and resource personnel for developing curriculum and material for history teaching. Mahima's most recent experience has been interning with Bellvue Arts Museum in Seattle, USA, a contemporary arts and crafts museum, for acquiring experience with museum and arts education for school children and adults.

K.M. Shrimali retired as Professor of History, University of Delhi. His important publications include *History of Panchāl* (in two volumes); *The Agrarian Structure in Central India and the Northern Deccan: A Study in Vākāṭaka Inscriptions; Constructing an Identity: Forging Hinduism into Harappan Religions; Dharma, Samaj aur Sanskriti; The Iron Age and the Religious Revolution.* Amongst several monographs edited by him are: *Essays on Indian Art, Religion and Society* (1987); *Archaeology Since Independence* (1996); *A Comprehensive History of India,* Vol. IV (jointly with Professor R.S. Sharma, in two parts). Currently, he is working on a multi-volume *Dictionary of Social, Economic and Administrative Terms in Indian Inscriptions* (a project of the Indian Council of Historical Research) and 'Geography of Early Indian Religions: An Exercise Towards Atlas of Early Indian Religions' (under Senior Academic Fellowship of the Indian Council of Historical Research). He has been associated with the activities of several leading organizations and academic bodies of professional historians and archaeologists and is committed to the dissemination of scientific and secular history through the teaching and writing of history—both at the academic level as well for common people.